*Confederate Settlements
in British Honduras*

To Donna, Tres, Mom, and Dad

and

In memory of Dr. Charles S. Davis,
historian, author, educator, and
inspiration to all aspiring historians

Confederate Settlements in British Honduras

Donald C. Simmons, Jr.

FOREWORD BY WILLIAM F. WINTER

McFarland & Company, Inc., Publishers
Jefferson, North Carolina, and London

Library of Congress Cataloguing-in-Publication Data

Simmons, Donald C., Jr.
    Confederate settlements in British Honduras / Donald C.
Simmons, Jr. ; foreword by William F. Winter.
        p.   cm.
    Includes bibliographical references and index.
    ISBN 0-7864-1016-7 (softcover : 50# alkaline paper) ∞
        1. American Confederate voluntary exiles— Belize — History —
2. Americans— Belize — History —19th century.   3. United
States— History — Civil War, 1861–1865 — Refugees.   4. Belize —
History —19th century.   5. Immigrants— Belize — History —
19th century.   I. Title.
    F1457.A5.S56   2001
    972.82'00413 — dc21   2001030376

British Library cataloguing data are available

Manufactured in the United States of America

On the cover: Members of the Pearce, Moore, and Mason families, and a
house servant (circa 1899) at the Pearce family home known as Fairview.
The Reverend Levi Pearce. (Photographs courtesy Robert D. Pearce and
Bert W. Pearce. Map ©2001 Art Today)

McFarland & Company, Inc., Publishers
Box 611, Jefferson, North Carolina 28640
    www.mcfarlandpub.com

Acknowledgments

It would be almost impossible to acknowledge all of the people who assisted my efforts. I owe my interest in history to my parents. My family stopped at every historic marker east of the Mississippi, and most of those west of it as well, during my childhood. Cecil Simmons, my uncle, introduced me to Belize. Many thanks are due my friend and mentor, Dr. Terence Tarr. With gratitude and admiration, I acknowledge his assistance, wisdom, and encouragement. Dr. Michael Pulman, Dr. Theodore Crane, and the other members of the faculty of the University of Denver deserve high praise for their objective criticisms and encouragement. Without the able assistance of the following librarians and archivists, I would not have written the first word: Charlie Brenner of the Eudora Welty Library; Nell Bassett, Mary Beth Green, and Becky Howell of the Troy State University Library; Pat Matthes and Gail Andrews of Mississippi University for Women; Carolyn Nault of Columbus–Lowndes County Public Library (Mississippi); Sherry DeRosia of the Church of Jesus Christ of Latter-Day Saints; Aileen Brooks of the Monroe County Library (Alabama); Victoria Reese of the Microfilm Library at the University of South Carolina; Kathy Bailey and the librarians at the Evans Memorial Library in Aberdeen, Mississippi; Hank Holmes of the Mississippi Department of Archives and History; Tara Zachary of the Charles W. Capps Archives and Museum at Delta State University; Linda Schneider of the Hill Memorial Library at Louisiana State University; Henry Fulmer of the South Caroliniana Library; Dr. Jerry Oldshue of the University of Alabama; and Francine Taylor and Mimi Jones of the Alabama Archives in Montgomery. The Reverend Murray Bullock of St. Paul's Episcopal Church and the Reverend Stiles B. Lines of the University of the South were helpful in the location of Episcopal church records.

The following citizens of Belize are to be noted for their cooperation and assistance: Charles Gibson, government archivist of Belize; the Honorable

Glenn Godfrey, former attorney general and minister of tourism and the environment; the Honorable Daniel Silva, former minister of state in the Ministry of Finance, Home Affairs, Defense, and Trade and Commerce; Judith Cayetano, formerly of the Belize Teachers College in Belmopan; and Macario Palma of Toledo, Belize, for detective work in local cemeteries.

Wallace Young, Claude Scarborough, Frank Mason, Colonel Robert Hardy, Bert Pearle, Charlie Pearce, Bo Devine, Lida Logan, and Dr. Ian S. Pearce generously provided family information. Marian McCutchon Yarborough of Pass Christian, Mississippi, provided a bounty of family information as well as many photographs for my research. I am grateful to Mary Lou Miller of the Metarie Cemetery in Louisiana for her contributions. To Agnes Man-Bourdon, I owe a debt of gratitude for her French translations. Mrs. T. Harry Williams of Baton Rouge, Louisiana, graciously provided information about her late husband's research. Barbara Doherty of New York University, Michael Camille of Northeast Louisiana University, Charles Yarborough of the Mississippi School for Math and Science, Dr. Harry Owens of the University of Mississippi, David Pendergast of the Royal Museum of Toronto, and Dr. Kit Carson Carter III were also instrumental to my work.

Funding is always crucial, and I thank my parents, who financed several trips to Belize, and the Southern Baptist Historical Library and Archives for assistance in the form of the Lynn E. May Research Grant. The University of Southern Mississippi Archives has agreed to accept and make available for future scholars all of my research and papers collected during many years of work on this project, and for this I am most grateful.

Finally, I would like to acknowledge the author of the foreword to this publication. A source of inspiration for many historians and genealogical researchers, Governor William F. Winter has dedicated much of his life to collecting, preserving, and promoting the history of Mississippi and the South. I am honored to have my friend join me in this project.

Contents

Acknowledgments   v
Foreword by William F. Winter   1
Preface   5

I. Belize City: Contraband Port and Haven for
   Refugees   7
II. Lure of the British Flag   19
III. Era of Group Migration to British Honduras   26
IV. Making the Trek Southward   34
V. Passage to British Honduras   41
VI. Plight of the Newly Arrived Immigrants   48
VII. Two Phases of Migration   54
VIII. Confederate Settlements in the Interior   63
IX. The Toledo Settlement   70
X. Waning of the Toledo Settlement   82
XI. Settlement at New Richmond   87
XII. Settlements in Northern British Honduras   93
XIII. Manattee and Other Settlements   100
XIV. Belize City at the Height of the Immigrant Influx   106
XV. Alternatives to Confederate Exile in British
    Honduras   116
    Conclusion   121

Appendix A. Arrivals at the Hotels 123

Appendix B. Passenger Lists Taken from Various Sources 124

Appendix C. Act 18 Vict., Cap. 18, as Published in
 Two Parts, 20 June 1868 and 27 June 1868, in the
 British Honduras Colonist and Belize Advertiser 131

Appendix D. Passenger Lists of Ships Arriving in
 New Orleans from Belize, Honduras 134

Bibliography 161

Index 168

Foreword

BY WILLIAM F. WINTER

Among the largely unheralded and unnoticed victims of every war are those legions of displaced persons whose lives have been interrupted, whose careers have been destroyed, whose families have been fragmented, and whose unhappy fate has been to roam the world to seek a new life. Such was the plight of a few thousand ex–Confederate Southerners who in the months after Appomattox chose to leave their beloved but shattered South and attempt to find refuge in places further south. Some fled to Mexico, Venezuela, Brazil, and the Caribbean islands. This book is the wrenching story of an estimated three to seven thousand who sought sanctuary in what was then the British colony of Honduras, now known as Belize.

For the most part those migrants were Louisianans and Mississippians who, in the wake of Robert E. Lee's surrender and the Federal occupation of their states, could not bring themselves to accept living under the governance of the United States, a country which they no longer regarded as their own. Many came from backgrounds of propertied affluence and political prominence. They were cotton and sugarcane planters from the rich farmlands of the lower Mississippi Valley, where slavery had flourished and created a way of life that these proud and still defiant rebels were loath to relinquish. In their desperate imagining, this Central American land represented an English-speaking enclave where the old Anglo-Saxon heritage could still be found and where they dreamed of reestablishing the socio-economic environment which they had enjoyed in the South before the war.

Despite entreaties from old Southern heroes, like Jefferson Davis and Lee, to stay and rebuild the South, these totally unreconstructed, stubborn defenders of the old order made it clear that they saw their only hope in a

1

life outside the United States. Some even dreamed of creating a cotton kingdom in a colony whose fealty was to the British monarchy, which many of them regarded as a form of government superior to that which prevailed in the "Yankee-controlled" democracy of their former country.

So, in the chaotic years between 1865 and 1870, a steady stream of vessels set sail from the Gulf Coast ports, most notably New Orleans, to transport this tide of voluntarily displaced persons to a strange and exotic realm to the south. There they found a generally hospitable reception from the people but not from the land itself. However much they sought to make it like the home that they had left, it was not Louisiana nor Mississippi nor, despite their Herculean efforts, would it ever be. With as much as 160 inches of rainfall a year in some areas, cotton bolls rotted in the fields. The tropical climate was found to harbor all manner of insects, and disease claimed many lives, including that of former Mississippi Governor John J. McRae, who died less than a month after his arrival in British Honduras in 1868.

There was even a misreading of racial mores in this new land, where a majority of the population consisted of former African slaves, who had been liberated in all British colonies over thirty years earlier. Most of the ex–Confederates found it difficult to accept the concept of racial equality as it was practiced in their newly adopted country, and there were a number of ugly incidents between the white Southerners and the black residents of the colony. Local newspapers sharply rebuked the new arrivals for their racial intolerance after one such unfortunate incident.

By 1870 it had become obvious that, onerous though it might be to accept, life in the postwar South was preferable to the inhospitable tropic wilderness of British Honduras. It is estimated that by this time only about one hundred ex–Confederates remained there. Those few who did remain were for the most part scattered, isolated from each other, and more than ever truly displaced persons living in permanent self-imposed exile from their homeland.

Through this intriguing but melancholy story there emerges a picture of more of the tragedy and pathos of the war and its aftermath. Told in part in the actual words of some of the men and women who made the disillusioning journey, this volume rescues from oblivion a chapter of history that for almost a century and a half has remained virtually unknown. Much has been written about the émigrés to Brazil. Next to nothing has been done until now to document and recount the efforts in British Honduras.

Dr. Donald Simmons has provided us in this book the rare opportunity to peer back through a newly opened window on a confusing and chaotic time. Because it was a period of turmoil and disorganization, the events of the years immediately after the Civil War have not been as well documented as those of the war itself. While the subject matter of this book cannot be considered as central to the story of that turbulent time, it is a particularly fascinating scene in a countless series of dramatic and largely tragic episodes that collectively make up the defining event of the American nineteenth century. As a vignette of the history of the period, it serves to remind us of how much human dislocation occurs in the cataclysm of war and how even today there are still lingering reminders in Belize of that long-ago time when a few thousand people from the South found a temporary home in a remote land.

The unsuspecting visitor there now finds familiar-sounding place names. There are a few remaining American surnames, although no distinctive American communities are intact. Perhaps the most lasting effect has been the development of a sugarcane industry that owes much of its existence to the imported knowledge and experience of the Louisiana planters. This volume is the result of the curiosity and diligence of Dr. Simmons, who discovered the historic background to the story quite by accident on a trip to Belize. His fascination with what he discovered has resulted in this stimulating and informative book.

William F. Winter is the former governor of Mississippi and serves as chair of the board of trustees of the Mississippi Department of Archives and History.

Preface

My introduction to the country of Belize occurred while I was an undergraduate student at the University of Mississippi. I must admit that, like many Americans, I had little knowledge of the tiny Central American nation prior to my decision to volunteer my services to Health Talents International, a church-funded organization based in Birmingham, Alabama. Facing the alternatives of a summer job or, worse, summer school and presented with the opportunity to travel widely in Belize, I opted to confront the unknown.

My appointed task was to travel the country to collect samples of the anopheles mosquito for use in research. The mosquitoes collected were tested for their resilience to DDT (dichloro-diphenyl-trichloro-ethane). Belizeans used DDT during the late 1970s and early 1980s, as did the southern section of the United States at one time, to control these mosquitoes, which are known to transmit malaria. The job was not always exciting, but I became well acquainted with the people and countryside of Belize.

Many of the scenes in rural Belize were reminiscent of my home in the southern United States. Several of the place and family names were strikingly similar to those of my home state of Mississippi. The more I thought about this, the more the close proximity of the country to the United States and particularly to the South made a possible past relationship between the two nations seem likely. Not understanding why any American would willingly choose to leave the United States, I let the notion pass. Sometime later, however, the similarities were brought back to mind during a class in graduate school. Picking up at random a book entitled *General Colin J. McRae: Confederate Financial Agent*, I had no idea of the consequences. The final pages of the book make reference to the general's life after the Civil War when he was among Southerners, primarily from Mississippi and Louisiana, who chose to settle in British Honduras rather than remain in the United States during Reconstruction. And so my search began.

5

I soon discovered that only a few secondary sources existed that made any reference to the Confederate exodus to British Honduras. It became apparent that New Orleans served as the major hub of all such activity and that 1866 to 1870 were the peak years. The New Orleans and British Honduran newspapers, passenger lists, and U.S. consular reports helped supply pieces of the historical puzzle. These same documents served to discredit many of the assumptions made by the few secondary sources available on this topic.

Visits to the former British colony revealed an array of complementary letters and other original sources, which contributed substantially to the research effort. Personal interviews were both helpful and disheartening, as family tales were often obviously fictional. The picture that emerged, however, was often as interesting as the tales of family legend. The following text is the result of more than fifteen years of research on the Confederate exodus to British Honduras.

CHAPTER I

Belize City: Contraband Port and Haven for Refugees

Belize, the former colony of British Honduras that became an independent nation in 1981, has a curious mixture of peoples and cultures. Throughout its colonial history, an array of peoples arrived to settle and make the land their home. Some came as pirates and conquerors, others were brought as laborers or slaves, and still others arrived seeking refuge from unbearable circumstances in their various homelands. This variety of immigrants has contributed to the cultural uniqueness of the country.

Prior to the arrival of the Europeans, Belize was inhabited by the Maya. The Maya developed extremely advanced cities and transportation networks. Their cities surrounded the temples which still dot the Central American landscape today. The height of Mayan greatness was reached some time before the birth of Christ. Historians can only speculate as to the causes of the decline of the Mayan civilization.[1]

The deterioration of Mayan society made the conquest of the area by Spanish explorers a relatively simple task. Belize was bypassed by most explorers. Although claimed by Spain, authorities did little to develop the territory. No Spanish settlements were established in what is now Belize. The wealth of gold in other parts of Latin America preoccupied the conquistadors, and they left the mosquito-ridden coast of the Caribbean to the natives.[2]

The arrival of the British in Central America did not occur until about 1603. The first Englishmen to settle the coast were pirates who used the country as a safe haven. Barrier reefs running parallel to the shore prevented the Spanish galleons from pursuing the much smaller pirate ships. A Scottish sea captain named Wallace is said to have established the contraband port and refuge for pirates that would later become Belize City.[3] Declining gold shipments and increased protection of shipping by the Spanish Crown soon forced the pirates to seek new professions. As the demand for wood and wood products increased, many turned to lumbering.[4]

Although the British were not officially given permission by the Spanish authorities to lumber in the area, the exportation of logwood and mahogany from the Central American coast to the British Isles proceeded steadily for some time. The Spanish, realizing that they were unable to police such activity effectively, eventually extended the wood-cutting concession for the area that is present-day Belize to the British in 1786. According to the Anglo-Spanish treaties, agricultural pursuits and the establishment of a government were forbidden. British subjects arriving in the wood-cutting settlement, however, ignored the demands of their Spanish landlord. A superintendent was eventually appointed by the Crown to maintain order and serve as administrator of the settlement. The laws were not those of England, however, but the traditional customs of the settlement, which were referred to as "Burnaby's Laws."[5] The settlement, as a result, was entirely self-governing prior to 1800.

The arrival and dispersion of people of various ethnicities occurred as the result of fluctuating economic conditions within the settlement. For years, the international market's demand for mahogany as well as the opportunity to sell weapons, much-needed food, and other commodities to warring neighbors proved to be the most prosperous business ventures available to settlers. Numerous other options were considered as alternatives to the precarious mahogany and arms trade; cotton, sugar, bananas, and citrus were all tried as substitutes with varying degrees of success. Sugarcane had been successfully planted throughout much of the colony but was considered by colonists, as late as 1865, a venture with little potential for profits.[6]

The potential for the commercialization of sugarcane production in the colony of British Honduras brought refugee Southerners from the United States as early as 1861, a year before colonial status was achieved. That group of refugee immigrants and others that followed — the focus of this work — added a distinctive flavor to the culture of the colony that is still noticeable today, more than 140 years later. While their efforts to establish large communities of Confederates prospering on sugar plantations failed miserably, the immigrants did establish a foundation for what is now the nation's primary agricultural industry — sugarcane production.

The close proximity, common language, and similar customs had always fostered the sense of a common bond between the settlements of

Central America.

British Honduras and the southern United States, and these ties were strengthened by the 1860s conflict known as the Civil War. During the early years of the Civil War, the British colonists rejuvenated the local economy by developing trade with the Confederacy. Facing declining timber resources, they were eager to benefit from the events occurring to the north, and the strategic location of British Honduras made the colony a prime site for the development of extensive trade in military hardware and supplies to ports along the Gulf of Mexico, in the southern United States, and Mexico. Until the U.S. naval blockade was able to stop the flow of such goods in May 1863, the U.S. representative in Belize City argued that it was the most important contraband port on the mainland south of Matamoros, Mexico.[7]

In September 1863 the women of Mobile, Alabama, marched down Dauphine Street, breaking open stores and taking food and clothing. Food riots and looting became a problem in many southern cities at the close of the Civil War. This illustration was originally published in the September 1883 issue of the Pictorial War Record. *(Courtesy Frank and Marie-Therese Wood Print Collections, Alexandria, Virginia)*

The commercial ties to the southern United States, which were established in 1861, encouraged sympathy for the plight of the colony's trading partner. The anti–Union sentiment in the colony was heightened in 1863 by the halt of illicit trade by Union blockades, which dealt a severe blow to the already weakened economy of British Honduras. The war's end, however, brought the promise of economic revitalization.

The final years of the conflict introduced a large influx of refugees from the war-torn southern states. The arrival of Civil War refugees caused many of the citizens of Belize to see new and promising possibilities for the future of the colony. The first known southerner to immigrate to British Honduras was an Episcopal priest, the Reverend R. Dawson, who, along with his entire family, arrived in early 1861. It is not known why Dawson left Mobile, Alabama, but he welcomed and advised many of his fellow countrymen as they arrived in the colony seeking refuge.[8] Dawson assumed a position of great prominence in the colony and is mentioned quite often in the correspondence of early arrivals in Belize City. He served as a driving force in the initial efforts to recruit Southerners to the colony. His prominence, however, diminished quickly, and he was replaced by more aggressive and outspoken men.

Other émigrés followed Dawson as the continued demise of the Confederate states brought great suffering throughout the war-torn South. Many white Southerners found themselves unable to protect or support their families as the Union armies, under the leadership of generals Ulysses S. Grant and William T. Sherman, burned and destroyed communities throughout the South. Desolate and demoralized, many began to seek refuge outside of the Confederacy. Boatloads of refugees followed Dawson and other early emigrants to British Honduras, Brazil, Mexico, Venezuela, and Cuba. Evidence suggests that perhaps as many as 16–18 percent of the families in the South considered leaving their homeland during the final years of the war.[9]

British Honduras eventually became one of the most popular destinations of Southerners in search of sanctuary from the perils of war. According to Charles A. Leas, American consul to British Honduras, Texans began to arrive in increasing numbers during the spring and summer of 1864. Leas reported to his superiors that many arrivals were declaring that the Confederacy was lost and expressing much resentment toward the U.S. government. Many planned to remain in the colony and establish cotton cultivation operations. Leas also informed Washington that some were in the interior seeking lands upon which to locate in early March of that year.

Leas makes no mention in 1864 of any Southerners other than Texans arriving from Matamoros before the war's end. Reports reaching the American consul's office suggested that there were thousands more in Texas who were trying to find passage to Belize City but they were held captive by the Union blockade. Leas indicated to his superiors that perhaps they should be allowed to flee since they were "not worth having as citizens and residents."[10]

Since none of the official consular reports make reference to specific numbers of arrivals in British Honduras, one can only speculate as to how many Confederate refugees arrived during this period or how many actually remained in the colony at the war's close. At least two Southerners had established soon-to-be successful sugar plantations north of Belize City as early as 1865.[11] They were probably in the minority as most went on to seek lands further south or returned home. Thus, no

A Baton Rouge family and their slaves comb through the rubble of a once-elegant home. More than a third of Baton Rouge was destroyed by Federal troops during the conquest and subsequent occupation of the capital city. (Photograph courtesy Andrew D. Lytle Collection, Mss. 893, 1254, Louisiana and Lower Mississippi Valley Collections, LSU Libraries, Baton Rouge, Louisiania)

communities of Southerners of any significant size existed in British Honduras in 1865.

Lee's surrender heralded a new era for the destitute South. An air of optimism swept through the southern United States. The hope of an amicable reconciliation turned many former rebels from thoughts of escape to the more pressing business of Reconstruction. Despite advertising campaigns on the part of those promoting Brazil and Mexico, Presidential Reconstruction under President Andrew Johnson was still a more acceptable alternative for most Southerners than leaving their homes for a foreign land. Instead of being tried as traitors, former belligerents not covered under the amnesty proclamation were granted pardons in very generous numbers by President Johnson, a fellow Southerner from the state of Tennessee. An average of one hundred pardons a day were granted by the president during the month of September 1865.[12]

Under Presidential Reconstruction, voters in Louisiana, Mississippi, and other southern states elected former Confederates in large numbers to local, state, and national offices. Lawmakers in several southern states wore Confederate uniforms while carrying out their official duties as representatives of the various state governments. In Mississippi, there was even debate regarding whether or not the American flag was to be raised above the state capitol in Jackson.[13] "Black Codes" were passed in the southern states that, for all practical purposes, reduced freedmen to a status comparable to slavery. For a very brief period until December 1865, when southern representatives to Congress were denied entry to the U.S. House of Representatives, it appeared as though things might not change so much in the southern states. Rather quickly, however, Southerners began to view themselves as outcasts in their own land and dominated, at least in their eyes, by their despised former enemy.

The change in national policy occurred soon after Republicans won the congressional elections of 1866. During the latter part of 1867 and throughout 1868, "Radical Reconstruction" was implemented by the Republican Congress, prompting the "era of group migration" to British Honduras and Brazil.[14] Radical Reconstruction appeared to be the beginning of the end for any hope of self-government for the still rebellious-at-heart white Southerners, who had no intention of being reconstructed. They watched in horror as President Johnson was forced to defend himself before impeachment proceedings, and to the consternation of many white citizens throughout the South, blacks were being registered as voters and elected to public office. Mississippians, in the fall of 1867, were represented by Blanche K. Bruce, a black man, in the U.S. Senate, a thought unimaginable just a few years prior.[15]

The carpetbaggers, Northerners who went to the South after the war, and scalawags, southern Republicans in control of the southern legislatures, enacted laws and increased taxes in such a manner that many former Confederates believed that achieving economic and social prosperity was no longer a possibility. With an estimated 10–15 percent of the potential white electorate disenfranchised through Reconstruction legislation and a large portion apathetic, the former Confederates faced what many felt were unbearable conditions.[16]

B. R. Duval of Virginia, founder of New Richmond, British Honduras, later described his situation in 1866:

> Soon after the surrender, I went to work and fixed up the saw mill, and hoped that at current rates, I might yet be able to save lumber enough to pay out. But lumber soon fell to a price not sufficient to pay expenses; and as soon as I saw this, I went to a most honorable lawyer, and asked him to make a deed of the most equitable character, and sell me out, for the benefit of my creditors. This was done, and we received only the allowance made by law to insolvent debtors.
>
> This was in May, 1866, and I was at a loss to know what to do. I could hear of no place where I could be supported, as a preacher, and my presiding elder told me that he knew not what to advise, as the times were such that he hardly knew how to advise himself.
>
> About this time, I had seen accounts in papers of a settlement of Southern people in Mexico.[17]

Charles Swett of Vicksburg, Mississippi, who traveled to British Honduras in 1866 for the purpose of locating lands for settlement, expressed similar sentiments that same year:

> It is regretted that the time of improvement in our circumstances is in the dim and distant future; so far, indeed, that we are unable to penetrate the gloom by which we are surrounded, and through which there is scarcely a gleam of light to direct us on our way. The work of the people in recuperating their condition after such losses as we have sustained, in a financial point of view only, must necessarily be slow, and require time for consummation; but with us it can be safely said there is no foundation on which to build.[18]

Most of the Southerners who eventually arrived in British Honduras found themselves in situations similar to that of Duval and Swett at the end of the war.

In spite of the difficult circumstances faced by most white Southerners, leaving the country was not popularly accepted by former compatriots or the southern press. Individuals who left were often ridiculed by former colleagues in arms for "fleeing like a common criminal."[19] The Jackson, Mississippi, *Daily Clarion* wrote, "It would be a blessing to our own land and useful to themselves, if the restless spirits, but lazy bodies, which are always complaining and fault finding, but never doing anything, should go to Brazil or Honduras."[20] The New Orleans *Daily Picayune* reflected the same sentiment as it requested that those with "Honduras on the brain" give up their "highly chivalric" disposition and help the South recover what had been lost.[21]

Union troops arriving in New Orleans with a demand for the surrender of the city were greeted with jeers and insults. Many citizens of New Orleans after the occupation of the city by Union forces refused to take an oath of allegiance to the United States. Some immediately departed for Mexico, eventually making their way to British Honduras. The illustration was originally published in 1862 as part of the Pictorial History of the American Civil War. (*Courtesy Frank and Marie-Therese Wood Print Collections, Alexandria, Virginia*)

Robert E. Lee, Jefferson Davis, P. G. T. Beauregard, and many other prominent former Confederate leaders called for submission to the U.S. government. Davis, former president of the Confederate States of America, in a letter to General Colin J. McRae, a fellow Mississippian and former Confederate financial agent in Europe, spoke of his deep regret that McRae would consider settling in a foreign land. He argued that a man of such talent was needed at home. General McRae's own brother, John J. McRae, a former governor of the state of Mississippi, also urged him to return to the United States.[22] Despite all efforts to stop the accelerating exodus, however, McRae and other Southerners ignored these requests and warnings from friends and family to begin the search for new homes abroad.

Jefferson Davis, former president of the Confederate States of America. (Courtesy Mississippi Department of Archives and History)

The era of group migration to British Honduras occurred at a time when Mexico, the early favorite for Confederate emigrants, was no longer considered a viable alternative. Many high-ranking Confederate officials had fled to Mexico after Lee's surrender only to find themselves in the midst of a civil war in that country. Within a year of their arrival, Southerners found that conditions had changed severely; the political situation in Mexico made it inhospitable for further immigration. Since most Confederates in Mexico had collaborated with Emperor Maximilian, who was executed by Benito Juárez in 1867, they were forced to flee or face severe retributions, including, possibly, death. A few did remain in Mexico, but the majority returned to the South.[23] Others made their way to British Honduras, the new haven for Confederates.

The failures of colonization attempts in Mexico were widely publicized throughout the United States and surely discouraged many who were considering a similar course of action. The *New York Times* reveled at the failures and proclaimed that it was "very glad to see the fact."[24] Newspapers throughout the South regularly reported political and military events in Mexico along with accounts of the "unheard of sufferings" experienced by former citizens.[25] Anti-emigrationists used such stories to dissuade others who were considering colonization efforts abroad.

Nevertheless, British Honduras and Brazil replaced Mexico by 1867 as the preferred destinations of emigrants. Accounts of the efforts to colonize Brazil and the undeniable successes of the cotton-producing Confederados (a term used to refer to the Confederate exiles of Brazil) are well known and have been widely publicized in the popular media in recent years. Surprisingly, little has been written about similar efforts in British Honduras where the potential for sugar production became the catalyst for immigration. Perhaps as many as seven thousand Southerners, a figure much higher than once estimated, may have arrived in Belize City during and after the war.[26] Such a large exodus surely makes the tale of Confederate settlement in British Honduras equally as intriguing as the more well known Brazilian account.

Notes

1. Benjamin Keen, *A History of Latin America* (Boston: Houghton Mifflin, 1996), 24–29.

2. O. Nigel Bolland, *The Formation of a Colonial Society: Belize, from Conquest to Crown Colony* (Baltimore: Johns Hopkins University Press, 1977), 17–20.

3. William Donohoe, *A History of British Honduras* (Montreal: Provincial Publishing, 1946), 27–28; Bolland, 21, 25.

4. Bolland, 25, 27.

5. Allen Burns, *History of the British West Indies* (London: George Allen and Unwin, 1954), 503.

6. Wayne M. Clegern, *British Honduras: Colonial Dead End, 1859–1900* (Baton Rouge: Louisiana State University Press, 1967), 43.

7. *Ibid.*, 20–26, 30.

8. Lawrence F. Hill, *The Confederate Exodus to Latin America* (Columbus: Ohio State University, 1936), 79; Belize Colonial Secretary's Office, "Memorandum of Revd. R. Dawson's Service for Pension," 11 November 187?, Public Archives of Belize, 107R681.

9. Donna D. Krug, "The Enemy at the Door in the Confederacy: A Crisis of Honor," paper presented at the annual meeting of the Southern History Association, Lexington, Kentucky, 9 November 1989.

10. Dispatches from U.S. Consuls in Belize, C. A. Leas to W. A. Seward, No. 141, 1 April 1864, FM T-334 Roll 3.

11. Hill, 78.

12. James M. McPherson, *Ordeal by Fire: The Civil War and Reconstruction* (New York: Alfred A. Knopf, 1982), 502–5.

13. David G. Sansing, *Mississippi: Its People and Culture* (Minneapolis: T. S. Denison, 1981), 202.

14. Eugene C. Harter, *The Lost Colony of the Confederacy* (Jackson: University Press of Mississippi, 1985), 37.

15. John K. Bettersworth, *Mississippi: Yesterday and Today* (Austin, Texas: Steck-Vaughn, 1964), 230; Sansing, 210.

16. McPherson, 535.

17. B. R. Duval, *A Narrative of Life and Travels in Mexico and British Honduras* (Boston: W.F. Brown, 1881), 5–6.

18. Charles Swett, *A Trip to British Honduras and San Pedro, Republic of Honduras* (New Orleans: George Ellis, Bookseller and Stationer, 1868), 6–7.

19. Andrew F. Rolle, *The Lost Cause: The Confederate Exodus to Mexico* (Norman: University of Oklahoma Press, 1965), 8.

20. "Who Might Emigrate," *Daily Clarion* (Jackson, Mississippi), 19 May 1867, 3.

21. "The Failure of Southern Colonization," *Daily Picayune* (New Orleans), 13 February 1868, 2.

22. Charles S. Davis, *Colin J. McRae: Confederate Financial Agent* (Tuscaloosa, Alabama: Confederate Publishing, 1961), 83–85.

23. Rolle, 182–87.

24. "The Honduras Colony," *New York Times*, 12 July 1868, 4.

25. "Emigration to Foreign Lands," *Daily Picayune* (New Orleans), 20 December 1866, 1(M).

26. William Dunn, "The Lost Confederates," *Detroit News Magazine*, 13 December 1978, 8, 14, estimated that 7,000 "expatriates fled to Belize." This estimate is perhaps questionably high. United States consular reports estimated that 1,200 arrived between 1 June 1867 and 1 June 1869, yet while published colonial reports of U.S. bound departures from the colony almost always match U.S. consular reports and primary sources, arrivals from the U.S., as reported by colonial officials and the U.S. consul, are typically under-reported. In some instances, shiploads of arrivals went unreported, an indication that colonial officials were intentionally concealing the information from U.S. officials.

CHAPTER II

Lure of the British Flag

The Victorian Age (1837–1901), during which Great Britain attained its "pinnacle of wealth and power," was a period of rapid decline for the British colonies of the West Indies and Caribbean.[1] The abolition of slavery, the emergence of free trade, and declining mahogany prices devastated the colonies of the region. The importance of England's colonies in America was overshadowed by developments in other parts of the expanding British Empire.

In response to economic decline in the Caribbean, the British initiated a consolidation of administrative responsibilities in an effort to cut costs. The Turks and Caicos Islands were established as a colony in 1848, as was the settlement at Belize in 1862. These moves were followed in 1871 by the inclusion of Antigua and Dominica in the Leeward Islands colony.[2] The reorganization not only reduced overall operating expenses, it also reduced the number of representatives of the Crown in the region. British Honduras, as a result, was now administered by a lieutenant governor who was subordinate to the governor of Jamaica. Limited self-rule was maintained in most colonies unless the situation required other arrangements. The Crown essentially avoided involvement in the affairs of the colonies of the West Indies and Caribbean during this period. The push for economic revitalization, as a result, was left to the inhabitants of the various colonies.[3]

Citizens of British Honduras who longed for economic revitalization observed events in the United States immediately following the Civil War with considerable interest. Most believed an influx of ex–Confederates to the colony would save them from economic ruin and, if numbers were great, set a course toward self-government. Lieutenant governor John Austin and several wealthy landowners spoke to the U.S. consular agent concerning such prospects on several occasions once it appeared the Confederacy was lost. Emigrants knowledgeable through years of experience in planting cotton, sugar, and tobacco were most desired by the colonial establishment. The hope was that the large tracts of cutover mahogany lands throughout the colony might be transformed by educated and industrious people into profitable plantations.[4] Desiring immigrants and getting them to settle in British Honduras would, however, prove to be two different matters entirely. Two factors inhibited the immigration of ex–Confederates: transportation barriers and exorbitant land prices.

Roads leading deep into the interior were virtually nonexistent. The rapid growth of underbrush made all road building and maintenance difficult and expensive. Efforts to establish roads were encouraged by the Crown, but financial assistance was rarely furnished. The few roads that existed were found near new settlements and led either to rivers or the coast. Officials understood the importance of roads to the interior, but little was done to improve conditions.

Travel overland by horse or wagon was not only tedious but also very expensive. Accounts of Southerners exploring the countryside rarely speak of overland travel. Water transportation, which proved to be much cheaper and quicker, was preferred by almost all even though floods, rapids, waterfalls, and rocks occasionally disrupted trade and communications. Travel by boat was the preferred conveyance for those searching for new homes in the interior of the colony.[5] Families that did eventually settle some distance from Belize City almost universally built homes near navigable waters.

Transportation to the colony itself became a popular topic of discussion at the close of the Civil War, as there was no regular steamship service before 1866 between Belize City and the United States. Early in that year, William S. Cary, who would eventually become a citizen of British Honduras, left Attakapas, Louisiana, where he had served as a corporal in the Confederate Army. He began preparations in New Orleans for the establishment of a regular steamship service from the port of New Orleans to Belize City.[6] His efforts were well received at both ends of the proposed route. Newspapers reported his actions with regularity as interest in his venture increased:

> We clipped the following from the *Planters' Banner*, Attakapas, Louisiana: When in the city lately, we met our old friend W. S. Cary, Esq., formerly of this parish, now a resident of Belize Honduras [*sic*]. Mr. Cary was one of our most active business men, enterprising, accommodating, and useful. He will create business wherever he goes. Few men of his means, which are extremely limited, could make themselves so useful in building up a new business point as Mr. Cary. He is untiring in his energies, and will patiently endure any amount of labor or fatigue to accomplish a worthy object. He is just the man for Belize Honduras.[7]

It is not known how Cary came to be interested in British Honduras or where he acquired his financial resources, but he established himself in an office on Carondelet Street in New Orleans. From there he addressed inquiries daily regarding trade, transport, lands, and other topics relating to the colony.[8] He apparently had quite a clientele as he purchased a half-interest in the steamer *Extract*, a vessel of considerable size at 288.6 tons, and soon made arrangements for regular transport service from New Orleans to Belize City. The steamer had been used previously by the U.S. Quartermaster Department during the Civil War before it was sold to private owners in March 1866.[9]

Under the most favorable weather conditions Cary hoped the voyage from New Orleans to Belize City could be completed in four days and in no more than two weeks during the hurricane season or other adverse weather.[10] He hoped that the short voyage would keep costs low, as well as provide numerous other advantages. After discharging emigrants and cargo arriving from New Orleans, the ship could be laden in Belize City with a cargo of tropical fruits, which would remain fresh during a short return, thus providing additional profits. British Hondurans, once news of the service to New Orleans was made public, were excited about the possibility of enjoying goods from New Orleans, which could be obtained much more cheaply than from other ports, as well as the new market for exports from the colony. Information, newspapers, and the mail might be received much faster than from New York or more distant ports. All of these positive attributes would, in turn, induce more Southerners to settle in the colony.[11]

Unfortunately for Cary and his investors, the venture would face numerous difficulties and was ultimately doomed to failure. After departing from New Orleans on her maiden voyage from New Orleans to Belize City in 1866, the ship encountered a terrible storm that lasted for four days, probably an early season hurricane. The storm caused much damage, including the total destruction of the rudder. Captain S. B. Caldwell and the ship's crew worked for three days outfitting a temporary rudder while the craft drifted in the Caribbean. With the temporary repairs finally complete, the captain and crew managed to guide the craft safely to the harbor at Havana, Cuba, where it was properly fixed. The voyage resumed a few days later, and the *Extract* arrived in Belize City on 11 July 1866.

The colony welcomed the steamship on that Tuesday morning with an air of great anticipation. Cary had not only managed to secure a regular shipping and transport service to Belize City, he also carried a number of Southerners hoping to make the colony their new home.[12] Contrary to the hopes of all concerned, however, this would be the last successful voyage of Cary's vessel. The *Extract*, on its second voyage, was wrecked when driven by heavy gales onto a coral reef near Mauger Kaye, British Honduras. Cary, who was not fully insured, was forced to abandon his attempt at establishing a regular transport service from New Orleans to Belize City. The vessel was eventually scrapped and sold piecemeal at public auction in Belize City.[13]

In spite of the much-celebrated (at the time) and tragic drama of William Cary's ship, the episode became a long-forgotten part of Belizean colonial history and has been overlooked by scholars. Yet, not only was the *Extract* the first regular transportation from the United States to British Honduras, it also carried a passenger who would forever transform the colony. James Mercier Putnam would in due time initiate efforts to bring thousands of Southerners to British Honduras. His exploits in the colony will be discussed later in greater detail.

High land prices, the other major barrier to southern immigration, troubled the colonial leadership more than transportation difficulties. For example, soon after the war, a Louisiana planter representing fifty families arrived for the purpose of purchasing land for a settlement. He apparently received a great deal of attention in the colony from those excited about the prospect of such a large influx of immigrants. After searching for some time throughout the British possession, he was astonished to find that the going rate for arable land was $5 an acre. After finding no relief from high land prices from the Crown, he eventually settled in Spanish Honduras.[14] Public lands were offered free to settlers in Spanish Honduras, and in Brazil, land sold for twenty-two cents per acre.[15] He was neither the first nor the last to arrive and after much consideration settle elsewhere. British Hondurans, fearing a great opportunity for the colony would be lost if action were not swiftly taken, called upon the legislative assembly and the governor to take steps to encourage immigration. The Crown and a small group of individuals who controlled most of the land were soon resented by the majority of the general public for their refusal to reduce land costs. This was apparently a common occurrence in Britain's American colonies. Land grants to "favourites of government," who were often nothing more than land speculators, were typical and much criticized. In fact, even the disposal of public lands for the expansion of new settlements in British Honduras was reserved, first and foremost, for Englishmen.[16]

Early in 1866, however, public pressure and the absence of purchasers forced some of the "selfish and unpatriotic" landowners to make symbolic gestures in the reduction of agricultural land prices.[17] Some immigrants were able to purchase land which had been cleared of mahogany for as little as thirty cents per acre.[18] Despite some decline in land prices in particular areas of the colony, however, the best lands along the coast and near navigable waterways still sold for a high premium.

Whereas prior to 1866, Southerners were given little more than an audience with the lieutenant governor, every effort was made to induce those arriving via the *Extract* to remain in the colony. In fact, the lieutenant governor placed the schooner *Aurora* along with the Crown surveyor, J. H. Faber, at their disposal. These actions were favorably received by the general populace of the colony. On their journey through the interior, the group of prospective immigrants inspected lands along every major waterway.[19]

The efforts of the Crown proved successful, in part. Two of the five men remained in the colony. The "enormous" price of land, generally around $5 per acre, still stood in the way of progress. At least two of the three who chose not to settle in British Honduras did so as a result of these land costs. Their plight received a great deal of notice from the colonial press in Belize City. The *Colonist*, a newspaper in Belize City, reported that one member of the group, a Mr. Arnut (also Arnoult), left the colony claiming that he had been deceived.[20] The newspaper also reported that Gabriel Laclaire Fuselier, who originated from the same Louisiana parish as William Cary, found relief from British Honduran land prices in the republic of Guatemala. The failure to recruit Fuselier, a highly respected member of Louisiana's prewar political machine and a senatorial delegate to the state's secession convention, was particularly devastating to the early colonization efforts. Several reports stated that many Southerners, including Fuselier, had settled in Guatemala near the border of British Honduras on good land purchased at nominal prices, despite concerns for personal safety. It was generally believed by colonists that Fuselier and other Southerners in Guatemala remained close to British territory so that protection would be available in the event of conflict or Indian uprising, both common at the time in neighboring countries.[21]

Arnut and Fuselier were used by those promoting emigration to British Honduras as examples of the foolishness often exhibited by the Crown. It was apparent to colonists that knowledgeable and experienced individuals who possessed capital were passing over British Honduras. The lure of the British flag was being obscured by the lack of reliable transportation and the high cost of land. Some citizens of the colony expressed outrage that the Crown, which did "not know the extent or limit of its land," would refuse to accommodate potential settlers while vast sections of the Crown's real estate lay undeveloped.[22]

The citizens of British Honduras who opposed the government's land policies felt betrayed by the Crown. It had been hoped that those immigrants arriving on the *Extract* would serve as a nucleus for agricultural settlements throughout the countryside. Others would naturally follow, allowing the colony to benefit from revenue collected, increasing trade, and a resulting demand for labor. The wreck of the *Extract* combined with frustration over land policies led to heightened criticism of the Crown. The *Colonist* lamented the loss of so many potential settlers:

> Thus the Colony suffers, although abounding in land more than sufficient for the requirement of its owners, laying waste and of no service. Can we be surprised at the backwardness or slow progress of British Honduras? Can any person resident and being cognisant [sic] of the tenure of the rich and fertile soil thus running waste, express astonishment? The astonishing and surprising part is, that the Crown remains content in its ignorance of what really has never been disposed of by it, resting (we assert iniquitously) satisfied that it never loses its right. The monopoly of land is, and will continue to be, the bane of the Colony — and until all the questions respecting and anent [sic] thereto, are fairly and honestly settled, we must continue to suffer.[23]

Other newspaper accounts also lamented the fact that Southerners would forgo a haven possessing the same language and customs as their native land for Portuguese-speaking Brazil. Not only were the colony's lands thought to be superior to Brazilian territory, but Brazil was also six times the distance from New Orleans.[24] A comparative analysis of the advantages of settling in Brazil versus British Honduras will be addressed in the final chapter.

Notes

1. Alan Burns, *History of the British West Indies* (London: George Allen and Unwin, 1954), 651.
2. *Ibid.*, 657–59.
3. *Ibid.*, 659.
4. Dispatches from U.S. Consuls in Belize, C. A. Leas to W. A. Seward, No. 141, 1 April 1864, FM T-334 Roll 3; "The Question of Opening Out Roads," *Colonist* (British Honduras), 10 March 1866, 3.
5. "The American News," *Colonist* (British Honduras), 5 August 1865, 2; "The Question of Opening Out Roads," 3.
6. C. D. [Christopher Hempstead], "British Honduras," *Daily Picayune* (New Orleans), 28 July 1866, 1(A); for information regarding Cary's service record or those of other Louisiana Confederates, refer to *Records of Louisiana Confederate Soldiers and Louisiana Confederate Commands*, comp. Andrew B. Booth (New Orleans: Louisiana Commissioner of Military Records, 1920).

7. "We Clipped...," *Colonist* (British Honduras), 25 August 1866, 6.

8. "Trade with Honduras," *Daily Picayune* (New Orleans), 9 March 1866, 2(M).

9. *Ships Registers and Enrollments of New Orleans, Louisiana*, prepared by the Survey of Federal Archives in Louisiana (WPA) (University, Louisiana: Hill Memorial Library, 1942), vol. 6 (1860–1870), 90. Previous scholarly works have failed to recognize the *Extract* as the first vessel to offer regular service to Belize City from New Orleans. The vessel sank during its second voyage; however, this was the first real effort to establish regular communication between the two cities.

10. "Trade with Honduras," 2(M).

11. "In Our Last Week's Issue...," *Colonist* (British Honduras), 21 April 1866, 2; "Rumors and Future Prospects," *Colonist*, 23 June 1866, 6; "The Steamer Extract," *Colonist*, 25 August 1866, 3.

12. T. E. Williams and others, "A Card," *Colonist* (British Honduras), 14 July 1866, 2; "On Monday Evening," *Colonist*, 14 July 1866, 3, 6.

13. C. D. [Christopher Hempstead], "Notice," *Colonist* (British Honduras), 25 August 1866, 2.

14. "There Never Was a More Favorable Opportunity...," *Colonist* (British Honduras), 24 June 1865, 2; "British Honduras," *Colonist*, 16 December 1865, 2; "We Anticipated...," *Colonist*, 23 December 1865, 2.

15. Swett, 106; Harter, 14.

16. C. E. Carrington, *The British Overseas: Exploits of a Nation of Shopkeepers* (Cambridge: Cambridge University Press, 1950), 349.

17. "British Honduras," *Colonist* (British Honduras), 16 December 1865, 2; "We Anticipated," 2.

18. Dispatches from U.S. Consuls in Belize, A. C. Prindle to W. A. Seward, 6 March 1868, No. 22, FM T-334 Roll 3.

19. "On Monday...," *Colonist* (British Honduras), 4 August 1866, 2; "We Understand...," *Colonist*, 21 July 1866, 2–3.

20. "It Is with Extreme Regret...," *Colonist* (British Honduras), 1 September 1866, 2–3; C. D. [Christopher Hempstead], "From Belize, Honduras," *Daily Picayune* (New Orleans), 14 June 1867, 1(A); "Journal of State Convention," *Louisiana History* 2, no.1 (1961), 3–5.

21. "It Is with More Than Regret...," *Colonist* (British Honduras), 13 October 1866, 2–3.

22. *Ibid.*

23. *Ibid.*, 1–2.

24. "The American News," *Colonist* (British Honduras), 5 August 1865, 2.

CHAPTER III

Era of Group Migration to British Honduras

In an effort to quell criticism and attract Confederate settlers to the colony, the lieutenant governor and the legislative assembly of British Honduras developed a more marketable and palatable alternative to their demand of $5 per acre for agricultural land. The scheme apparently worked because almost overnight, those who had been their most outspoken critics began singing their praises. Instead of requiring payment for lands before settlement, as had been the standard practice in the colony prior to that time, the colonial government announced its intent to "give land" in various amounts to settlers for five years. The condition for land ownership was that upon completion of the five years in residence, the settler would be obligated to pay $1 per acre per year for the next five years. Southern immigrants arriving in Belize City after 1866, under the delayed payment option, enjoyed the luxury of living on land at no expense for the first five years of residence in the colony. Such an alternative was extremely enticing for families with little or no resources. Capital could be used for the commencement of planting operations rather than for the purchase of land. The Crown, meanwhile, still received the required $5 an acre.[1]

One of the early outspoken proponents of reduced land prices was Christopher Hempstead, an American who had lived in Belize City for several years and was a well-respected resident. Hempstead, after serving as U.S. consul at Belize during the administration of President James K. Polk (1845–1849), remained in the colony and became a British subject. He made no secret of his pro–Southern sentiment during the Civil War nor of his desire to attract Confederate immigrants at the war's conclusion.[2] A respected and well-known member of the colony's business community, Hempstead was known for his passionately critical discourse regarding land prices in the colony.[3] Once the Crown resolved the land question, he turned his attention to the business of luring fellow Southerners to British Honduras. Less than one month after the Crown announced the more liberal land policy, Hempstead withdrew as one of the most vocal critics of the Crown to become one of its most ardent supporters.

Letters from Christopher Hempstead began to appear in Louisiana newspapers in July 1866. Addressing primarily sugar planters, he argued that planters could no longer expect to make a living in the United States. British Honduras would now be the place for sugar planters from Louisiana and Texas. The following is an excerpt from one such letter:

> But even admitting, for argument sake, (which I can not believe is correct,) that what you say is true, viz: That there are no causes for the old sugar planters to leave the United States, and that in "your great and good country" there is room and opportunity for industrious persons to make fortunes and to do as they formerly did under the old state of affairs, what chance has a sugar planter in the United States to make a fortune, or even a living, at sugar making now? With an excise duty of three cents a pound on all he makes, and with enormous taxes on all he eats, drinks or wears, and with only five or six weeks to take off his crops—which he has to plant every year—compared to this colony where planting will suffice for ten years, and where the tenth crop will produce a better cane, giving a larger yield of saccharine matter than any crop in Louisiana or Texas under the most favorable circumstance.[4]

He also spoke of the ease with which "a gentleman" might establish himself in the colony. For example, he stated that on payment of $16, one could become a naturalized British subject. Moreover, agricultural goods necessary for sugar cultivation, he reported, were admitted duty free. The government of British Honduras was as "liberal as any in the world."[5]

Hempstead's vivid descriptions of the colony's wealth and advantages attracted the attention of many frustrated sugar farmers in the war-torn states of Louisiana and Mississippi. During the later years of the Civil War, General Benjamin F. Butler's occupying army had initiated policies that transformed slaves on Louisiana sugar plantations into wage laborers and leased abandoned plantations to northern investors.[6] High rates of interest, tremendous increases in taxes, and increasing labor costs were prevalent, particularly in the sugar-producing states of the lower Mississippi Delta region following the war. Carpetbaggers and large corporations replaced many Southerners as the owners of the larger sugar-producing estates after 1865.[7] Southern planters began to seek new opportunities as their businesses failed and creditors foreclosed on mortgaged property. The correspondence of Hempstead and others in British Honduras sent through newspapers and to individuals found a growing and increasingly receptive audience as the severity of Congressional Reconstruction policies was realized. The promise of free land for five years under the protection of the British flag was an irresistible proposition for someone inextricably in debt. As conditions worsened for the former Confederates in the fall of 1866, the era of group migration began for British Honduras.

Promoting the colony would have had little effect, however, if regular communication with New Orleans had not resumed. The wreck of the *Extract* in 1866 forced would-be immigrants to embark upon the difficult and expensive task of chartering a vessel in order to reach the colony. There remained little hope of a large influx of Southerners under such conditions.

James M. Putnam, one of the passengers who arrived via the *Extract*, was the first to endeavor to renew ties to New Orleans. Before the Civil War, Putnam operated as a businessman in New Orleans, primarily in the cotton trade. He achieved some notoriety during the war when he set fire in 1862 to the large supply of cotton and sugar warehoused in New Orleans rather than allow Union forces to seize it. When he was captured, still in possession of the order to destroy the cotton, Colonel Putnam was sent to a federal prison. From that point until his arrival in British Honduras and residence on Ambergris Cay, his activities remain unknown.[8]

Putnam returned to New Orleans from Belize City as an agent of colonial businessmen and enticed the owners of the steamer *General Sherman* to allow it to sail to British Honduras in an attempt to reestablish service to that port. Putnam and agents of the vessel arrived at Belize City aboard the steamer in March 1867. They spoke to the inhabitants and merchants of Belize City about the possibility of a government subsidy to establish regular steamer service. Putnam stated in a public meeting that present conditions in the United States were such that there was a considerable desire among the "industrious classes" in Louisiana and surrounding states for emigration. He argued that if a regular transportation service were available, large numbers would settle in the colony. Those present at the meeting were receptive to Putnam's proposal, and a request was sent to Lieutenant Governor Austin and the house of assembly for the appropriation of money for a contract service to New Orleans.[9] The assembly would not meet until the first of May, however, so no official action could be taken.

The agent of the *General Sherman* informed the residents of the port that the ship would not return in May unless the sum of $2,500 was guaranteed. He also remarked that an annual subsidy of $30,000 would be necessary to secure year-round service. In addition to the subsidy, passage each

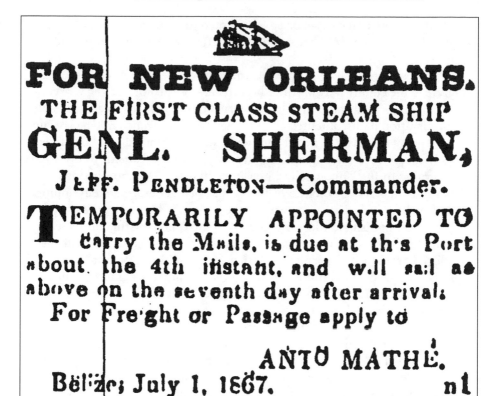

FOR NEW ORLEANS.
THE FIRST CLASS STEAM SHIP
GENL. SHERMAN,
JEFF. PENDLETON—Commander.

TEMPORARILY APPOINTED TO carry the Mails, is due at th's Port about the 4th instant, and will sail as above on the seventh day after arrival. For Freght or Passage apply to

ANTO MATHE.

Belize; July 1, 1867.   n1

The Commercial Adviser, *a British Honduran newspaper, closely followed the activities of the* General Sherman *as well as the passengers it delivered to the colony. Advertisements promoting the new steamship service from New Orleans to Belize City were prominently featured in the publication during the summer of 1867.*

way would be $50 in gold. Freight charges would be $1.50 for dry barrels and $2 for wet barrels. Believing agricultural immigrants were the key to the colony's future economic success and fearing the continued lack of such service to New Orleans, the merchants of Belize City collectively paid the $2,500. The decision to pay the *General Sherman* had been a hasty move, however, one they would soon regret.

Regular steamship service did begin in mid–1867, but it was the *Trade Wind*, not the *General Sherman*, that received the contract. The *Trade Wind* of New Orleans, which underbid the *General Sherman*, agreed to carry passengers and the mail for $20,000 annually, two-thirds of the original sum requested by the *General Sherman*. Under the contract, in addition to the subsidy paid by the colonial government, passage aboard the *Trade Wind* was set at $40 in gold, $10 less than the fare demanded by the *General*

Sherman. The latter vessel briefly attempted to compete without the subsidy, but withdrew by August 1867 after attracting few passengers and little cargo.[10]

Putnam's prognostications regarding the desire of Southerners to emigrate to the colony were apparently correct. A. C. Prindle, acting vice consul for the United States in Belize, reported in August 1867 "a considerable immigration of discontented citizens" now that the *Trade Wind* had begun its regular rounds. He noted that with each docking came about thirty individuals extremely hostile toward the U.S. government. Many were returning to the United States, however, disappointed and discontented. No settlements nor colonies of the former belligerents were developing, and he believed, despite reports to the contrary, that only a few would remain in British Honduras.[11] Lieutenant governor Austin and the colonial assembly also were becoming increasingly concerned that despite their efforts, permanent agricultural settlements would not be established. A large sum of colonial funds, including the subsidy for regular steam service, had been invested in a venture which did not as yet appear to be producing the desired results.

In a bold move to ensure successful settlement of the colony and deter further criticism, the lieutenant governor entered into a contractual agreement with James Putnam and four other Southerners. In exchange for a large grant of Crown land the individuals would recruit Southerners to settle the colony. Under the terms of the contract, signed in July 1867, Putnam, along with David Walker Foster, William Abel Howard, Maunsel White Chapman, and Robert Lears Weir, agreed to introduce fifty planters and laborers along with their families into the colony within two years and at least two hundred other persons within five years. Putnam and his associates were to settle immigrants on the lands given to them by the Crown or on other "lands within the said district or region." Failure to introduce the specified number of settlers as agreed under the terms of the contract would make the grant null and void.

The grant of land, known as the Icacos Grant, included all unclaimed property bordered on the north by the Monkey River and or the parallel of north latitude 16°33', on the south by a straight line from Point Icacos (Ycacos) to the mouth of the Deep River, and then up the river to the north latitude 16°20'. The borders to the west and east were the Guatemala border and the Atlantic Ocean, respectively.[12] The Crown did, however, reserve the rights to minerals and use of all navigable bodies of water.

The colonial press immediately applauded Lieutenant Governor Austin for his efforts to colonize the country, but it was rumored that he did not receive such favorable reviews from private landowners in the colony, land speculators, and his superiors in London. Her Majesty's colonial and foreign secretaries were quoted in the colonial newspapers as having immediately reprimanded him for the act which was "disapproved, and is at an end." Lieutenant Governor Austin was soon recalled, reportedly as a result of his actions.[13] The *British Honduras Colonist and Belize Advertiser* defended the actions of Austin:

> We know not what are the limits placed on the Lieutenant Governor's authority in the granting of lands, but we presume his power is extensive as that conceded to Colonel McDonald and his Successors Superintendents of the Colony; and if such be the case, then his authority to confer grants on behalf of the Crown can not be fairly called in question; and we wish all grants made had been as much for the benefit of the colony as the one to which we have referred.[14]

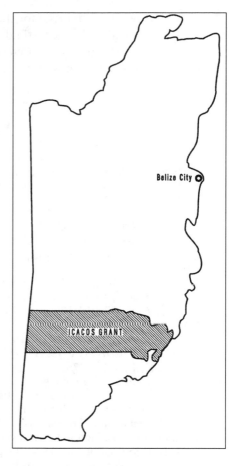

The Icacos Grant.

The legality of the right to confer land grants on behalf of the Crown, when questioned, was ultimately interpreted by the Crown in the same manner as it had been by the press. The Icacos Grant was recognized by Austin's successor, although the confusion over the 300,000-acre grant and its questionable legality troubled those contemplating settlement in the colony. News of the incident quickly spread throughout the United States.

Evidence suggests, and the reported rumors appear to confirm, that Austin was recalled as a result of the land grant. It is also likely, however, that the decision to recall Austin from the colony was also influenced by the failing colonial economy. The decline of mahogany prices on the world market had continued to devastate the colony.[15] Many colonists, especially landowners, had become increasingly critical of Austin and demanded action from officials in London. The timing of the change of administration was interpreted as a reprisal for the lieutenant governor's liberal grant of land. Landowners who were still determined to sell property at $5 an acre could not have been more pleased with Austin's removal. The unfortunate set of circumstances, however, dealt a severe blow to future settlement efforts.

Notes

1. C. D. [Christopher Hempstead], "British Honduras," *Daily Picayune* (New Orleans), 28 July 1866, 1(E); C. D., "British Honduras," *Daily Picayune*, 22 August, 1866, 1(E); Hempstead revealed his identity in the 17 September 1868 *Daily Picayune*.

2. Dispatches from U.S. Consuls in Belize, A. N. Miller to W. A. Seward, 3 September 1866, FM T-334 Roll 3.

3. "We Anticipated...," *Colonist* (British Honduras), 23 December 1865, 1; C. D. [Christopher Hempstead], "Belize, British Honduras," *Daily Picayune*, 7 July 1866, 1(E).

4. C. D. [Christopher Hempstead], "British Honduras," *Daily Picayune* (New Orleans), 22 August 1866, 1(A).

5. C. D., "British Honduras," *Daily Picayune* (New Orleans), 28 July 1866, 1(A).

6. John Mack Faragher, Maria Buhle, Daniel Czitrom, and Susan Armitage, *Out of Many: A History of the American People* (Upper Saddle River, New Jersey: Prentice Hall, 1997), 517.

7. Daniel G. Rosenberger, "An Examination of the Perpetuation of Southern United States Institutions in British Honduras by a Colony of Ex-Confederates," Ph.D. dissertation, New York University, 1958, 331–33.

8. *War of the Rebellion: Official Records of the Union and Confederate Armies*, ser. 1, 15:495 (Washington, D.C.: Government Printing Office, 1880–1901); Charles S. Dwight, Journal of Charles S. Dwight, 1867–1869, entry dated 21 April 1868, manuscript collection, South Caroliniana Library.

9. Minutes from "A Meeting of Merchants and Other Inhabitants of Belize Held in Mr. Cramer's House," 1? March 1867, Public Archives of Belize, 94R48. Putnam and Cary at some point became business partners and maintained a "commercial firm" until it was dissolved on 6 September 1867. A notice of dissolution by mutual consent was published in the 14 September 1867 issue of the *British Honduras Colonist and Belize Advertiser*. Putnam, Cary, and one other individual also purchased Ambergris Cay, now a major resort area.

10. C. D. [Christopher Hempstead], "From Belize, Honduras," *Daily Picayune*, 22 May 1867, 2(E); Dispatches from U.S. Consuls in Belize, A. C. Prindle to W. A. Seward, No. 1, 1 July 1867, FM T-334 Roll 3.

11. Dispatches from U.S. Consuls in Belize, A. C. Prindle to W. A. Seward, No. 2, 9 August 1867, FM T-334 Roll 3.

12. Letter written by Governor Robert Longdon to J. H. Faber, Crown surveyor, 16 August 1869, Public Archives of Belize, 107R349.

13. "Telegraphic Intelligence," *Mobile Sunday Times*, 27 October 1867, 3(M); Dispatches from U.S. Consuls in Belize, A. C. Prindle to W. A. Seward, No. 3,

1 October 1867, FM T-334 Roll 3; "Important," *British Honduras Colonist and Belize Advertiser*, 7 September 1867, 2.

14. "The Telegrams," *British Honduras Colonist and Belize Advertiser*, 14 September 1867, 2–3.

15. Wayne M. Clegern, *British Honduras: Colonial Dead End, 1859–1900* (Baton Rouge: Louisiana State University Press, 1967), 42–43.

CHAPTER IV

Making the Trek Southward

The process of leaving the United States was undertaken in various ways depending upon individual circumstances. For many it was a much-deliberated act that required planning for the relocation of an entire family including, in some instances, former black slaves. Other emigrants, of course, who were either single or perhaps wanted for war crimes gave the matter less forethought. There was no uniformity of wealth nor status among those seeking refuge in the British colony.

In preparation for the move, Southerners reviewed a barrage of often contradictory information about the British colony. Newspapers, magazines, flyers, and other publications circulated throughout the southern United States containing information of interest to potential immigrants. For example, the *Daily Picayune* published more than twenty letters written by either Christopher Hempstead or James Putnam between 1867 and 1869 that spoke favorably of the colony. T. C. Brewer, formerly of Alabama, B. R. Duval, formerly of Virginia, and many others also sent numerous pieces of correspondence to newspapers in their home states promoting the colony and predicting favorable future economic and political development. The following are the concluding remarks of one letter sent home to family in the United States:

> To sum it up: I claim for British Honduras, the following advantages over any of the central and South American countries:
>
> 1st. A stable government.
> 2. Entire freedom of speech, religion and of the press, and security of life and property.
> 3. A common language and common faith.
> 4. A system of labor already established, which needs only to be turned into different channels.
> 5. A country more open and less encumbered with dense tropical vegetation.

6. The fact that it is one of the healthiest, if not the very healthiest locality on the Atlantic seaboard.
7. Speedy and easy communication with Europe and the U.S. and a ready market for produce; steamers now run regularly once a month to New Orleans, and bring over crowds of prospecting Southerners, each trip.[1]

The letter, written by Maunsel Chapman, formerly of New Orleans, clearly outlines the major topics addressed in correspondence to potential settlers.

Although not mentioned in the preceding quotation, the price and or availability of land was also a topic addressed in most correspondence and publications. Reports varied considerably even within the same newspaper. The availability of game, the beauty of the wilderness, navigable waterways, and the attractiveness of Belize City were also often discussed. Descriptions of the fertile soil and the ease of agricultural pursuits typically followed such discourse. Almost all correspondence warned, however, that despite the potential for financial success under these conditions, those not willing to engage in manual labor should stay home. Potential settlers were also warned not to come to British Honduras without sufficient resources to survive at least a year, a warning often ignored.

Once established in the colony, many of the same individuals sending correspondence home returned to their former communities in efforts to encourage neighbors and family to follow. Levi Pearce of the Toledo Settlement in southern British Honduras returned to Mississippi and Louisiana on several occasions to successfully recruit new settlers. Coffee, cane, cotton, tobacco, hemp, and rice from the colony were displayed throughout the southern United States. James Putnam became a regular exhibitor at the annual Louisiana State Fair in New Orleans. Putnam's display included, in addition to the agricultural products, several specimens of wood, minerals, and shells from the colony. The fair exhibit was apparently well received and attracted considerable attention from attendees.[2] Putnam used the exhibits to promote his own efforts to relocate Southerners. The event became increasingly popular and as such served as an excellent forum for promoting the colony. Newspapers in British Honduras published reactions to the display of their produce and goods. The *British Honduras Colonist and Belize Advertiser* reprinted the following article, originally published in the *New Orleans Times*:

> State Fair–British Honduras.— The products of British Honduras, now on exhibition at the Fair Grounds, are attractive and worthy of notice. The sugar is of enormous size. Planters should see it. Beside[s] specimens of coffee, rice, Sisal hemp, tobacco and tropical fruits, there are over

sixty varieties of native wood, all valuable and all worth seeing. Go and
see them. ...

Much interest was manifested at the display of the productions of
British Honduras—a subject now attracting great attention in the Southern United States. This collection is very complete, and we shall take
an early opportunity of treating it more in detail. Notwithstanding the
fact of this department being well filled, daily additions are yet being
made.[3]

DeBow's Monthly Review, a well-known magazine of the time that was
published in New Orleans, began reporting Putnam's actions in 1867. The
Review stated that even though it did not encourage citizens to leave their
homes, interest necessitated addressing the topic. *DeBow's Monthly Review*
published five articles and one editorial between December 1867 and March
1869 that addressed colonization efforts in British Honduras. Four of the
articles were written by Chief Justice Robert Temple of the colony. He
addressed several topics in his articles, including colonial history, trade,
and natural resources. The editorial published by the magazine was a comparative study of the southern emigration to Brazil and British Honduras,
which spoke favorably of the latter. Information relating to settlement in
the British colony, although not always accurate or consistent, was available in quantity to those considering it as an option.

While most reports were honest in their efforts to recruit settlers, one
publication received almost universal criticism for its misleading and exag-
gerated reports of the wealth of resources available in the colony. C. T.
Hunter, manager of British Honduras Company Limited and under great
pressure from stockholders in England to sell company lands at a huge
profit, published what was to become known as "Mr. Hodge's Pamphlet."
The pamphlet, which promoted the interests of the colony's second largest
landowner, was distributed by its author throughout the southern states.
It apparently misled many and outraged colonists.

Those sincerely interested in the well-being of the colony were dis-
turbed by the "highly colored" facts contained in the publication. One
critic of Hunter assailed the portrayal of British Honduras as an "Eden."[4]
This misleading account, along with others that surely existed, frustrated
many potential settlers. One individual who referred to himself as "G"
returned to his home in the United States after spending time in the colony
and published a cautionary letter in the *Mobile Tribune* advising against
settling in British Honduras.[5]

The long-term ill effect of this misleading information on the efforts
to attract immigrants is obviously difficult to estimate. The reports of "G"
and others who returned home frustrated did not encourage potential

No. 12285

CERTIFICATE OF SHARE.   £5.

THE

British Honduras Company, limited,

Incorporated pursuant to the Joint Stock Companies' Acts, 1856-7.

No. 12285

CAPITAL,
£100,000.

IN SHARES

of £5 each.

This is to certify that John Campbell, Esq., *of* 26, Old Broad Street, London, *is the Proprietor of the Share Number* 12285 *of the* BRITISH HONDURAS COMPANY, LIMITED, *subject to the Regulations of the said Company, and that there has been paid up in respect of such Share the full sum of Five pounds.*

Given under the Common Seal of the said Company, the 1st *day of* June *in the year* 1863.

SECRETARY.   DIRECTORS.

British Honduras Company stock certificates like this one, purchased in 1863 by John Campbell of London, became a popular investment in London financial circles once news that former Confederates, knowledgeable in the production of sugar, were considering settlement in the colony following the close of the Civil War. (Author's collection)

settlers to consider the colony. Ignoring all warnings, some did decide to emigrate and settle on land owned by the British Honduras Company Limited.

Once the decision to move was made, however, individuals became more concerned with making the necessary arrangements for the trek to the jungles of the Caribbean. Most families left during the winter months after gathering the year's crops, selling property, and settling accounts with creditors. Upon arrival in New Orleans and other ports throughout the southern states, preparations immediately began for the voyage. Passage aboard the *Trade Wind*, the colony's regular steam service from New Orleans, was the preferred mode of transportation but was by no means the only option. The schooners *Cecilia* and *Fancy* (agent: E. R. Poole of

166 Common Street, New Orleans) and the steamship *Mexico* (agent: B. L. Mann and Co. of 33 Magazine Street, New Orleans) were regularly chartered for voyages to Belize City.[6]

Even though New Orleans was the main hub of emigration, the practice of chartering vessels from ports all along the Gulf Coast was evidently common. General Colin J. McRae suggested to his friends a chartered schooner from Pascagoula, Mississippi, as the best means of passage to his new home.[7] Sailing vessels were preferred by the less well financed since they were much cheaper than the steamer *Trade Wind*. Sailing vessels were much slower and smaller, however, and some were forbidden by U.S. Customs officials to carry passengers. Emigrants opting for sailing vessels were sometimes forced either to stow away or to wait to be picked up somewhere down river, thus allowing the ship to receive clearance to leave port from the U.S. officials without complication.[8] This suggests that estimates of the number of Southerners who emigrated may be far too low. Passenger lists read by the U.S. consular agent in Belize City indicated that an average of fifty Southerners per month arrived during the years 1868 and 1869, while thirty per month had arrived during 1867.[9] Official reports suggest that about fifteen hundred reached the colony, but other evidence indicates that perhaps three times that number arrived during that period. General McRae, one of the most prominent settlers, was not recorded on any passenger list of incoming vessels. He arrived in October 1867, and yet his entrance to the colony was not known to U.S. officials until months later. If McRae could avoid the notice of U.S. officials for such an extended period, surely other far less well known Southerners went totally unrecorded.[10] T.C. Brewer, a hotel owner in Belize City, estimated one thousand settlers were in the colony prior to the group migrations, an observation that clearly questions the reliability of the U.S. consul reports,[11]

Whatever the number of emigrants to British Honduras, the influx of travelers into New Orleans, a way station on the trek southward, fostered several business opportunities for the city's entrepreneurs. Industrious New Orleans merchants quickly catered to the specific needs of those leaving for Belize City. While booking passage and awaiting the departure of the previously mentioned vessels, wealthier emigrants resided at the St. Charles and St. James hotels. Guest registers printed in newspapers and diaries show the St. Charles, which was much more moderately priced than the elegant St. James, was the favorite of the two, which is verified by supplemental information.[12] It was noted that Varina Howell Davis, former first lady of the Confederacy, entertained guests on the way to Belize City at the St. James; the implication of this, of course, is that only the affluent could afford such extravagances as those provided by the staff of the St. James.

Merchants in New Orleans offered a variety of goods and services to travelers about to embark upon the voyage for Belize City. New Orleans newspapers regularly published advertisements specifically targeting the emigrant:

> British Honduras — Before you leave the Crescent City for Belize, Honduras, call at Blelock's and supply yourself with some of their late and attractive books, which they call your attention to in this morning's Picayune. They have just received Jean Inglelow's new volume of poems, entitled "A Story of Doom" — besides innumerable other attractive new books for summer reading. Blelock is always ahead. Go to Blelock's. Our friends in the country can buy book[s] from this house at publisher's prices, and have them sent by mail, post paid.[13]

Most leaving New Orleans for Belize City were, of course, interested in more practical items than the latest book of poetry. Yet this does highlight the extreme diversity of those embarking for Belize City. While some individuals were begging and borrowing to finance the trip, others were pursuing more leisurely activities.

One other business worthy of note is that of J. Avet located at 60 Old Levee, a few blocks from the New Orleans Post Office, where he exchanged U.S. currency for the currency of British Honduras.[14] The colonial assembly had enacted legislation which created the British Honduran dollar in 1864. The currency, according to law, was equal to four English shillings, which at that time placed the value of the colonial dollar at 97.5 cents U.S.[15] It was not in the best interest of the potential emigrant to embark upon a venture to British Honduras in possession of U.S. dollars. The American currency had a history of extreme instability on the world market in comparison to the British Honduran dollar, which was tied to the relatively stable English pound.[16] The exchange and speculation of monies was apparently a lucrative business for Avet, although his exact fees for the transaction are not recorded. He advertised frequently in the newspapers of New Orleans.

Notes

1. Maunsel W. Chapman, "British Honduras," *Livingston Journal* (Alabama), 22 June 1867, 1.

2. "Emigration to Honduras," *DeBow's Monthly Review* 6, no. 3 (March 1869): 262.

3. "Louisiana State Fair," *British Honduras Colonist and Belize Advertiser*, 29 February 1868, 3.

    4. "Mr. Hodge's Pamphlet," *British Honduras Colonist and Belize Advertiser*, 14 September 1867, 3; A Louisiana Planter, "A Merchant of This Town...," *British Honduras Colonist and Belize Advertiser*, 14 September 1867, 3.
    5. CANDOR, "We Have Been a Good Deal Amused...," *British Honduras Colonist and Belize Advertiser*, 21 September 1867, 3.
    6. James M. Putnam, "Homes in British Honduras: Free from Taxation," *Daily Picayune* (New Orleans), 7 February 1869, 4(M); George W. Hynson, "Honduras," *Daily Picayune*, 12 June 1869, 7(M); E. R. Poole, "Honduras," *Daily Picayune*, 3 March 1868, 7(M); Poole, "Belize Honduras," *Daily Picayune*, 16 September 1868, 8(M).
    7. C. J. McRae, "British Honduras," *Mobile Daily Register*, 28 September 1868, 2(M).
    8. Duval, 43.
    9. Dispatches from U.S. Consuls in Belize, A. C. Prindle to W. A. Seward, No. 64, 7 April 1869, FM T-334 Roll 3; Dispatches from U.S. Consuls in Belize, A. C. Prindle to W. A. Seward, No. 2, 9 August 1867, FM T-334 Roll 3.
    10. Dispatches from U.S. Consuls in Belize, A. C. Prindle to W. A. Seward, No. 10, 6 December 1867, FM T-334 Roll 3; Lawrence Hill in 1936 published *The Confederate Exodus to Latin America*, which speculates that U.S. Consular estimates were considerably low.
    11. T. C. Brewer, "Letter from British Honduras," *Mobile Daily Register*, 8 June 1868, 2.
    12. Swett, 2.
    13. "British Honduras," *Daily Picayune* (New Orleans), 31 July 1867, 3.
    14. J. Avet, "Belize Honduras," *Daily Picayune* (New Orleans), 25 January 1868, 1(E).
    15. Dispatches from U.S. Consuls in Belize, C. A. Leas to W. A. Seward, No. 158, 7 May 1864, FM T-334 Roll 3.
    16. For more information about the monetary history of the United States during this era, refer to Walter T. K. Nugent, *The Money Question During Reconstruction* (New York: Norton, 1967).

CHAPTER V

Passage to British Honduras

With the necessary supplies purchased and monies exchanged, emigrants awaited the departure of their selected vessel from New Orleans. The *Trade Wind* advertised departures on the third Wednesday of each month at 5:00 P.M.[1] The *Trade Wind* and the *General Sherman*, during the few months that it provided regular service to Belize City, departed from the wharf at the foot of Erato Street.[2] Smaller sailing vessels which were sometimes chartered for passage from New Orleans to Belize City could always be found at Picayune Tier, located opposite the French Market.[3]

Within an hour of the scheduled time of departure, emigrants, their families, and friends assembled at the appropriate wharf to say their last goodbyes. Despite high spirits and the prospect of success and happiness in a new country, Southerners often reported lamenting leaving their homeland. Colonel R. T. Johnson, formerly of Desoto, Louisiana, described his departure:

> Old friends came on board to bid us farewell with their parting blessing; the steam is up — the bell rings— one hearty grasp of hand — friends part, perhaps forever — there is a waving of hats from on board and on shore — then comes the suppressed anguish of heart as your country, in the distance, recedes from view.[4]

The suffering and devastation faced during the war and Reconstruction that followed caused the emigrants to resent the U.S. government but not their former home. The hated and despised "Yankee," who was still viewed as the enemy by many arrivals in British Honduras, had destroyed their old way of life and now ruled the South. Most Southerners upon leaving their homes reminisced about the Old South which no longer existed. Colonel Johnson and many others expressed a desire to recreate, or at least preserve, part of the Old South in British Honduras. For blacks who traveled to British Honduras from the South with their former masters, the colony promised freedoms not guaranteed in the United States until many years later.

Any painful emotion felt by Southerners, both black and white, as they left the United States were soon forgotten as the perils of the voyage became apparent. Stories of the trip to Belize City speak repeatedly of the hardships faced during the passage. Weather conditions often delayed the passage and also made the ocean voyage almost unbearable. The Gulf of Mexico and the North Atlantic annually experience an average of 8.45 major hurricanes and severe tropical storms.[5] The regularity of rough seas caused by the storm systems only served to accentuate the commonly experienced symptoms of seasickness.

On several occasions the vessels were attacked by members of the various factions of the civil war that was still ongoing in Mexico. The stop at Utilla, Mexico, a regular way station on the trip, turned deadly on several occasions. The *General Sherman* and the *Mischief* were attacked on at least one occasion, engaging in an extended firefight which resulted in the loss of two of the crew aboard the *Mischief* and the total destruction of the vessel. Survivors reported that "sharks were as thick as bees" and expressed amazement that more were not lost. The "Spanish soldiers" were said to have fled into the brush almost as quickly as they appeared, leaving the "houses full of holes where the fight took place."[6]

References to the nausea, dizziness, and lethargy resulting from the perpetual motion of the ship were often mentioned in correspondence relating events of the passage. The cramped quarters of the *Trade Wind* and other such vessels did little to relieve the suffering. Alcoholic spirits were suggested by more experienced travelers as a means of thwarting the effects of the unending swaying of the ship. Champagne, the preferred antidote of some, was said to work well, but as one traveler pointed out, finances were "not in as healthy a condition as in former days."[7] Therefore, most passengers either had to rely on less expensive spirits or some other remedy. Despite all efforts, however, few travelers completely avoided seasickness.

On several voyages, overcoming seasickness became a trivial matter compared to the scourge of deadly infectious diseases that appeared on board. A yellow fever epidemic broke out in New Orleans in 1867 which caused considerable loss of life. Emigrants awaiting their departure were infected with the disease that reached full vehemence during the voyage. The infectious disease, transmitted by mosquitoes, caused a great deal of apprehension among passengers and crew as its origin was unknown at that time.

The vomiting, hemorrhaging, jaundice, and other symptoms displayed by victims of yellow fever horrified fellow passengers. The bodies of those victims who died were thrown overboard and their personal effects delivered to the appropriate U.S. representative in Belize City. Christopher A. Hatch, a well-known and respected initiator of Confederate emigration to British Honduras, was one of the unfortunate victims. A former resident of Morehouse Parish, Louisiana, Hatch secured permission for the settlement of what would eventually become the Toledo Colony.[8] He died of yellow fever while on board the *Trade Wind* during his return to the colony that was to have been his permanent residence.[9] The death of Hatch was considered a great loss and was widely publicized throughout the colony.

Vessels arriving in Belize City carrying infected passengers were quarantined by colonial port authorities until it was deemed appropriate for them to enter the colony. Even under the most extreme circumstances, the personal comforts of passengers were of secondary concern to the authorities. On one occasion, in October 1867, the *Trade Wind* arrived carrying three bodies and did not enter the port. Passengers and freight were loaded onto another vessel where they remained under quarantine as the steamer, running behind schedule and pressured to fulfill the terms of its contract, returned to New Orleans.[10]

The yellow fever epidemic in New Orleans (1866–1867) had hardly subsided when cholera emerged to plague the city.[11] The disease, which is characterized by serious intestinal disorders, soon found victims aboard the *Trade Wind*. The results were horrific as one passenger described his voyage of 23–30 November 1867:

> The passengers without exception, I think, disgorged from their stomachs the last morsel of food contained in that receptacle [*sic*]; and from the heaving, crying, groaning and writhering [*sic*] I witnessed, I thought some of them discharged their chitlings [*sic*] as well as their breakfast; your correspondent was so disgusted at the scene around him that he found it impossible to vomit the bile from his stomach and consequently was sea-sick through the trip. On Wednesday, a little child of Mrs. Potts died, and was shrouded, and after the reading of the church service, was cast into the briny deep to make food for fishes. After a passage of eight days, we landed on British soil to behold the most beautiful country in the world.[12]

Fortunately, for most traveling to their new home, the incidence of yellow fever and cholera outbreaks remained occasional. However, the potential for horrific occurrences similar to the one mentioned above concerned all. The successfully completed voyage, one without disease, illness, or fatalities, was such a blessed occurrence as to warrant coverage by the press in both countries.

The more typical voyage avoided loss of life but was still a less than pleasant experience. The steamships and sailing vessels of the day were not known for their comforts. Movement was limited under the cramped conditions.[13] Passengers were often packed together on board small vessels in numbers considered unsafe by U.S. port authorities. Lack of sanitary conditions aboard such crowded ships facilitated the spread of infectious diseases. Except for religious services, which were held with regularity, social activity aboard ship was minimal during the passage. Most passengers remained in their quarters, hoping for a safe and short trip.

Meals were occasionally the subject of complaint. One former Louisiana resident commented that those "accustomed to metropolitan dinners" found shipboard fare less than desirable.[14] Fishing aboard the vessels was apparently common, and catching a shark for the entertainment of the children occurred on at least one occasion. Samuel McCutchon's wife, Adele, referred to the grouper caught by the crew as "fine eating and a beautiful fish."[15] Complaints about the ship and crew were surprisingly few, however, as most expected only the successful and safe completion of the voyage.

Arrival in Belize City, which occurred after four to thirty days at sea, depending upon the type and condition of the vessel as well as the weather conditions, was a welcome event. An air of exaltation enveloped the ship as land was finally sighted. After dropping anchor within a half mile of Belize City, the immigrants awaited the arrival of colonial officials who sailed out to meet them in smaller vessels.[16] Once the passengers and crew were cleared by the appropriate authorities, all were ferried to land.

The immigrants rejoiced as they reached the shore. They had left behind a land which seemed to hold no hope for the future and before them lay a land believed to hold new and great opportunities. Many of those arriving in the colony had held positions of status and authority in the late Confederacy. Although sometimes destitute, with little or no apparent means of supporting themselves, the immigrants only saw the wealth of opportunity available to them in the British colony:

> I could not say when my foot touched British soil, "my foot is on my native shore, my name's McGregor"; but I felt free forever; — joyously free. I did not feel entirely as a stranger, because here I heard spoken my native language, the language of Shakespeare, and of Byron; because I was in the midst of a people whose remote ancestors are my ancestors and whose history and tradition are linked together until time shall cease to exist. I feel free here because freedom is not a mockery under a gov-

ernment which originated trial by jury, and habeas corpus; and whose baron ... at Runnymede, forced the king to sign the written deed of magna charta, the basis of English liberty. Flags were flying from the different consulates, and I caught the glimpse of the United States flag, but not with the same emotions which fired with national pride, the heart of him who wrote "The Star Spangled Banner." No; the rememberance [sic] of "The Bonnie Blue Flag," though furled and laid aside perhaps forever, is dearer to my heart, with its clustering associations, than the flaunting flag of the United States, once the pride and boast of every true American, but now the emblem of Radical oppression.[17]

The immigrants were soon to discover that, contrary to their expectations, the British government did not interpret "freedom" in the same way as they had in the Old South. A conflict of cultures, which will be discussed later in detail, would eventually emerge.

The citizens of British Honduras viewed the arrival of the immigrants in a different light. Curious onlookers gathered to view the families in exile as they arrived in the city. The sight of individuals formerly of such high status carrying all of their worldly possessions touched many. Some residents of the colony, after observing the pitiful lot that was arriving in Belize City, requested that action be taken to protect the newcomers. The new arrivals, unfamiliar with the colony, were known to be easy targets for swindlers. Efforts were made to organize an "immigration committee" which would furnish the immigrants with appropriate accommodations along with useful and reliable information, thus keeping them from being harassed.[18] The *British Honduras Colonist and Belize Advertiser* published the following description of the arrival of immigrants from one colonist's point of view:

> Every vessel which arrives from New Orleans brings its full complement of passengers, all or nearly all of whom are persons seeking homes and places of settlement in foriegn [sic] lands, and many if not most of whom remain amongst us as permanent residents, prepared to accept thier [sic] new, and for many of them who have seen better and happier days, trying positions, with manly fortitude under present difficulties, and with trust and confidence in their future fortunes and prospects. There is something at once touching and exhilirating [sic] in the sight that meets the eye on the public warf [sic] of Belize every time a vessel arrives from New Orleans, for these immigration is displayed in its most interesting, if not always its most attractive forms. The man who was once the owner of numerous slaves and estates in Georgia, Carolina, or Louisiana, the spoilt child of fortune, brought up in the lap of luxury, who with all the fiery [sic] of the "chivalrous South" rush'd con amore into the late desparate [sic] struggle for independence and came out ruined in fortune

and estate, but neither bankrupt in energy nor broken in spirit, some time and not unfrequently stands before one, probably with his household treasures around him and those the richest and the most precious gems of all his worldly belongings— his wife, his daughters, or sisters![19]

The correspondent vividly recreates the scene as colonists welcomed the "spoilt" Southerners to the British possession. Most colonists realized that life for the new immigrants would be a difficult one. The harsh environment was a far cry from the "lap of luxury" to which many of the new residents had been accustomed. Unfortunately, despite the efforts of several colonists who realized the difficulty of such a transition, no immigration committee was ever appointed. Immigrants were left to seek out information as best they could under the circumstances.

Most immigrants arriving in the colony sailed directly from ports in the United States as described above. A few exceptions reached Belize City via Britain, France, Spanish Honduras, and Mexico. These nations, except Spanish Honduras, had served as safe havens for Confederates at the close of the war. Attempts at colonization in Mexico and Spanish Honduras failed miserably, and those emigrants who were determined to remain abroad found British Honduras to be more palatable than returning to the United States.

Notes

1. Swett, 14.
2. "For Belize, Honduras," *Daily Picayune* (New Orleans), 5 March 1867, 11(M).
3. "Belize, Honduras," *Daily Picayune* (New Orleans), 21 February 1867, 07(M); "Honduras," *Daily Picayune*, 3 January 1868, 7.
4. R. T. Johnson, "British Honduras," *British Honduras Colonist and Belize Advertiser*, 29 August 1868, 3.
5. Brian R. Jarvinen, Charles J. Neumann, and Arthur C. Pike, *Tropical Cyclones of the North Atlantic Ocean, 1871–1986* (Asheville, N.C.: National Climatic Data Center, 1988), 2.
6. Adele Destrehan McCutchon to Samuel McCutchon, letter dated 6 November 1873. Located in the personal collection of Marian McCutchon Yarborough of Pass Christian, Mississippi.
7. Swett, 16.
8. "Memorable Events...," *British Honduras Colonist and Belize Advertiser*, 11 April 1868, 3–4.
9. "Deaths," *British Honduras Colonist and Belize Advertiser*, 16 November 1867, 2.
10. Dispatches from U.S. Consuls in Belize, A. C. Prindle to W. A. Seward, No. 3, 01 October 1867, FM T-334 Roll 3.

11. Perseverance, "The Present and Future," *British Honduras Colonist and Belize Advertiser*, 13 June 1868, 3.

12. A Passenger, "Steamer *Trade Wind*," *British Honduras Colonist and Belize Advertiser*, 7 December 1867, 3.

13. Swett, 17; Johnson, 3.

14. Johnson, 4.

15. Adele Destrehan McCutchon to Samuel McCutchon, letter dated Thursday AM. Located in the personal collection of Marian McCutchon Yarborough of Pass Christian, Mississippi.

16. Johnson, 3.

17. *Ibid.*, 3.

18. "The Arrival...," *British Honduras Colonist and Belize Advertiser*, 7 December 1867, 2–3.

19. "Since the Departure...," *British Honduras Colonist and Belize Advertiser*, 11 April 1868, 2.

CHAPTER VI

Plight of the Newly Arrived Immigrants

According to the 1861 census, 25,635 citizens were residing in the colony of British Honduras when the first immigrants from the southern United States arrived. The influx of Southerners had a tremendous impact as the number of immigrants climbed into the thousands, perhaps reaching as many as seven thousand. Consequently, the port town of Belize City was unable to provide even temporary accommodations for all of the new arrivals.[1] Although the colonial capital had a concentrated population of eight thousand, Belize City boasted only two hotels and a few shops.[2] Those immigrants arriving in 1866 aboard the *Extract* had only two choices for lodging: The Hotel, owned by John McKenzie, located at the corner of Orange Street and Water Lane, and the very new Belize Hotel, owned by Joseph Brackman, located at the corner of Orange Street and Duck Lane.[3] During the era of group migration, the demand for lodging in Belize City was so great that immigrants were often forced to advertise in the local newspapers for private accommodations and room and board in private homes. By the same token, as the demand by immigrants for used bedsteads and mattresses grew, British Hondurans regularly advertised such items for sale in the same chronicles.[4]

Almost overnight, however, the sleepy little port was transformed into a boom town. Taverns and shops sprang up at every corner, all ready to attend to the needs of the new arrivals. Escalating demand for quarters encouraged the establishment of three new hotels in the city. All were owned by exiles from the United States and were exceptionally popular with the Confederates. The largest and most expensive of the new hotels was appropriately known as the Southern Hotel and Restaurant. Rooms rented for $10 (B.H.) per week, board included, or $1.50 (B.H.) per day.[5] The proprietor, W. S. Weir, owned a great deal of land in the colony and was on good terms with the governor. Thus, numerous land and other business transactions transpired at this hotel/restaurant.

The American Hotel, owned by Mrs. A. Foote, a recent immigrant herself from St. Mary's Parish, Louisiana, was about the same size but slightly less expensive than the Southern Hotel. Foote advertised "Large and airy Rooms, civil and attentive servants, and a table well supplied with all the Market affords" for the sum of $9 (B.H.) per week. Meals at Foote's establishment cost fifty cents (B.H.), twenty-five cents less than the cost at the Southern Hotel.[6]

The third and smallest establishment in the colonial capital that accommodated travelers was Brewer's Hotel, located on Orange Street. Captain T. C. Brewer, the owner, found great favor among Southerners as he was said to be not only an "ex–Confed" but also "a gentleman." The former Wilcox County, Alabama, native offered "sleeping apartments" that his patrons described as "neat, airy, and comfortable."[7] Brewer's hospitality was noted in much of the correspondence to family and friends back in the United States. The prices for services rendered at Brewer's Hotel are unknown as he did not advertise his rates in the press.

Upon securing temporary shelter, immigrants turned their attention to the pressing need for permanent housing. The first order of business for most immigrants was a visit to the offices of James Mercier Putnam.[8] Putnam was so heavily involved in the establishment of Confederate colonies that most, if not all, immigrating Southerners made his acquaintance either in person or through the mail.

Putnam earned quite a reputation in the colony and the southern United States while serving as manager of the Putnam Immigration Association Limited and agent in charge of the sale of lands for the firm of Young, Toledo and Company of Belize. As has been previously mentioned, he was also an exhibitor at the Louisiana State Fair and was held in high regard throughout the colony. The Putnam Immigration Association offices were located on Albert Street on the south side of Belize City where he also sold general merchandise, dry goods, and agricultural implements.[9] Putnam was not the only agent to sell lands to southern immigrants, but his association so dominated the market that the impact of his competitors was of little consequence.

Once suitable property was located for the immigrant, arrangements were made for those who could afford to purchase land. The specific terms of land transactions varied depending on the location and the seller. Nothing could be done in the way of buying land, however, without the consent of the Crown. The rights and privileges of aliens were severely restricted by law, and ownership of land was limited solely to British

JAMES M. PUTNAM,   WM. S. CARY,
formerly of New Orleans, La.   formerly of St. Mary, La.

Putnam & Cary,

General Commission, Receiving

AND

Forwarding Merchants,

ARE prepared to fill orders for all kinds of Sugar Machinery, and procure the services of the most efficient and reliable Sugar-makers, Kettle-setters, Cooper, Engineers, Brick-makers, etc., etc., for those in want of them, having a large acquaintance with the Sugar-planters of Louisiana, many of whose Estates are now unoccupied, we feel confident that we can procure the best quality of Second-hand Machinery, on the most advantageous terms. All other kinds of Machinery, Agricultural Implements, Western Produce, and Articles of Merchandise, will be purchased in New Orleans or New York on orders.

Office on Albert Street,
South Side Belize.
Sept. 22nd, 1866.

After his failed effort to establish regular steamship service from Belize City to New Orleans, William Cary joined forces with James Putnam in a commercial endeavor that provided immigrants with much-needed agricultural implements and machinery. This advertisement, describing how they planned to provide the colony with goods "on the most advantageous terms," appeared in the Colonist *on 29 September 1866.*

citizens. Most Southerners came to the colony intending to purchase property and establish permanent residence. In order to do so, they were required to go through the process of naturalization.[10] Since the governor had the power to deny entry to the colony and refuse applications for naturalization, his approval had to be obtained by whatever means. Hence, an introduction to and a positive reception with the colonial governor was required of arrivals wishing to purchase land.

Many of the former Confederates appeared before the lieutenant governor of British Honduras in possession of letters of introduction from prominent individuals: the British consul in New Orleans; the well-respected Prussian consul at Belize, Mr. Dieseldorff; or a London businessman with several associates in the colony, to name just a few.[11] Putnam often accompanied immigrants to the offices of His Excellency's colonial government as they paid their respects to the lieutenant governor and requested asylum. James Robert Longdon, who replaced Lieutenant Governor Austin prior to the era of group migration, was reluctant to offer any hope of special consideration to Southerners. Bearing in mind that many believed Austin had been dismissed for giving special inducements, Longdon was not anxious to repeat the mistake. Despite his caution and reluctance in assisting the immigrants, Longdon did become good friends with many of the new residents. Correspondence of Southerners always referred to the representative of the Crown in the most positive manner. One immigrant, Charles Swett, described his interview with the lieutenant governor as follows:

> While we were not discouraged by the interview, we can say that Governor Longdon did not at once accept as fact the many reports concerning the great agricultural and planting properties of the Colony, but gave us every reason to believe that what could be done by the government, in conformity with its laws, to promote the welfare of emigrants, would be done, but at the same time would offer no extraordinary inducements to emigrants.[12]

Unfortunately, several additional disappointments awaited southern immigrants. Naturalization in British Honduras did not provide the full protection of British citizenship as many were led to believe. Outside the borders of the colony, the British government offered none of the guarantees or protections associated with citizenship.[13] In addition, there were several restrictions within the colonial boundaries. Naturalized subjects residing in the colony were not allowed by statute to vote in elections for members of the colonial assembly, and they were not eligible to become members of the legislative body under Act 18, as passed by the colonial government. The only exceptions were given to those individuals "expressly allowed" and "specially exempted in and by the certificate of naturalization."[14] The limitations disappointed many who had hoped to secure the full privileges and protections of British citizenship promised in newspapers throughout the United States which had for years published reports assuring "all immigrants" "the rights and privileges of British subjects on the payment of $16."[15] None of the propaganda made reference to the limitations placed on naturalized subjects.

Even though many felt disappointment upon discovering they had been misled regarding the full extent of citizenship available in the colony, the news did not deter those determined to remain in British Honduras from applying for citizenship. The colony was deemed a welcome reprieve when compared to the Republican-controlled government in the United States. More than a few Confederates arrived in Belize City expressing a new outlook on the role of government. Some were indeed quite outspoken about their newfound belief, inspired by the situation in the United States, that nations could only be properly governed by an emperor or king. These immigrants felt the most violent hostility toward the government of the United States and intended never to return. The U.S. commercial agent characterized them as individuals who would be "miserable" under any circumstances.[16]

Upon receipt of the application for naturalization, the colonial secretary investigated the applicant to ensure that all requirements had been met and that all fees had been paid. The application called for the declaration in writing of age, profession or trade, duration of residence in the colony, and the grounds on which the rights of a British subject were sought. Applicants approved by the colonial secretary and governor were issued a certificate of naturalization with the stipulation that within sixty days of the issue date, the applicant would take the following oath:

> I [name] do sincerely promise and swear that I will be faithful and bear true allegiance to her Majesty Queen Victoria, and will defend her, to the utmost of my power, against all conspiracies and attempts whatever, which may be made against her person, crown, or dignity; and I will to my utmost, endeavor to disclose and make known to her Majesty, her heirs and successors, all treasons and traitorous conspiracies which may be formed against her or them; and I do faithfully promise to maintain, support, and defend; to the utmost of my power, the succession of the British Crown, which succession, by an act, entitled "an act for the further limitations of the crown, and better securing the rights and liberties of subjects," is and stands limited to the Princess Sophia Electress of Hanover, and the heirs of her body, being Protestants, hereby utterly renouncing and adjouring [sic] any obedience or allegiance into any person claiming or pretending a right to that crown, so help me God.[17]

The certificate of naturalization declared that upon taking the oath, the new citizen was entitled to the rights and privileges of a British subject "during the time he may reside or remain within the limits of the colony." According to the U.S. commercial agent in Belize, Americans who took the oath did not seriously consider the impact of the contract and still claimed the rights and privileges of American citizens.[18] Several apparently told the U.S. representative that they eventually intended to return home as soon as the "transition state through which our country [is] passing [is] over."[19] Even for those who would have preferred to remain in the United States, the turmoil and uncertainty of Reconstruction was more than many Southerners were willing to endure.

Notes

1. Swett, 84.
2. "Southern Emigration: Brazil and British Honduras," *DeBow's Monthly Review* 4, no. 6 (December 1867) 542.

3. Henry Schurer, "To Let," *Colonist* (British Honduras), 14 July 1866, 2; Joseph Brackman, "The Belize Hotel," *Colonist*, 29 July 1865, 1.

4. G__S__; or; The Asylum of Refuge, "For Sale," *Colonist* (British Honduras), 17 March 1866, 1.

5. W. S. Weir, "Southern Hotel-and-Restaurant," *British Honduras Colonist and Belize Advertiser*, 14 September 1867, 1.

6. Mrs. A. Foote, "American Hotel," *British Honduras Colonist and Belize Advertiser*, 2 November 1867, 1.

7. Swett, 72.

8. *Ibid.*, 21.

9. James M. Putnam and Wm. S. Cary, "Putnam and Cary, General Commission, Receiving, and Forwarding Merchants," *Colonist* (British Honduras), 29 September 1866, 1. Putnam became sole owner of the merchandise and dry goods establishment when Cary withdrew in 1866.

10. Dispatches from U.S. Consuls in Belize, Albert E. Harlan to John Davis, No. 20, 30 May 1883, FM T-334 Roll 4; Dispatches from U.S. Consuls in Belize, A. C. Prindle to F. W. Seward, No. 15, 10 January 1868, FM T-334 Roll 3.

11. Dispatches from U.S. Consuls in Belize, A. C. Prindle to W. A. Seward, No. 10, 6 December 1867, FM T-334 Roll 3; Swett, 14.

12. Swett, 21–22.

13. Dispatches from U.S. Consuls in Belize, Albert E. Harlan to John Davis, No. 20, 30 May 1883, FM T-334 Roll 4; Swett, 22.

14. "The Following Is a Copy of Act 18 Vict., Cap. 18," *British Honduras Colonist and Belize Advertiser*, 20 June 1868, 2; Act 18 Vict., Cap. 18, in its entirety is in appendix C.

15. C. D. [Christopher Hempstead], "British Honduras," *Daily Picayune* (New Orleans), 28 July 1866, 1(A).

16. Dispatches from U.S. Consuls in Belize, A. C. Prindle to Hamilton Fish, No. 95, 12 April 1870, FM T-334 Roll 4.

17. "The Following is a copy of Act 18 Vict., Cap. 18," 2.

18. Dispatches from U.S. Consuls in Belize, Albert E. Harlan to John Davis, No. 20, 30 May 1883, FM T-334 Roll 4.

19. Dispatches from U.S. Consuls in Belize, A. C. Prindle to F. W. Seward, No. 15, 10 January 1868, FM T-334 Roll 4.

CHAPTER VII

Two Phases of Migration

The Confederate migration to British Honduras is divisible into two clearly distinct phases. The first, lasting six years (1861–1867), was characterized by an amiable political and social climate in British Honduras. The war's end fostered renewed hope for the future of the ailing colony. Like gold at the end of a rainbow, immigrants arriving from the southern United States were believed to be the key to future economic success for British Honduras. Lieutenant Governor John Austin and most colonists succumbed to the vision and hoped for the arrival of thousands of settlers from the United States, men with the vigor and money to transform the colony, who would save it from certain ruin.[1] Unceasingly, efforts were made to accommodate and acclimate the Southerners arriving in increasing numbers.

In an attempt to seduce wavering immigrants, public pressure forced landowners, including the Crown, to sell lands for more acceptable terms. The lieutenant governor went so far as to give consent to the legislative assembly's contracts for transport: one for regular steamship communication with New Orleans[2] and the other for the navigation of the Belize River. Fear that large numbers would not settle in the colony unless regular transportation service to bring them was available prompted the first contract. The creation of New Richmond required the establishment of regular service between Belize and the envisioned upriver Confederate settlement. The terms of the contract called for a subsidy of $100 (B.H.) per trip to be paid to the operator of the service.[3] Moreover, government vessels and the Crown surveyor were available free of charge to those immigrants who wanted to scout along other rivers in the colony.[4]

Needless to say, Austin became especially popular among members of the Confederate community in the colony. He entertained Southerners at parties and dinners with regularity. As in the olden days, the songs "Bonnie Blue Flag" and "Maryland! My Maryland" concluded the festivities on many occasions.[5] Austin and his daughters were known to visit the new residents and to be quite complimentary about the progress being made toward settlement. As has been previously stated, however, Austin's generosity contributed to his removal from the office of lieutenant governor. The recall of Austin in 1867 was a severe blow to efforts to settle the colony and ended the first phase of Confederate migration to Belize. The second phase (1868–1870) can best be characterized as a period in which the colonists became increasingly hostile toward the immigrants. The transition between the first and second phases of immigration is best identified by the change of official responsiveness to the arriving Southerners. James Robert Longdon, who replaced Austin, found any desire to assist Southerners tempered by the knowledge of the fate of his predecessor. Longdon was quick to inform new arrivals that no special consideration would be afforded them. He was even somewhat reluctant to encourage agriculturalists to settle within the colony. One of the first Southerners to appear before the newly appointed lieutenant governor, Charles Swett of Vicksburg, Missis-

"Maryland! My Maryland" often filled the night air of Belize City during the height of the Confederate migration. The song, written during the Civil War by a Marylander living in Louisiana, concluded festivities at the home of Lieutenant Governor John Austin on at least one occasion. Such friendly associations between the Confederates and the government of British Honduras troubled A.C. Prindle, the U.S. consul in Belize City, and his superiors in Washington. (Courtesy Maryland Historical Society)

sippi, stated, "While we were not discouraged by the interview ... Longdon would offer no extraordinary inducements to emigrants."[6] While the correspondence of Southerners rarely referred to Longdon unfavorably, he never received exceptionally favorable reviews as had Austin.

Southerners also found the citizens of the colony less receptive by 1868. Some settlers did establish themselves as prominent agriculturalists

and businessmen as had been hoped, yet they were in the minority. Many
arrived in Belize with little or no money despite stern published warnings
that none should consider attempting settlement without ample funds for
a year or more without an income. Even those possessing sufficient funds
at the time of their arrival in the colony sometimes found themselves destitute after having fallen victim to swindlers, the forces of nature, or poor
business practices. The poor soon roamed the streets of Belize City seeking any means of sustenance. Some resorted to selling furniture or personal items in order to purchase passage back to the United States, yet
others with no such property became a nuisance to colonial officials and
citizens alike.[7] The *Trade Wind* remedied the problem on at least one occasion by offering free passage home to the destitute as an act of charity.[8]

The problem of lawlessness and disrespect for people of color, however, proved to contribute much more to increased resentment of Southerners than did vagrancy. The immigrants soon discovered that, contrary
to their expectations, British Hondurans did not interpret freedoms in the
same manner as those embracing the customs of the ante-bellum South.
This fact apparently led to a great deal of animosity on both sides. The
controversy often revolved around the issue of race and social equality.
The newcomers from the South, who had just fought for four years in an
effort to preserve the "peculiar institution" of slavery, now found themselves subject to a government that espoused, at least officially, the concept of racial equality. The British had outlawed slavery in all possessions
many years before, in 1834, and officially recognized men of color as equal
in status to whites. Men of color owned property and, in theory, could
rise without hindrance to prominent positions in society.[9]

The majority of Southerners living in British Honduras refused to
associate with anyone of even a trace of color and explained any signs of
industry or intelligence on their part as being a result of "a strong dash of
the Anglo-Saxon's blood."[10] Even Europeans who associated as equals with
people of color were considered offensive and unworthy of association.[11]
This attitude on the part of Southerners did little to encourage good relations and literally outraged some colonists:

> When on an altercation taking place at Manatee [*sic*], between a laborer
> and his employer, (an Immigrant from the Southern States,) the latter
> deliberately went into his house, brought out a double barrelled gun, and
> followed the man to his own door, threatening "if he never shot a nig-
> ger before, he would shoot one then," which bringing on a struggle, the
> cap went off, but fortunately without any discharge following, or the
> result might have been fatal to one or other of them. Now we would have
> these Southern gentlemen to understand that there is one rule more

inflexible than another wherever British law obtains and British feeling exists, it is that the use of deadly weapons shall not be resorted to for the settlement of private or personal, real or imagined wrongs.

Our laws will not permit, public feeling will not endure it; and if the persons who immigrate to our shore in search of homes, or for business, or pleasure cannot keep their violent and lawless passions under control, it would be for better that they remained under the tender and merciful care of Major-General Butler and the Authorities who have succeeded him in the Southern States than come here to disturb our repose and to raise up a feeling against them in the breasts of the people of the Colony, which might be productive of very serious consequences.

We highly esteem and honor the real chivalry of the South, as much as we admire and respect the enterprise, energy and intelligence of the North, but we have no sympathy with or feelings in favor of the Rowdies of either section of the Union; and we warn and caution them before hand that if they are not careful how they conduct themselves especially with clubs, cut-glasses, and deadly weapons in their hands they will be in as serious trouble on a small scale as ever they were in Texas, Louisiana, or Virginia on a larger one.[12]

Incidents similar to the one in Manattee were reported with regularity by the colonial press. It is obvious from the passage above that some colonists were deeply troubled and angered by the actions of some Southerners.

Much of the Confederate correspondence with relatives and friends in the United States contained some mention of race relations. One writer explained that despite the fact that the population of the colony was overwhelmingly "colored," all were polite, neat, and "well behaved." A typical Southerner justified this observation by stating, "The negros [had] been thrown into very intimate relations with foreigners of high rank, which beside exercising a refining influence upon them [had] taught them to venerate their social superiors."[13]

Reaction to this more tolerant atmosphere varied from one of intrigue to extreme hostility. The presence of "negro police officers" and black customs officials walking the colonial capital startled and troubled many. Not all Southerners were outraged, however, by the much more liberal attitudes toward race promoted in the colony. The following is a portion of W. A. Love's perceptions of Belize City and his reaction to those of color:

This is quite a city, ahead of any we have in Mississippi, in nearly every respect. The buildings are good, neat, and some of them fine. There are said to be about 7,000 inhabitants, about 4,000 negros, near 3,000 colored, and about 250 whites. The negros and colored people are very polite to white people, and the subject of social equality does not seem to have entered into the minds of either the black, colored, or white race.— Nearly all the police and customs house officers are black or colored, and they are as polite and as affable a set of officers I ever saw. I attended church at the Wesleyan chapel yesterday. The congregation was large — all black and colored — and a more decent and well behaved congregation I never saw anywhere.— They gave me a seat between an old woman and a young man, both coal black, and in front of me a young woman set, well dressed, with a fine waterfall, and sang from the hymn book like a "sure enough lady." The choir was fine, nearly all of them being coal black the performer on the melodeon and one or two others being colored. The young of both sexes were well dressed, some splindidly [sic], and looking more like ladies and gentlemen than you could well imagine.[14]

Love, a former member of the Mississippi House of Representatives, was quite taken by what he saw in the colony, but others were not so impressed with the black population of the colony. One was quite adamant in stating that he did not intend to settle among the "negroes" but among his fellow compatriots, and he would not be fooled by this "charade of equality." He enclosed the following message to his friends in Aberdeen, Mississippi:

> As you may be aware, a large majority of the people are blacks, but like our slaves, in former times, they are simple, confiding and respectful in their intercourse with the whites. They are, as a class, far more honest and intelligent than the liberated slaves of the U.S. It must be confessed, that the Southerner will at first, experience a certain degree of repugnance, when he finds the negro raised to a certain extent to quasi equality with himself. But let him suspend his judgment for a season, and he will learn that the equality is more apparent than real.[15]

To the surprise of many Southerners who came to British Honduras, the equality was real, at least when compared to the United States of the 1860s. Although racism remained a problem in the colony, the British Honduran government would not tolerate overt mistreatment of citizens, black or white. Racial animosity created quite a bit of conflict and eventually contributed to the growing resentment of Southerners by many British Hondurans.

It was only outside of Belize City that Confederate communities were able to survive while maintaining their old customs and values. In the interior of the colony, the settlers were not so restricted by the perceived overbearing English influence. Ironically, for those whose families remained and prospered, the goal of maintaining cultural and racial isolation was lost in future generations. Most descendants of the Confederates who remain in Belize today are a mix of many races and cultures.

Another aspect of living among the English also caused Southerners a great deal of consternation: they were referred to as "Yankees" by British colonists. This outraged Southerners, who considered the reference an insult since they interpreted a Yankee to be a native or inhabitant of a northern U.S. state, especially one of the states siding with the Union in the recent "war of Northern aggression." The English, apparently unaware of the offensiveness of the term, persistently referred to all coming from the United States as Yankees. The absence of distinction among Americans on the part of colonists offended Southerners who protested angrily. In fact, anything associated with the northern states or the U.S. government was despised and the target of much ridicule. The U.S. consul reported that because he flew the nation's flag he was the target of much hostility.[16] The following are two letters which engage the debate regarding the appropriate usage of the term Yankee. The first was written by a Southerner in Belize and displays the extreme hostility exhibited toward the lack of distinction. The second letter, probably written by the U.S. consul since he believed no other loyal Americans resided in the colony[17], was a response to the first.

> Mr. Editor,
>   I perceive that the inhabitants of this Colony, persist in calling Southern persons who visit here Yankees.
>   For their information I will state that the people of the New England States, of the United States of America, were previous to the late Confederate struggle for liberty called Yankees, and since that period all those who lived in aH [sic] the Northern States were so called.
>   The name is derived from the Indian word exankee, meaning coward slaves, and was applied by the people of Virginia, while a colony of Great Britain, to the people of Massachusetts, for refusing to aid them in a war against the Savages, and afterwards applied to all the New England States, from the diminutive size of the combative organs of that people, and their whining ways to make themselves hateful.
>   CONFED.
> Belize, 22nd July, 1867.[18]

> To the Editor of the B.H. Colonist.
>   Belize, 26th July, 1867.
> Mr. Editor:
>   One of your readers has not been a little tickled at an explanation of the word "Yankee" which appeared in the Com. Adv. of the 24th instant. American people from the U. States are certainly, called "Yankees" from no disrespect, any more than persons from the West of Europe are in the East called Franks, and there seems to be no help for it, for the present.

The Indian word "Exankee" Eshankay, has this very remarkable feature, that although I have acquaintance with that language it stands in my knowledge as the Third beginning as it does with Ex. One is Eex you, plural of Ech Thou, a pronoun. The other is Ex, signifying a gentleman's garment, commonly named inexpressibles, but fashionably called "Pants."

Taking the word as a veritable third, I demur to the explanation "Confed" has given, that it means coward slave, nevertheless. For reasons I beg to submit. The first is that judging from other names which they have given they were rather deft at the practice, and the Indians intercourse with the people would not warrant it, besides late events that have occurred prove it quite a misnomer. There may however be some discrepancy in the spelling, such as an "a" for a "u"; thus "Exunkee." In this form I am prepared to confirm the Indians wisdom in his application of names.

Thus Ex. Pants, pockets of course, large and well filled. Unkel, may be taken as the nearest Indian spelling for "Uncle." So the cute Indian by the name would seem to intimate, that Uncle Sam's pocket had been found more than a match for them in their struggles for independance [sic], driving them from their homes and hunting grounds in dismay.

Some expounders of the word "Yankee" have given it as a corruption of the word "English" putting their personal pronoun Y.He. as a prefix. Just as in the East Irish, Scott [sic] and English are called "Bengees." I beg to close my communication Mr. Editor with a proposition, which I am persuaded this community would greatly relish. That since the matter of Slavery has now become a thing of the past, that like the New Testament the term Slave should never appear in the pages of our Journals.

CONFAB.[19]

The first letter highlights the frustration of Southerners at being called Yankees, as well as their extreme contempt for New Englanders. The response of the U.S. consul, if that is indeed who penned the second letter, surely confused the English colonists and frustrated the Southerners residing in the British possession. The entire issue only served to alienate Southerners from their colonial hosts and to encourage them to seek association with their compatriots either in the interior or back in the United States.

During the second phase of the Confederate migration, few settlers, if any, settled in Belize City. Settlements in the interior were established and, as one immigrant stated, all were able to "choose [their] society among our friends and neighbors."[20] The number of Southerners in Belize City declined rapidly after 1868 as most returned to the United States homesick and unable to assimilate, while only a small portion remained in the city or settled in the interior. The U.S. consul in British Honduras reported in January 1868 that "many of them admit that the Flag of their Nationality, never has looked to them, so beautiful as now."[21]

W. J. S. Scobell, editor of the *Commercial Advertiser*, left the colony aboard the *Trade Wind* in April 1868.[22] W. S. Cary, who initiated the steamship service with New Orleans, and his family left in February 1869.[23] T. C. Brewer and his wife, Anna, closed their hotel and departed Belize City in June 1869.[24] Like most who went to British Honduras, the Brewers returned to the United States and were living near their former pre-war residence in Alabama by 1870.[25] Scobell, Cary, and the Brewers were accompanied by a deluge of immigrants opting to return to their former homes.

Of course, not all immigrants from the United States were unable to assimilate, and not all were violent individuals. The Hempsteads, for example, remained in the colony and were much-respected members of the community of Belize. Reverend Dawson, the highly esteemed Episcopal/Anglican minister, eventually retired from the priesthood to garden outside of Belize City until his death.[26]

Association with those of color was not universally offensive to all Southerners. A small fraction actually spoke favorably of British Honduran society. One commented that in British Honduras, "You hear nothing of 'manhood' or 'universal suffrage'; for to exercise the right of ballot requires an educational and property qualification. Radical ignorance and brutality are not substituted for virtue and intelligence."[27] Colonel J. F. Harrison, formerly of Tensas, Louisiana, carried an "American citizen of African descent" with him to British Honduras. William Owens, a former slave of the colonel, chose to accompany his former master to the colony.[28] This fact is not surprising to those aware of the close relationship a few Southerners had with their former slaves. Some Confederates and their descendants who remained in the colony married "Spaniards" and Native Americans.[29]

Notes

1. Dispatches from U.S. Consuls in Belize, C. A. Leas to W. A. Seward, No. 141, 1 April 1864, FM T-334 Roll 3; "The Question of Opening Out Roads," *Colonist* (British Honduras), 10 March 1866, 3.

2. C. D. [Christopher Hempstead], "From Belize, Honduras," *Daily Picayune* (New Orleans), 22 May 1867, 2(E); Dispatches from U.S. Consuls in Belize, A. C. Prindle to W. A. Seward, No. 1, 1 July 1867, FM T-334 Roll 3.

3. C. D. [Christopher Hempstead], "From Belize, Honduras," *Daily Picayune*, 20 July 1867, 1(E); "How Things Look in British Honduras," *Daily Picayune* (New Orleans), 23 July 1867, 1(M); Philip B. Duigan, "British Honduras," *Daily*

Picayune, 31 January 1868, 1(M); C. D. [Christopher Hempstead], "From Belize, Honduras," *Daily Picayune*, 14 June 1867, 1(A).

4. "On Monday...," *Colonist* (British Honduras), 4 August 1866, 2; "We Understand...," *Colonist*, 21 July 1866, 2–3.

5. AMIGO, "From British Honduras," *Montgomery Weekly Advertiser* (Alabama), 18 June 1867, 3; "From Belize, Honduras," *Daily Picayune* (New Orleans), 14 June 1867, 1(M).

6. Swett, 21.

7. Duval, 65–66.

8. Dispatches from U.S. Consuls in Belize, A. C. Prindle to F. W. Seward, No. 15, 10 January 1868, FM T-334 Roll 3.

9. Dispatches from U.S. Consuls in Belize, A. C. Prindle to Hamilton Fish, No. 88, 29 January 1870, FM T-334 Roll 3.

10. R. T. Johnson, "British Honduras," *British Honduras Colonist and Belize Advertiser*, 29 August 1868, 3.

11. Dispatches from U.S. Consuls in Belize, A. C. Prindle to Hamilton Fish, No. 88, 29 January 1870, FM T-334 Roll 4.

12. "It Is with No Little Regret," *British Honduras Colonist and Belize Advertiser*, 24 October 1868, 2.

13. Maunsel W. Chapman, "British Honduras," *Livingston Journal*, 22 June 1867, 1.

14. W. A. Love, "Social Customs in British Honduras," *Hinds County Gazette*, 9 August 1867, 1.

15. Chapman, 1.

16. Dispatches from U.S. Consuls in Belize, A. C. Prindle to Hamilton Fish, No. 95, 12 April 1870, FM T-334 Roll 4.

17. Dispatches from U.S. Consuls in Belize, A. C. Prindle to Hamilton Fish, No. 88, 29 January 1870, FM T-334 Roll 4.

18. CONFED, "Mr. Editor," *Commercial Advertiser*, 24 July 1867, 2.

19. CONFAB, "To the Editor of the B.H. Colonist," *British Honduras Colonist and Belize Advertiser*, 27 July 1867, 3.

20. Chapman, 1.

21. Dispatches of U.S. Consuls in Belize, A. C. Prindle to F. W. Seward, No. 15, 10 January 1868, FM T-334 Roll 3.

22. "Passengers," *New Orleans Crescent*, 16 April 1868, 1.

23. "Passengers per Steamship *Trade Wind*," *Daily Picayune*, 9 February 1869, 7.

24. "The Following in the List of Passengers," *Daily Picayune*, 12 June 1869, 9(M).

25. According to the U.S. Census, Brewer and his wife were living in Dennards Bluff, Monroe County, Alabama, in 1860.

26. Hill, 79; see also Belize Colonial Secretary's Office, "Memorandum of Revd. R. Dawson's Service for Pension," 11 November 187?, Public Archives of Belize, 107R681.

27. Johnson, 3.

28. Swett, 21.

29. Personal communication with Wallace Young, 31 December 1989, Punta Gorda, Belize; Dwight, journal entry dated 10 November 1868.

CHAPTER VIII

Confederate Settlements in the Interior

Eleven Confederate settlements in the interior of British Honduras have been documented, and many more probably existed for brief periods. The Toledo Settlement, near Punta Gorda along the Rio Grande, was the most successful and survived as a cohesive community well into the twentieth century. The others achieved varying degrees of success. Three settlements developed in the northern portion of the colony. Two along the Mexican border, one at Corosal and the other at Orange Walk, survived through assimilation with nearby inhabitants. One small community along the Belize River, New Richmond, survived until 1876. South of Belize City, settlements were much more numerous. Manattee River, Middle River, Moho River, the Rio Grande, Mullins River, Deep River, and South Stann Creek, were all targets of Confederate efforts to establish themselves in the colony.[1]

From the beginning, most Southerners were much more interested in settling in the interior rather than near Belize City. Colonial officials encouraged this interest by offering special incentives to immigrants with agricultural inclinations. Encouraged by a Southern settlement led by Cole Chamberlain, formerly of Natchez, Mississippi, located along South Stann Creek, the colonial government exempted immigrants arriving after 31 December 1866 from land tax[2] and all import duties for a period of three years.[3] There were several stipulations, of course. An immigrating planter had to prove ownership of land and show adequate evidence of intent to establish himself as an agriculturalist. No stock, furniture, or agricultural implements exempt from import duties could be sold for a profit.[4]

The decision to grant remission was the subject of much deliberation by the colonial treasurer and collector of customs, the Honorable Thomas Graham,[5] who was known to be less than receptive to such requests. On

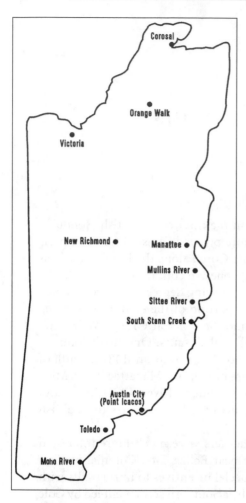

one occasion when Graham denied Joseph Benjamin, who was the younger brother of Judah P. Benjamin, the former Confederate secretary of state, a request for exemption of duties, outraged Belize City businessmen contacted the lieutenant governor for an appeal. The incident, it was argued, must be immediately corrected so that Benjamin could report to his many friends in the United States in a favorable manner.[6] There is no evidence to suggest that Graham overturned his decision at the request of the lieutenant governor. Joseph Benjamin did eventually settle in the colony and did engage in agricultural pursuits. The incident, however, proved that despite the status (social or monetary) of southern immigrants, colonial officials were reluctant to grant special considerations.

One surprising aspect of the British Honduran attempts to encourage an influx of agricultural immigrants was the promotion of cotton as the crop of choice. Many early arrivals apparently planned to plant cotton throughout the colony,[7] and *Colonist*, a newspaper in Belize City, encouraged the notion that it could be successfully produced in British Honduras. The *Colonist* featured articles heralding the increasing demand for cotton in Europe.[8] Portions of a book entitled *Agriculture in British Honduras*, written by Captain W. G. Stovall, were published in the newspaper. The book, which was also advertised in the publication, served to corroborate the belief that cotton was the crop best suited for the colony. The entire text was devoted to cotton production. One chapter discussed the selection of cotton seeds best suited for the soil and climate of British Honduras. Others were discourses on "Breaking Land," "Planting Cotton,"

Confederate settlements in the interior of British Honduras.

and "Cotton Concluded." Only one chapter referred to the planting of corn while no reference was made to the planting of sugarcane.[9] The focus of Stovall's book is somewhat surprising in light of the impact sugar would have on the local economy in later years as the colony's major export. Yet there were obvious reasons why cotton was promoted instead of sugar.

The colony had been in need of immigrants for some time by 1865, and the desire for exiles from the United States only intensified with the realization of a southern defeat. Prior to the U.S. Civil War, agriculture had transformed the southern region of the United States into one of considerable wealth. The planters of the South were predominantly cotton farmers, thus the colonists believed that promoting cotton as the crop of choice in British Honduras would attract Confederate immigrants. The colonists and government officials refused to acknowledge in publications that cotton had never been profitably produced in British Honduras.[10] There is no documented evidence that any southern immigrant, or anyone else, ever successfully planted and harvested cotton in sizeable quantities anywhere in the colony.[11] Several individuals commented that it grew well and yielded a "superior quality" of cotton,[12] but, unfortunately for those who tried planting cotton in the colony, worms and rains diminished the possibility of profitable ventures.[13]

Sugarcane eventually became the crop of preference for southern immigrants. The move toward the planting of sugarcane was in motion even as colonial officials and colonial newspapers continued to promote the potential of cotton. Sugar had been exported from the colony in small quantities as early as 1862. The limited success had not met expectations, however, and the government pronounced the cultivation a failure.[14] The haste on the part of the government was soon realized as a handful of Southerners who arrived in 1864, a year before the end of the Civil War, demonstrated sugar's profitability. The *Colonist* by April 1866 was praising "those energetic Southerners" who were "waking up" the Spaniards "from their lethargic habits" by producing exportable quantities of sugar.[15] The article was presumably referring to the agricultural success of John Wallace Price, formerly of Louisiana, and others who arrived in the colony in 1864.[16] His estate at "Tower Hill" quickly became one of the leading sugar producers in the colony and contributed to the move toward a sugar-dominated economy. Promoters of cotton abandoned their efforts once reports of profitable sugar production surfaced in 1866. In fact, James Putnam, who promoted the colony extensively through his Putnam Immigration Association, did not even refer to the product in flyers and advertisements while sugar, corn, and rice were frequently mentioned.

The move toward sugar intensified the ties between British Honduras

Shaded areas indicate known parishes of origin for Louisiana Confederates who emigrated to British Honduras. Evidence suggests that West Feliciana and perhaps three other parishes may have also been originating parishes of Confederates in British Honduras.

and the state of Louisiana. The planters of Louisiana before 1860 had produced about 95 percent of the total national output of sugar.[17] Conveniently, New Orleans, the state's major port, was also the closest U.S. port to Belize City. The realization that sugar was the crop of the colony's future served as a catalyst for interest in steamship connections with New Orleans. The state was full of frustrated sugar planters desirous of escaping the carpetbagger governments. High interest rates, increased taxes, and rising labor costs were bankrupting planters throughout the state. Promoters of immigration to British Honduras found a growing and receptive audience in Louisiana as the severity of Congressional Reconstruction was realized.

Letters, books, and advertisements promoting British Honduras during the era of group migration always compared its sugar production to Louisiana's. Statements similar to the following were not uncommon:

> I will give the notes of one of the best practical Louisiana sugar planters I know: "Sugar canes are better and finer than in Louisiana, the juice is richer, say from 11½ to 30% as it comes from the mill. With less water and less gum. Consequently evaporates in less time and is more easily clarified. Sugar is easily made of good quality — even canes 2 years old made good sugar."[18]

Shaded areas indicate known counties of origin for Mississippi Confederates who emigrated to British Honduras.

R. F. Gray of the sugar region of Louisiana made this observation. He traveled extensively throughout British Honduras and was amply qualified to draw such a comparison.

Efforts to target potential immigrants from the sugar-producing state were so concentrated that few displaced Southerners outside Louisiana were initially attracted to the colony. In fact, only a handful were from areas other than Louisiana or the surrounding states. Almost all exiles to arrive in British Honduras from states other than Louisiana had either family, political, or business ties to the state.

Geographic proximity surely played an important role but was by no means the only reason Southerners selected the British colony as a haven of exile. Large numbers of Southerners from many states went to Brazil and Venezuela after the war. Most of those who went to Venezuela were from the states of Kentucky and Missouri.[19] One can conclude, therefore, that geographic proximity was a minor factor in the decision to settle in a particular country when compared to effective promotional efforts.

While Brazilian promoters targeted the entire South and Venezuelan promoters concentrated efforts in Kentucky, British Honduras cultivated the interest of sugar planters of the Deep South. Geographic locale combined with the fortunate coincidence that Louisiana and British Honduras were both ideal sites for sugar production fostered an unusual bond between the two. The bond was a marriage of convenience.

Notes

1. Scholars have confused the numerous settlements, which is understandable since several are referred to in documents in various ways. For example, "the Putnam and Cary plan on land between the Monkey and Deep rivers" and "the Icacos Grant" are the same. Refer to Michael Anthony Camille, "Historical Geography of Toledo Settlement, Belize, 1868–1985: A Transition from Confederate to East Indian Landscapes," M.A. thesis, Louisiana State University, 1986, 18. The "Reverend B. R. Duval plan" and "New Richmond" on the Belize River are also the same settlement. In an effort to avoid further confusion, this text will refer to the aforementioned lands as the Icacos Grant and New Richmond.

2. Minutes from the meeting of the Legislative Council, 16 March 1868, Public Archives of Belize, 104R1-4.

3. Lieutenant Governor James R. Longdon to unknown person, 6 April 1868, Public Archives of Belize, 97R370; "From Belize, Honduras," *Daily Picayune* (New Orleans), 22 May 1867, 8; James M. Putnam, "British Honduras, Central America," *Daily Picayune*, 2 August 1867, 1(A).

4. "From Belize, Honduras," *Daily Picayune* (New Orleans), 22 May 1867, 8.

5. Dispatches from U.S. Consuls in Belize, A. C. Prindle to W. A. Seward, No. 55, 2 January 1869, FM T-334 Roll 3.

6. Letter written by John Hodge to Lieutenant Governor James R. Longdon, 3 April 1868, Public Archives of Belize, 97R366 (661).

7. Dispatches of U.S. Consuls in Belize, C. A. Leas to W. Seward, No. 131, 10 March 1864, FM T-334 Roll 3.

8. "Prospects of the Cotton Trade," *Colonist*, 17 March 1866, 1.

9. "Agriculture in British Honduras," *Colonist*, 8 April 1865, 4; Captain W. G. Stovall, "Indian Corn or Maize," *Colonist*, 11 March 1865, 2.

10. "Rumors and Future Prospects," *Colonist*, 23 June 1866, 6.

11. Wayne M. Clegern, *British Honduras: Colonial Dead End, 1859–1900* (Baton Rouge: Louisiana State University Press, 1967), 43.

12. D. W. Foster, "British Honduras," *Livingston Journal* (Alabama), 8 June 1867, 1.

13. Duval, 41.

14. David M. Pendergast, "The 19th-Century Sugar Mill at Indian Church, Belize," *Industrial Archaeology* 8 (1982): 62–63.

15. "It Has Constantly Been…," *Colonist* (British Honduras), 28 April 1866, 2.

16. Foster, "British Honduras," 1.

17. Joseph Karl Menn, "The Large Slaveholders of the Deep South, 1860," Ph.D. dissertation, University of Texas, 1964, 5; William J. Cooper, Jr., and Thomas E. Terrill, *The American South: A History* (New York: McGraw Hill, 1991), 187–88.

18. R. F. Gray, "British Honduras," *Opelousas Journal* (Louisiana), 4 July 1868, 2.

19. "Southerners in Venezuela," *Daily Picayune*, 7 May 1867, 2; see also A. J. Hanna and Kathryn Hanna, *Confederate Exiles in Venezuela* (Tuscaloosa, Alabama: Confederate Publishing, 1960).

CHAPTER IX

The Toledo Settlement

The Toledo Settlement, located between the Rio Grande and the Moho River, is the best known and was the most successful of the Confederate settlements in British Honduras. Originally known as the "Hatch Colony," named after Christopher Asa Hatch of Morehouse Parish, Louisiana, and also referred to during the early years of settlement as "Cattle Landing,"[1] the community at its height comprised some sixty-six permanent settlers.[2] It was Hatch who selected the site and returned to the United States to recruit settlers. Hatch's role in founding the settlement was soon forgotten, however, as he was never to see his dream realized. He fell victim to yellow fever while returning to the British colony after an extended recruiting trip throughout much of Mississippi and Louisiana.[3] The Reverend Levi Pearce, formerly of Sharon, Mississippi, eventually replaced Hatch as leader of the Confederate settlers in the southernmost part of the colony.

It is not known at what point, or if, Hatch and Pearce were introduced or became acquainted. Hatch fell victim to yellow fever prior to the arrival of Pearce in British Honduras, which would lead one to presume that the two met while Hatch was traveling throughout the South in 1867 seeking recruits for his settlement. Levi Pearce and a group of friends arrived in Belize City on 5 January 1868,[4] only to discover that Hatch had died a month earlier. While A. H. Hatch, the son of Christopher Hatch, and others who arrived in Belize City aboard the *Trade Wind* embarked for the site selected by the elder Hatch, Pearce and the following group of individuals contacted James Putnam and began making preparations to explore the southern coast of the colony in search of a suitable place for settlement:

Name	Former Home in the U.S.
Col. J. F. Harrison	Tensas, Louisiana
Daniel Swett	Vicksburg, Mississippi
Dr. G. P. Frierson	DeSoto, Louisiana
Dr. G. A. Frierson	DeSoto, Louisiana
Dr. R. F. Gray	Opelousas, Louisiana
Capt. W. Buckner	Tensas, Louisiana
J. S. Peak	Chicot, Arkansas
E. V. Frierson	DeSoto, Louisiana
T. C. Frierson	DeSoto, Louisiana
T. F. Owen	Catahoula, Louisiana
Thomas Kane	Jackson, Louisiana
T. P. Morris	Batesville, Arkansas
Charles Swett	Warren Co., Mississippi

Putnam, land agent for Young, Toledo and Company of Belize, who had arranged for the sale of the Toledo site to Hatch one year earlier, was more than happy to assist the group with introductions and preparations for the expedition into the interior of the colony.[5]

Pearce apparently found no lands better than those near Toledo. He and the others traveled for almost two months throughout the British colony, along with a stint in Spanish Honduras, without finding a better site. He abruptly left the group he was traveling with in San Pedro Sula, Honduras,[6] on 20 January 1868 and one month later in a letter from Toledo informed James Putnam of his intent to settle there.[7]

Those Pearce left in Spanish Honduras returned to the United States impressed with what they had seen in the colony but not enough to consider settlement. Charles Swett described the lands of British Honduras as follows:

> The cahoon palm, which is received as a sure indication of rich land was found growing on soil both wet and dry, rich and poor. That there is high land in British Honduras cannot be questioned, but it is not on the coast, nor is it on the rivers within fifteen or twenty miles of the coast, anywhere south of Belize that was visited by us, except at "All Pines" and "Seven Pines," and we were informed the best lands could be found in that part of the colony. We examined the lands on the rivers; and as far as examined, they are generally flat, and present every indication of being subject to overflow.[8]

Swett and the others who began the trip from the United States with Levi Pearce were also probably discouraged by the realization that the climate made the land unsuitable for planting cotton. Evidence suggests that sugarcane, the emerging crop of choice in the colony, was unfamiliar to several in the group.[9]

Undaunted by the reluctance of his fellow travelers, Pearce arrived in Toledo to be welcomed by a fledgling settlement founded by the younger Hatch and his associates. Temporary housing was still being erected on the coast while a survey of the selected site four or five miles inland was being completed. The group, despite an outbreak of cholera which killed six within the first month, maintained a positive spirit as they awaited more arrivals. Levi Pearce found the following heads of families located at Toledo on 22 February 1868, making preparations for the settlement:

Name	Former Home in the U.S.
F. M. Pearce	Madison Co., Mississippi
J. A. Watrous	Monroe Co., Mississippi
Horace Hatch	Monroe Co., Mississippi
A. Ward	Harrison, Texas
A. H. Hatch	Morehouse Pa., Louisiana
C. J. Hatch	Morehouse Pa., Louisiana
J. E. Hatch	Morehouse Pa., Louisiana
E. C. Dexter	Morehouse Pa., Louisiana
James Foley	Natchitoches, Louisiana
G. W. Sherrod	Natchitoches, Louisiana
Danl. Brown	Natchitoches, Louisiana
W. Williams	Caddo, Louisiana
W. G. Williams	Caddo, Louisiana
Jas. Gray	Caddo, Louisiana[10]

The immigrants waited on the coast, not far from Toledo, for more than a month while property boundaries were established for twenty-seven families. J. E. Smith and Thomas Henderson, both apparently from the United States, led the party of surveyors, which included C. S. Dwight of South Carolina and Henry K. Farrar of Mississippi. Records indicate that James Putnam chose to have the settlement surveyed into one-mile tracts using the township range system of the United States instead of the metes-and-bounds system common to the colony. Most of the survey work was completed by 22 March 1868, and families began clearing the lands and building houses about that time even on lands not yet surveyed. Henderson stated that the lands on T.1.N.R.1.E. (Township 1 North, Range 1 East), where the Mason, Pearce, Watrous, Payne, and Copeland families eventually established themselves, was "excellent farm land" and "well watered." Each head of family initially purchased 160 acres of land as a homestead.[11]

The first year was extremely difficult for the arrivals from the United States. Little money was available for large and impressive homes and plantations. Only a few of the settlers were able to make full payment for their land purchases. The majority obtained land on the deferred payment plan under which full ownership would be realized in ten years. Forty-three additional immigrants joined the settlement in mid–March. Mostly women and children, the group arrived in Toledo on 5 March aboard the steamer *Enterprise*, which had been chartered by James Putnam.[12] In a letter to Lieutenant Governor Longdon on 27 March 1868, the settlers boasted of initial efforts to open sixteen plantations and the purchase of four thousand acres of land.[13] Either these figures are inflated, or a large number of settlers withdrew within the first few months. In an official statement one year later, the local magistrate reported only twelve families had opened lands near Toledo.[14] Evidence suggests that as many as sixteen families left the settlement during the first twelve months of their residence. It is likely that a number of the settlers, despite the warnings of Putnam and Pearce, arrived without funds sufficient for support of their families for at least a year.

While the lands were being surveyed, the men built a road which extended four miles inland to Toledo.[15] The road was vital to the community. While experimenting with crops and clearing fields, the people of Toledo resorted to the export of bananas as a source of revenue. The close proximity of New Orleans made the crop marketable. Bananas grew wild around Toledo and were a dependable source of income. The disadvantage to dependence on bananas, however, was that they had to be delivered to ships on the coast when ripe regardless of the season or weather. The road became impassable during the rainy season, thus eliminating this vital source of revenue for many months of the year.[16] Frustrated with the condition of the road from Toledo to the coast, which was essentially a logging path, the settlers petitioned the lieutenant governor and house of assembly in 1869 for the construction and maintenance of a road which would "no doubt be found to be indispensable to the extension of agriculture." The house of assembly was receptive to the petition and set aside $500 for the construction of a road sixty feet in width and three and one-half miles long "running up in a westerly direction between the Moho and Rio Grande Rivers."[17] Despite the improved roads, however, the export of bananas was eventually discontinued in favor of more traditional southern crops.

The settlers along the Rio Grande experimented with several crops during the first planting season. Sugarcane, corn, rice, yams, and plantains were planted by all of the families. Other crops tested included beans, peas, tomatoes, okra, cabbage, turnips, cucumbers, oranges, apples, coffee, and pineapples. The unfamiliar climate caused considerable frustration as efforts to identify profitable agricultural pursuits commenced.[18] The average annual rainfall in the southern region of the colony was about 160 inches, nearly three times the rainfall typical in Louisiana and Mississippi. Piled trees and brush, as one settler noted, did not burn as easily as expected, and fire "did not burn off as much as it generally [did]." The moisture reportedly caused the tomatoes to rot at a much faster rate than in the southern United States.[19]

Insects proved to be a foe equally as formidable as the rains. While carrying on daily tasks, the settlers confronted bottle flies and sand flies. These bloodsucking insects along with mosquitoes were said to be most active when the winds were calm. Z. N. Morrell, formerly of Texas, made the following comments about the annoying insects along the Rio Grande:

> I will first state there is one heavy draw-back to this country — that is the sandflies. It is due to my friends that I should state when I first wrote home to Texas, I did not know that there were mosquitoes, bottle flies, or sand flies, in British Honduras. But a calm ensued, and the wind from the Northwest came up, and brought with it a few mosquitoes, very few compared with parts of Texas and Louisiana, the bottle fly answering to the Buffalo gnat, although not quite so severe, were quite numerous. But the sand flies mustered their forces their numbers were legion, somewhat like the black gnat of Texas, they bite keen and sharp, but when the trade winds are in motion, all these insects are still.[20]

The Reverend Morrell, like so many other settlers, apparently arrived in British Honduras unaware of the annoying insect population. The pests were never mentioned by promoters of the colony but were a frequent topic in the correspondence of settlers.

Equally troubling insects for the newly arrived immigrants were the red ants. The ants destroyed vines and many of the vegetables planted before the crops reached maturity. Leafy vegetables and gourds seemed best suited to survive the effects of insects, according to the settlers, and produced large healthy yields. Turnips, mustard, cabbage, cucumbers, squash, beets, beans, and pumpkins were said to be the most "vigorous" of the provision crops.

Agricultural products planted for commercial purposes also received mixed reviews in the Toledo Settlement. Corn was cultivated in a variety of ways. It was believed after the first year of planting that corn "kept clean with the hoe" did not fare as well in the climate as corn left to compete with the vegetation. Corn planted in December, January, June, and July apparently matured much better than that planted in other months. Rice planted in August was also said to do well. A tobacco crop planted by a settler from Virginia was a complete failure. Exposure to the extremely bright sun killed the entire crop as soon as it germinated and the young plants appeared. A second attempt proved somewhat more successful as the young plants were protected under a shelter until large enough to withstand the hot sun.

A few stalks of cotton were planted that first year with limited success. The primary concern of those considering it for large-scale production was when to plant so maturity would be reached during the dry season. The dry season in the southern part of the colony lasts from February through April, although even this period is regularly interrupted by storms.[21] The ever-present threat of rains damaging cotton crops discouraged those contemplating it as a means of livelihood. Some Southerners planted cotton for a few years, but they eventually concluded that the climate made a profitable harvest impossible.[22]

Settlers soon discovered that sugarcane was the crop "par excellence" of the region.[23] It could be planted at any time of the year and harvested at any time as well. All believed that the sugarcane would grow for fifteen to twenty years without replanting. One settler at Toledo stated that he was "of the opinion men [in British Honduras] can live with less labor than any place I ever saw."[24] Many colonists, Confederate and otherwise, were encouraged by the success of sugar-planting Southerners along the Sittee River. Colonel Samuel McCutchon of Sittee, formerly a Louisiana sugar planter, produced seventy-five tons of sugar during the spring that the Toledo colony was being settled. Sugar soon became the mainstay of the Toledo Settlement.[25] Sugar was not subject to the environment as were cotton and bananas, and it could be produced easily and stored. Sugar manufacturing in Toledo began in a primitive manner. The earliest mills were small, turned by mules or horses, and the juice was boiled in open pans. Only ten or twelve barrels of sugar could be produced daily using this method. By 1890, steam-driven mills were being used, and more than five hundred tons of sugar was being produced annually.[26] The investment in sugar production was a profitable one for the new residents of Toledo.

The first year was one of considerable activity for the settlers. Not only were crops planted and homes built, but also a church and school were erected. Young, Toledo and Company donated the lumber for the floor of the church.[27] Presumably in appreciation of the donation, the name Hatch Colony was replaced by Toledo Settlement in honor of Philip Toledo of the aforementioned company. The settlement was being referred to in numerous pieces of correspondence as the Toledo Settlement by April 1868, and it has maintained that name to the present. Prior to the erection of the church, the Reverend Levi Pearce held services in the homes of the settlers.[28]

The unfamiliar environment combined with homesickness to extract a terrible toll from the Toledo Settlement during that first year. The remoteness of the settlement caused many to desire to return to the United States. The knowledge that New Orleans was only a few weeks' travel away surely tempted many as transplanted cultures and traditions failed to meet expectations. Of the original fourteen families to settle at Toledo, only four remained eighteen months later. A. Ward of Harrison, Texas, left in May 1868 and was followed by one member of the Hatch family from Morehouse Parish, Louisiana, in September of that year. The year 1869, however, was one of mass exodus back to the United States. James Foley of Natchitoches, Louisiana, led the way in January. James Gray and W. Williams, both of Caddo, Louisiana, along with Gray's three children abandoned their efforts in March. George C. Hatch left in late April or early May and was followed a month later by five more members of his family. They were accompanied by G. W. Sherrod. Daniel Brown and his family concluded the departures of 1869. The remainder of the Hatch family left in March 1870. Not only did the original families leave, they took with them other more recent immigrants. The Frasten, Morrill, Mooring, and Eldredge families also left during the aforementioned period along with J. Glasscok and M. E. Chick.[29] The remaining Pearce, Watrous, Foster and Dexter families found the situation increasingly critical by the end of 1868. New families had recently arrived, among them the Copeland and Lester families, who were to become prominent members of the community, yet the early rate of attrition called for some sort of response.

Levi Pearce and James Mercier Putnam were sent to the United States during the final months of 1868 in an effort to recruit new settlers and thus save Toledo. Putnam advertised in newspapers throughout the South: "Homes in British Honduras Free from Taxation,"[30] while Pearce traveled from state to state promoting his cause. His expenses appear to have been paid by Young, Toledo and Company.[31] The steamship *Mexico* was chartered in February 1869, and preparations were made for a party of emigrants destined for Toledo.

Pearce and Putnam achieved considerable success in their efforts to recruit newcomers. A rejuvenating party of immigrants arrived in Belize City aboard the *Mexico* and the *Trade Wind*, which also carried a circus, during the first week of March 1869. The party of seventeen aboard the *Mexico*, all destined for Toledo, along with an undisclosed number of settlers aboard the other vessel, had experienced a horrendous voyage marked by frequent heavy gales. The entire party suffered from seasickness during the passage. The new recruits were evidently as unimpressed with Toledo as had been the bulk of the original settlers. At least nine of the seventeen passengers arriving aboard the *Mexico* were back in the United States one year later.[32]

Housing during the first twenty years for those who remained was primitive. Using the resources available in the immediate vicinity, the buildings erected were essentially thatched huts. It was only after the community established a successful sugar trade that more conventional housing became practical. The homes were built on stilts in an effort to better preserve the inhabitants and their personal belongings from insects and the elements.[33]

Some of the settlers hired laborers from Guatemala and Spanish Honduras during the first few years in an effort to quickly move toward the large-scale production of sugar.[34] The local "natives," many of whom were of African descent, refused to work for the Southerners. There was apparently a great deal of animosity between the two groups. The Catholic priest at the neighboring village of Punta Gorda sent a letter to the lieutenant governor regarding encroachment. He requested that the colonial government take some action to protect the village's inhabitants and their lands from the intruders.[35] There is no evidence of any action on behalf of the colonists by the government.

The Confederates soon discovered, however, that the workers from Guatemala and Spanish Honduras did not meet their expectations. Wages were $6–10 a month for up to three years. Depending upon the terms of the contract, some paid half of the wages in food and supplies and the other half in money. A rare exception paid the total wages in cash. Contracts for employment were signed before the local magistrate or representative of the Crown. The Southerners soon discovered that the system did not allow the control of laborers afforded by the slave system to which they had been accustomed in the ante-bellum South.[36] The Spanish-speaking laborers' attrition rate soon became a major problem for the settlers. Laborers refused to work the long hours and under the harsh conditions demanded by their employers. They often fled to Guatemala to avoid punishment by colonial authorities for violating their contracts. The remote settlement offered no recourse for the employer when the problem first became apparent as there was no local magistrate available to enforce the laws. An appeal from the settlers of Toledo, made only three months after the settlement was established, requested that the lieutenant governor appoint a "board of police" for the welfare of the community.[37] The response was a rapid one. D. W. Foster was appointed justice of the peace for the Southern District only a short time later.[38] The choice of Foster, a

Southerner who had been in the colony for some time, was well received by the residents of Toledo.

The difficulty of acquiring labor for those who could afford it, and the lack of money for those who could not, forced the settlers at Toledo to initially work and cultivate the land themselves, something most were not accustomed to doing back in the United States. Faced with dense forest and undergrowth, which required removal before planting could commence, the settlers resorted to a variety of Native American methods to clear the new fields. Larger trees were felled on smaller trees that had been weakened by ax or machete. Using larger trees to knock down smaller ones accelerated the clearing of lands. Some of the wood was used for building material, but most of it was burned or left to decompose.[39]

The settlement at Toledo survived despite the obstacles presented by the environment. Success was not achieved, however, without personal sacrifice and determination. Levi Pearce and his followers found comfort and strength in their religious convictions. It was a central part of their existence. With a few exceptions, all who remained after 1870 were Methodists. Pearce, an ordained minister of that denomination, was a natural leader. The church served as a meeting place and community center. Toledo, as a result, has been historically known as a Methodist community with strict prohibition on the practice of other faiths. The deeds to the school, church, cemetery, and parsonage were specific regarding this matter. Doctrines other than those of the Methodist faith were not allowed to be openly professed, and the sale or consumption of intoxicating liquors were also forbidden.[40] While Methodism unified the settlement, thus ensuring its survival, it also isolated Toledo from its neighbors, discouraged the migration of possible settlers of other sects, and segregated the community from fellow Southerners in other parts of the British colony. Former Confederates of Catholic, Jewish, Episcopal, and other faiths avoided Toledo in favor of other parts of the colony.

The Reverend Z. N. Morrell, a Baptist preacher, attempted to establish a Baptist church at Toledo in 1868, but failed. Despite the fact that he was said to have been the first to "raise the standard of the cross in Texas," his efforts went unrewarded in the Methodist community.[41] He had been in poor health for some time prior to his arrival in British Honduras and complained that he was unable to travel well "for want of proper conveyances." Hostility toward his faith by the Methodist community in Toledo combined with the difficult traveling and the "most troublesome" insects and vampire bats were more than the reverend and his flock could tolerate. Morrell left the colony with his dozen followers from six southern states almost as quickly as he appeared.[42] There are no records of other faiths attempting to establish themselves in Toledo after the Baptist fiasco.

Methodism became so entrenched in Toledo that by 1875 it is believed that of all the community members, only Mr. Perrett, a Louisiana Roman Catholic, was not affiliated with the church. The high moral standard of the community was presented by those residing in Toledo as the reason for the total absence of violent crime. Moreover, only two divorces existed in the history of Toledo prior to 1930. This could be easily explained, according to the residents, as one of the divorces involved "the daughter of Mr. Parrett [Perrett], the Catholic." The Perrett family endured further alienation from the community because of the operation of a distillery which produced spirits to be sold elsewhere in the colony. The use of alcohol was believed to promote the development of immorality and thus explained the short-comings of those outside the Methodist faith.[43]

The Reverend Z. N. Morrell, a Baptist preacher, attempted to establish a Baptist congregation at Toledo, British Honduras, in 1868. Despite the fact that he was said to have been the first to "raise the standard of the cross in Texas," his efforts went unrewarded in the predominantly Methodist community. Morrell left the colony with his "ten or twelve" followers soon after his departure from Toledo. (Drawing from Morrell's book, Flowers and Fruits, courtesy Southern Baptist Historical Library and Archives)

Notes

1. Thomas Henderson [A. A. E.], "Memorable," *British Honduras Colonist and Belize Advertiser*, 11 April 1868, 1; Dispatches of U.S. Consuls in Belize, A. C.

Prindle to W. A. Seward, No. 6, 4 December 1867, FM T-334 Roll 3. Previous scholarly works have stated that the Reverend Levi Pearce was the individual who initiated the Toledo Settlement. The efforts of Christopher Asa Hatch have until now been overlooked along with the fact that it was originally known as the Hatch Colony.

  2. Letter written by settlers at Cattle Landing to Lieutenant Governor J. R. Longdon, 27 March 1868, Public Archives of Belize, 97R583-585 (also cited as 97R321).

  3. Henderson, 1; Dispatches of U.S. Consuls in Belize, A. C. Prindle to W. A. Seward, No. 6, 4 December 1867, FM T-334 Roll 3.

  4. Desmond Holdridge, "Toledo: A Tropical Refuge Settlement in British Honduras," *Geographical Review* 30, no. 3 (3 July 1940): 378; Camille, M.A. thesis, 19.

  5. Swett, 20–23.

  6. *Ibid.*, 43–48.

  7. Letter written by settlers at Cattle Landing to James Mercier Putnam, 22 February 1868, published in *British Honduras Colonist and Belize Advertiser*, 29 February 1868, 2.

  8. Swett, 80.

  9. Swett, 7. In early diary entries Swett makes numerous references to cotton as the "staple crop." No mention of cotton is made after his arrival in Belize.

  10. Letter written by settlers at Cattle Landing to Putnam, 2; the original letter is located in the Public Archives of Belize, 101R137.

  11. Letter written by Thomas Henderson [A. A. E.] to James Mercier Putnam, 22 March 1868, published in *British Honduras Colonist and Belize Advertiser*, 11 April 1868, 2; Dwight, journal entry dated 16 December 1867 and 11 March 1868.

  12. "Memorable Events," 1–2; Swett, 73.

  13. Letter written by settlers at Cattle Landing to Lieutenant Governor J. R. Longdon, 27 March 1868, Public Archives of Belize, 97R321.

  14. David W. Foster, "Statement Touching the Settlement of Toledo," Public Archives of Belize, 107R271.

  15. "Memorable Events," 1–2.

  16. Rosenberger, 184.

  17. House of Assembly Message N. 11 to Governor Longdon, 15 March 1869, Public Archives of Belize, 107R271.

  18. Foster, 107R271.

  19. *Ibid.*

  20. Letter written by Z. N. Morrell to James Mercier Putnam, 14 April 1868, published in *British Honduras Colonist and Belize Advertiser*, 25 April 1868, 2.

  21. Foster, 107R271.

  22. Z. N. Morrell, *Flowers and Fruits from the Wilderness; or, Thirty-Six Years in Texas and Two Winters in Honduras* (Boston: Gould and Lincoln, 1873), 375; Camille, M.A. thesis, 26; Camille, "Historical Geography of the U.S. Confederate Settlement at Toledo," 40; Clegern, 43.

  23. Foster, 107R271.

  24. Letter written by Morrell to Putnam, 2.

  25. Letter written by R. F. Gray to the *Publishers Journal* of British Honduras and reprinted in *Opelousas Journal*, 4 July 1868, 2. Gray visited Toledo and received

correspondence from Samuel McCutchon while visiting the All Pines Sugar Estate owned by Antonio Mathe.

26. Rosenberger, 187–90.

27. Letter written by settlers at Cattle Landing to James Mercier Putnam, 2.

28. "Memorable Events," 1–2.

29. Information regarding the dates of return to the United States is based upon records detailed in *Passenger Lists of Vessels Arriving at New Orleans*, National Archives and Records Service, M259, Rolls 50–54. For more information, refer to appendix D.

30. James Mercier Putnam, "Homes in British Honduras," *Daily Picayune* (New Orleans), 7 February 1869, 4(M).

31. Camille, "Historical Geography of the U.S. Confederate Settlement at Toledo," 40; Holdridge, 378–79.

32. Dispatches of U.S. Consuls in Belize, A. C. Prindle to W. A. Seward, No. 62, 10 March 1869, FM T-334 Roll 3; "Steamship *Mexico*" and E. C. Duff, "Personal," *British Honduras Colonist and Belize Advertiser*, 6 March 1869, 3.

33. Rosenberger, 197.

34. "Memorable Events," 1–2.

35. W. C. Genon to Lieutenant Governor Longdon, 18 April 1868, Archives of Belize, Belize City, 97R423 (in French).

36. Gray, 2.

37. Letter written by James Mercier Putnam to Lieutenant Governor Longdon, 13 April 1868, Public Archives of Belize, 97R405.

38. Dispatches of U.S. Consuls in Belize, A. C. Prindle to W. A. Seward, No. 55, 2 January 1869, FM T-334 Roll 3. The information regarding Foster was taken from a copy of the *British Honduras Almanac* included in the dispatch. Foster also served as Board of Health representative from the Southern District of the colony.

39. Rosenberger, 183.

40. *Ibid.*, 201–2.

41. J. W. D. Creath, "Elder Z. N. Morrell" and Z. N. Morrell, "British Honduras," *British Honduras Colonist and Belize Advertiser*, 11 April 1868, 2.

42. Morrell, *Flowers and Fruits from the Wilderness*, 370, 380, 382.

43. Rosenberger, 196, 202.

CHAPTER X

Waning of the Toledo Settlement

While Toledo managed to survive in spite of continuing adversities, the residents were fighting a losing battle. Only the following families remained in Toledo after the arrival and departure of the second wave of immigrants: Foster, Pearce, Lester, Watrous, Mason, Moore, Copeland, Johnston, Wilson, Shaver, and Perrett (also Perret, Perrette, or Parrett).[1] Colonel R. G. Shaver left in 1871, when his farm and the Perrett farm were destroyed by fire. The newspaper reported that everything was burned, including "houses, furniture, and canes." Shaver left the colony a broken man, but Perrett fought to recover and rebuild his home in Toledo. While these losses were "most distressing to the new settlers," those who decided to remain managed to survive in spite of such adversities.[2]

The residents of Toledo eventually grew tired of struggling with the local labor force and began, in 1872, to import East Indians (from India via Jamaica) to work the plantations. Forced to labor under conditions strikingly similar to those of slaves in the United States prior to the Civil War, indentured East Indian workers in British Honduras were essentially at the mercy of their employers. Although paid a wage of about $7–11 a month and given room and board, the "coolie" was not allowed to leave the estate without the express written permission of his employer.[3]

This cheap labor, however, proved to be of little value as subsidized sugar beet production in Europe steadily forced the market price of sugar to new lows. A severe blow to Toledo's economy was rendered in 1874 with the lifting of a three-cent-per-pound tariff on imported sugar.[4] Sugarcane production declined as a profitable business venture once the imported product could be sold more cheaply than its domestic competition. Several more families were forced by the economic circumstances to return to the United States during the late 1870s.[5]

Members of the Pearce, Moore, and Mason families, and a house servant enjoy a sunny afternoon (circa 1899) at the Pearce family home known as Fairview. (Photograph courtesy Robert D. Pearce and Bert W. Pearce)

Those who remained despite the destruction of the sugar industry in British Honduras were forced to resort to other business activities for sustenance. Mahogany cutting, banana farming, livestock raising, and apiculture were considered. Mahogany cutting was, of course, nothing new to the British colony. The mainstay of the colony until about 1850 had been the sale of this valuable timber. Most of the best wood near Toledo had been cut prior to the arrival of the Confederates, so settlers pursuing this venture had to relocate to other areas of the colony. One such Toledo resident, James Gabrouel Johnston, the son of J. H. and Louise Perrett Johnston, moved to Monkey River where he made his fortune in mahogany.[6]

The relocation of settlers from Toledo proved to be a terrible blow to the cohesiveness of the heavily Methodist, Confederate community. To further worsen matters, the period of prosperity was short lived. The outbreak of World War I abruptly ended demand for timber, and like sugar, mahogany became a worthless commodity. For example, the members of the Pearce family lost $114,000 when a mahogany deal fell through in 1914. With no buyers available because of the war in Europe, the wood was left to rot where it lay.[7]

While World War I destroyed the mahogany market, it created demands for food staples. The price of pork rose in relation to the ever-decreasing supply in Europe. Cheap molasses, corn, and potatoes were readily available for the fattening of hogs. Eggs from Toledo were shipped to Belize City weekly. Traffic in these goods eventually declined as the international conflict subsided.[8]

Banana harvesting as a source of additional revenue was resumed during the 1880s in an attempt by the Toledo families to diversify the local economy. The crop had always served in difficult times as a supplementary income for Toledo as little additional effort was required for the continuance of the trade. The crop was said to bring $250 per acre annually during the final decades of the century. A United Fruit Company steamer brought freight and mail to Toledo, while bananas and other produce were loaded prior to departure for export via Belize City. The end of World War I coincided with the end of the banana trade. After 1920, the United Fruit Company discontinued service to the area as dealing in such small quantities was no longer considered profitable.[9]

While most of the community at Toledo struggled to maintain a stable income, at least one family apparently found financial relief through apiculture. Jay B. Copeland became quite the successful beekeeper by 1880. He managed to successfully produce honey for profit with regularity, but his business endeavor attracted little interest from other members of the community. Swarming, stinging insects apparently held little appeal for the other residents of the settlement. Undaunted by the cool reception from his neighbors, Copeland went so far as to try to encourage other Southerners with interests in bee culture to settle in British Honduras. The following is an excerpt from a letter from Copeland to an individual in Monroe County, Florida:

> The climate is well suited to Bee Culture, and there are numberless honey-producing plants and shrubs scattered throughout our forests. Anyone coming from Florida, where orange growing is so extensively undertaken and so well understood could scarcely fail to do well in this colony, where the orange, lime, shaddock, citron, banana, etc., grow luxuriantly without cultivation.[10]

There is no evidence that he had any success recruiting others to engage in apiculture in the colony, but his idea eventually proved its merit as honey is now one of Belize's major exports. Copeland died sometime in the 1890s and was buried on the farm he called "Orange Grove." As late as the 1990s, John Alfred Young, a descendant of Perrett, continued the legacy of Copeland's efforts by maintaining a number of hives on his family farm.[11]

The decline of Toledo was greatly influenced by economic forces, but they were by no means the only reasons for the settlement's misfortunes. The determination of the ex–Confederates to maintain the customs and traditions of the southern United States isolated the community and contributed to the deterioration of Toledo. Racial intermarriage and social mixing was not permitted during the early years of the settlement. Caucasian citizens have always been in the minority in British Honduras, and the segregation imposed by the residents of Toledo created a great deal of resentment toward them throughout the colony. Another contributing factor was that parents sent their children, male and female, to live with family and friends in the

The Reverend Levi Pearce, a Methodist minister from Sharon, Mississippi, traveled throughout the South after the Civil War, recruiting Southerners for settlement in British Honduras. (Photograph courtesy Robert D. Pearce and Bert W. Pearce)

United States and to attend schools there. Having been indoctrinated at an early age with the customs of the Old South, the children were easily integrated into the culture of the southern United States. As a result, the large majority of those sent to school in the United States married Southerners and remained there to pursue careers and rear families.[12] Only a few returned to live in British Honduras, and those who did often maintained a second residence in the United States where they also claimed citizenship.

The result of this outward migration was a steady decline in the population of Toledo. With only limited opportunities available in Toledo, the youth had to look elsewhere for economic opportunity. Today only a small handful of Confederate descendants live in or near Toledo. John Alfred Young, Pierre Perrett's great-great-grandson, was the only descendant in 1990 who still maintained a farm and permanent residence on lands purchased by the Confederates of Toledo.[13] Frank Mason, grandson of James Rogers Mason, spent half of the year in Toledo and half in Florida.[14] Very few of the original settlers or their descendants remained in Toledo until their deaths. Even Levi Pearce, "aged minister of the gospel," went home for his final days. Pearce and his wife left the settlement they helped to create in favor of Jackson, Louisiana, in 1891. He, like so many others, simply wanted to die "at home" in the United States.[15]

Notes

1. Rosenberger, 177.

2. "Fire," *New Era* (British Honduras), 13 May 1871, 7.

3. Camille, "Historical Geography of the U.S. Confederate Settlement at Toledo," 40; Rosenberger, 189–90.

4. Rosenberger, 220; Camille, 41.

5. Camille, 41.

6. "Last Will and Testament of James Gabrouel Johnston" and "Petition for Probate of Will," *Probate Records*, 1925, No. 24, General Registry of Belize; personal correspondence with Wallace Young of Punta Gorda, 1 January 1990.

7. Personal correspondence with Frank M. Mason of West Palm Beach, Florida, 21 August 1990.

8. Rosenberger, 241–42; Camille, M.A. thesis, 59–60.

9. *Ibid.*, 51.

10. Jay B. Copeland, "Correspondence," *Belize Advertiser*, 25 June 1871, 2.

11. Personal correspondence with Wallace Young of Punta Gorda, 1 January 1990.

12. Rosenberger, 192–95, 349.

13. Personal correspondence with Wallace Young of Punta Gorda, 1 January 1990.

14. Personal correspondence with Frank Mason, 21 August 1990.

15. W. L. C. Hunnicutt, "Rev. Levi Pearce," *Christian Advocate* (New Orleans), 6 October 1892, 1.

CHAPTER XI

Settlement at New Richmond

The settlements near New Richmond, which included the McRae Estate, did not manage to achieve the permanence of Toledo, but they did survive for a short period with limited success. Named after the capital city of the defeated Confederacy, the settlement of New Richmond, as envisioned by its founder, was to be a city of the future which would "excel in wealth, wisdom, and prosperity its namesake in Virginia."[1] Unfortunately, the New Richmond of Confederate County, British Honduras, fell miserably short of the dream. The concept of New Richmond was developed by Methodist minister B. R. Duval, who was from Petersburg, Virginia. Duval, his wife, three daughters, and one son had originally settled in Mexico with General Sterling Price,[2] but they were forced to flee at the end of the emperor's reign.[3]

After returning to New Orleans and finding little promise of permanent employment, Duval decided to travel to British Honduras in hopes of finding a better life. He boarded the *Trade Wind* for Belize City, and soon reaching the colonial capital, he joined a party of Southerners on a venture up the Belize River. On that voyage, he was very impressed by the lands he passed:

> In all this region the pasturage is very superior, and any amount of cattle and hogs could be raised. About one hundred and forty miles above Belize the northern and southern branches unite, and about three miles above the fork, on the northern branch, is the place which I have selected for my home.[4]

The site he chose is along what is now known as Labouring Creek where it is intersected by Cut and Throw Away Creek.

Having now made a selection for a homeplace, Duval returned to Belize City to make the necessary arrangements with Lieutenant Governor Austin for the purchase of the land on credit and at low rates. He also negotiated terms for his fellow countrymen who might settle around him. His plan was to promote this new and improved New Richmond throughout the southern United States in an effort to recruit those who might be of like mind and "in need of a little impetus."

Duval returned to New Orleans via the *Trade Wind* on 13 June 1867,[5] and he wrote an article for the *Crescent*, a New Orleans publication, detailing observations about the British colony and encouraging correspondence by those interested in such an endeavor. The results of the article were promising. About two hundred individuals responded to his call. Most stated their intentions of settling in British Honduras at the end of the year, that is, as soon as the cotton crop could be sold. The minister was delighted by the overwhelming response. Accompanied by his family, Duval left for Belize City to begin preparations for the establishment of New Richmond.[6]

The Duvals rented a house in Belize City. Shortly thereafter, he began making arrangements for the commencement of a regular steamboat service to the proposed settlement upriver.[7] In an unusual show of support, the legislative assembly and Lieutenant Governor Austin passed an act giving him the exclusive monopoly of navigation on the Belize River for a period of five years.[8] In addition to the monopoly, he was also given a $100 subsidy per trip for the first six months of his endeavor.[9] He made two trips upriver before being forced to abandon his efforts. The government in England formally revoked the privilege of the monopoly with the removal of Lieutenant Governor Austin.[10] This action by the Crown was a severe blow to Duval's undertaking and reportedly caused many to reconsider moving to the colony.

Still determined to realize the dream of New Richmond, the minister and his family embarked upriver for their new home. They established themselves in a house which had previously been used as a trading post. The buildings were made of wood poles tied by vines and covered with a roof of leaves. The dirt floors served as havens for all varieties of insects, including fleas.[11] Duval promptly went to work clearing an area for the planting of corn. He employed local Mayas to assist him with the clearing and to repair houses for the expected influx of immigrants. Plantains and bananas, in great abundance, were cultivated so that all who came would be supplied with food as well as shelter. In compensation, the Native Americans received $5 a month and a supply of rations. Duval, understandably, preferred employing Native Americans rather than paying "the Africans" $9 plus supplies, including flour.[12] The family supplemented its supply of food crops with game from the forest, along with hogs and fowl received in trade from the Indians. Duval found the meat of the tapir and the iguana particularly appealing. He compared the iguana to poultry. The minister refused, however, to eat howler monkey which he said "looked to [*sic*] much like a child for [his] use."[13]

Soon after his arrival Duval was joined by General Colin J. McRae and others, who settled to the south of New Richmond near Cotton Tree Bank on Saturday Creek. The estate purchased by the general, known even today as McRae, consisted of eighteen square miles of land extending all the way north to the Cut and Throw Away Creek.[14] The total purchase price for the large estate was $3,500 (U.S.), which was a very good price compared to the then-current market prices within the colony.[15] He probably purchased the land from private landowners as such a large purchase from the Crown would have been noted by the U.S. consul.

Before coming to British Honduras, McRae had served as the Confederate financial agent in Europe during the Civil War. He was wanted by U.S. authorities for the sale of government property, and, unlike many other former belligerents, he was not to be pardoned. The charges against him were so extensive that he would not even consider a brief visit to the United States.[16] Jefferson Davis, former president of the defunct Confederate States, tried to dissuade McRae from going to Central America. Davis recommended New Zealand, a site he thought held much more promise. In spite of Davis's diligent efforts to discourage the general, McRae opted to settle in British Honduras anyway.[17]

McRae and Joseph Benjamin, the younger brother of former Confederate Secretary of State Judah P. Benjamin, operated a cattle, mercantile, and mahogany business from McRae Estate located along Saturday Creek. The two also operated a store at Puerto Cortez.[18] Joseph Benjamin borrowed $25,000 from his older brother for his business venture in British Honduras. Benjamin apparently had difficulty managing his finances as he eventually

General Colin J. McRae settled to the south of New Richmond, British Honduras, on an estate where he operated a cattle, mercantile, and mahogany business until his death in 1876. Wanted by U.S. authorities for actions committed during the Civil War, McRae refused to consider even a brief visit to his family in Mississippi. (Photograph courtesy Alabama Department of Archives and History, Montgomery, Alabama)

lost all of his brother's money.[19] He withdrew a short time later, selling his interest in the business to McRae, who continued alone.[20]

Joseph Benjamin remained in British Honduras after leaving McRae, developing quite a reputation for disrespect of the law. Within six months of arriving in the colony, Benjamin was found guilty of "trespass for assault and battery" for which he was required to pay $500 damages. While serving as the manager of Trial Farm Estate, sometime later, he assaulted a Mr. Oswald during an argument over cattle. The *British Honduras Colonist and Belize Advertiser* added to the report of the proceedings: "NOTE.— Club Law may be all very well for some countries, but it will not do for British Honduras."[21] Despite the notorious actions of Joseph Benjamin, his family remained well respected in the colony. The retirement of his brother from public life in 1881 was extensively reported in the colony as it was said to be of interest to many colonists.[22]

While Duval did have such notable neighbors as McRae and Benjamin, there is no record of settlers he recruited. The families who had responded so enthusiastically to his article in the *Crescent* lost their cotton crops in the fall of 1867 and could not afford to resettle. Duval was devastated, both emotionally and financially, after living two years in the British colony. He decided to return to Richmond, Virginia, in November 1869. With no money for boat fare to Belize City, he was forced to sell furniture to raise funds. Once in the colonial capital, he could not afford fares for his family and had to leave them there until he could raise the necessary money in Virginia for their departure to the United States.[23] Upon his return to the United States, Duval summarized his experience:

> I have no furniture worth naming; our supply of clothing is very limited, and what I wear is not worth giving away, having done good service before it was given to me. I have no horse, no watch, nor even the means of moving our things to another part of the town, much less to a circuit. But on the other hand we have reason to be thankful to our Heavenly Father, that we have had a full average of the worlds comforts, and no deaths, and but a little sickness in my immediate family, for twenty years; and considering the benefits of our observations and experiences in foreign lands, especially to the children, we do not regret our course for the last four years.[24]

With the departure of Duval, McRae and a few families were all that remained as the sole reminder of what might have been. Gelene Armor, McRae's niece and daughter of James Armor, a Confederate Navy paymaster, moved to British Honduras to live with the McRaes after the death of her father. She was a resident of McRae Estate from her early childhood until she was in her late teens, when she returned to Mobile, Alabama.[25]

The McRaes attracted considerable attention from the colonial press in 1868 when John J. McRae, former governor of the state of Mississippi and older brother of Colin J. McRae, arrived for a visit. The older McRae played a prominent role in the early development of the state of Mississippi. Considered by many to be one of the most successful pre–Civil War governors, McRae was actively involved in developing Mississippi's transportation system, specifically the railroads. Also a proponent of education, Governor McRae was intimately involved in establishing the school in Oxford that would eventually become the University of Mississippi.

The family celebration at the governor's arrival was short lived, however, as he soon became gravely ill and died a few days later. He was buried on the McRae Estate. News of Governor McRae's illness and death was widely reported in British Honduras and the United States.[26]

Colin McRae, who never returned to the United States, died at his estate in 1876. His property in British Honduras was then transferred to his sister, Catherine Hempstead, who leased it to tenants as late as 1894.[27] There is no evidence that members of the McRae family maintained a residence in the colony after the general's death.

Notes

1. C. D. [Christopher Hempstead], "From Belize, Honduras," *Daily Picayune* (New Orleans), 20 July 1867, 1.

2. Duval, 5–7.

3. *Ibid.*, 20–21.

4. *Ibid.*, 40–41.

5. Refer to the appropriate passenger list in appendix D.

6. Duval, 42–43.

7. "How Things Look in British Honduras," *Daily Picayune*, 23 July 1867, 1; Duval, 47.

8. C. D., "From Belize, Honduras," *Daily Picayune*, 20 July 1867, 1.

9. Rosenberger, 152.

10. *Ibid.*, 153.

11. Duval, 48–50.

12. *Ibid.*, 58.

13. *Ibid.*, 52–53, 55. Duval and others often referred to "baboons" in their writings. It is assumed that they were referring to the howler monkey, a genus of Central American monkeys similar in appearance to the baboon, a larger African and Asian primate.

14. "Estate of Colin J. McRae Late of Saturday Creek," *Probate Records*, Office of the General Registry, Belize City, Belize. General McRae also had property in Alabama and Mississippi, which somehow escaped the notice of federal authorities.

His will was probated in Jackson County, Mississippi, Deed Book 2, 238. Refer to *Colin J. McRae* by Charles Davis; the *British Honduras Colonist and Belize Advertiser* of 13 June 1868 reports that Colonel Mechlin, Captain DeShields, Messrs. Borders, Carroll, Dixons, and Mayo were on the "western frontier" with Duval and McRae.

15. Dispatches from U.S. Consuls in Belize, A. C. Prindle to F. W. Seward, No. 22, 6 March 1868, FM T-334 Roll 3.

16. Charles S. Davis, *Colin J. McRae: Confederate Financial Agent* (Tuscaloosa, Alabama: Confederate Publishing, 1961), 87.

17. *Ibid.*, 86.

18. *Ibid.*, 87; There has apparently been considerable confusion regarding the final destination of Joseph Benjamin. Even the most recent scholarly works place him in Spanish Honduras instead of British Honduras.

19. Eli N. Evans, *Judah P. Benjamin: The Jewish Confederate* (New York: Free Press, 1988), 381.

20. Davis, 87.

21. "Monday September 21st," 3 October 1868, 3. Benjamin, upon his arrival in the colony, unsuccessfully sought a position managing a sugar estate. Refer to John Hodge to Lieutenant Governor James R. Longdon, 3 April 1868, Public Archives of Belize, 97R366 (661).

22. "Mr. Benjamin, Q.C.," *Belize Advertiser*, 28 March 1883, 3.

23. Duval, 53–54, 65–66.

24. *Ibid.*, 69.

25. Claude Scarborough of Columbia, South Carolina, and descendant of Gelene Armor, 11 February 2000 telephone interview with author.

26. Davis, 87–88.

27. Davis, 88. Probate records in Belize City conflict with McRae family records regarding the date and year of McRae's death.

CHAPTER XII

Settlements in Northern British Honduras

Initially three sites enticed ex–Confederates to the northern portion of the colony. Corosal, Orange Walk, and Victoria were selected for settlement, but only the community at Orange Walk lasted any length of time.[1] Settlers in the northern region of the colony faced a different environment than did their counterparts settling farther south. Moreover, the Icaiche Indians from Mexico frequently terrorized inhabitants along the colony's northern border and contributed to the ultimate failure of most settlement efforts in this region.[2]

While little is known about Victoria beyond the simple fact that a group of Confederates initiated efforts to settle there, much more information is available regarding the community which established itself near the town of Corosal. Captain Armand T. Beauregard, younger brother of the famous General P. G. T. Beauregard, led the way for fellow exiles when he purchased the well-established San Ramon Estate on 30 April 1868 for the sum of $7,969 (B.H.). He paid almost one-third of the amount in cash with the rest to be paid in installments over a five-year period.[3] The estate, which comprised some 640 acres, had one mile of frontage on the seashore at the mouth of the New River.

Captain Beauregard conducted a number of agricultural pursuits on his estate. More than seventy acres were planted in sugarcane which, when ready for cropping, could be properly processed onsite at his own mill. The estate also maintained a still for the production of rum. Beauregard, as a Catholic, had none of the reservations regarding the consumption of alcohol so evident among the citizenry of the Toledo Settlement. He also dabbled in the livestock industry as the San Ramon Estate provided an extensive grazing range for cattle, horses, and mules.[4]

A number of other families arrived at Corosal in 1868, including those

Sugar mills similar to this one at Indian Church, Belize, which is now barely recognizable through the underbrush, are the only visible reminders of the Confederate plantations that once dotted the countryside. Prior to the organization of the predominantly Confederate "flying cavalry," which forced the surrender of the last of the renegade Indian war parties in the colony, production at the Indian Church mill was frequently halted by Indian raids. (Photograph courtesy William Parker)

of Dr. Mark Allen of New Orleans, Louisiana; Dr. Lewis Hobbs Hill of Morehouse Parish, Louisiana; and Dr. Ade Wilson of Long Beach, Mississippi. The Hills and Wilsons are said to have sought refuge in Corosal after being forced out of their homes in Spanish Honduras by "a revolution."[5] Hill and Wilson were married to two sisters whose maiden name was Otterson.[6]

Those who arrived in Corosal soon discovered that the area was no haven for the war weary. Indian raids on the people of Corosal and Orange Walk were a common occurrence. When Beauregard and his fellow exiles arrived in the Northern District, a frontier force led by John Carmichael, captain of the militia, patrolled the area. While this did not completely halt the raids, the settlers were at least protected by the colonial government. But, when the decision was made to withdraw the militia in early 1870, Corosal lay defenseless and open to attack.[7] Dr. Mark Allen, his wife, and two daughters fled the colony in September 1869. They were followed by Mrs. Beauregard in late December of the same year. Captain Beauregard himself soon withdrew to New Orleans just ahead of an attack.[8] The Wilsons and Hills, meanwhile, sought refuge within the colony, eventually arriving in Toledo.[9] The militia had barely withdrawn when Corosal was occupied by a 116-member Indian fighting force from Mexico.[10] Unlike the settlers at Orange Walk, the confederates at Corosal opted to surrender their homes rather than fight, once again, to defend them against a formidable enemy.

There were several former Confederates who settled along the New River near Orange Walk. John Wallace Price of Algeries, Louisiana, has become perhaps the most legendary of the group.[11] Price, along with E. Boudreau, H. J. Archer, Kevlin,[12] Doirn, Dagle, and Doughty, purchased large tracts of land for sugar plantations along the New River.[13] Price became a well-known individual in the colony within a few years. The colonial press lauded his success in the cultivation of sugarcane. The *New Era*, in 1871, stated that Price had produced at least two tons of sugar per acre for the past season.[14]

While Price's success in agricultural pursuits is worth noting, it was his fighting ability which brought his longer-lasting fame. Price had considerable experience in the art of modern war. He served in a Louisiana artillery company and in the Confederate Medical Department during the Civil War. Avoiding capture until the very end, he was taken prisoner in the final month of the conflict.[15] Following his parole in Richmond, Virginia, Price embarked for British Honduras, where he purchased what was soon to become Louisiana Farm at Tower Hill.[16]

The arrival of the Confederates was welcomed not only by other area settlers but by the British Honduras Company as well. Indian raids in February 1867 had resulted in the deaths of two of the company's employees and the halt of sugar manufacturing in the area.[17] Price joined the "flying cavalry," as did a number of Confederates around Orange Walk. The group of volunteers was to act as a backup for the militia should the Indians invade the area. The compensation one received for services in this unit included $30 a month, a horse, and all "necessary accouterments" required for such service. The colonial government worked to recruit the well-trained Confederate veterans and even advertised this opportunity in the United States as part of its effort to entice potential settlers.[18]

The battle that won Price a place in the history of British Honduras occurred in August 1872. The same Indian force which had expelled Captain Beauregard and other Confederates from Corosal in 1870 invaded the area near Orange Walk on 31 August 1872 in an attempt to surprise the Queens West Indian regiment stationed there. The garrison was easily surrounded by the Indian force which initially tried to burn the buildings being used by the soldiers as safe havens. The officer in command was wounded along with fourteen others, and two were killed. The entire regiment would have been doomed were it not for the arrival of the predominantly Confederate flying cavalry. The group of ex–Confederates attacked the Indians from the rear, killing at least fifteen and wounding many others, including the chief, who died soon after. The Indians' defeat was so decisive that the new chief sued for peace with the British government.[19] John Wallace Price, E. Boudreau, and H. J. Archer[20] were the heroes of the "most famous episode" of the Indian wars in the Northern District.[21]

When a cholera outbreak in the town of Orange Walk was in full fury and a large number of citizens were dying in January 1868, Price volunteered his services. The following is an excerpt from an article about the terrible scourge facing Orange Walk and Price's response to the situation:

> J. W. Price Esquire, of Tower Hill ... guaranteed to cut down and fence in at his own unaided cost a piece of ground somewhat less than a mile distant from Orange Walk, on the road leading to Tower Hill, for the interment of persons dying of Cholera, and also provide a cart for the removal of corpses.[22]

This is just one example of the great lengths to which Price was willing to go in order to help residents of his new community. He was known to have considerable compassion for his fellow man. The cholera outbreak subsided almost as rapidly as it had appeared, but its effect on the colony was not forgotten.

Belize's largest sugar manufacturer is now located outside of Orange Walk, just a short distance from Louisiana Farm, the plantation once owned by John Wallace Price, formerly of Louisiana. Confederates opened much of the area surrounding Orange Walk for the cultivation of sugar, thus introducing that part of the colony to what is now the major agricultural export of the nation of Belize. (Photograph courtesy William Parker)

As in the rest of the colony, with Toledo as the exception, no community of Confederates survived in Orange Walk. The descendants of Price and Kevlin still remain in the colony, but they are the only known remaining Confederate descendants from Orange Walk. The other families eventually gave in to homesickness and over the years returned to the United States.[23]

The Confederate settlement of Orange Walk has been overlooked by contemporary scholars. The sugar industry begun by the Confederates was important to the economic development of British Honduras, but their contributions to the colony has not been noted in histories of the colony and the nation of Belize. Confederates opened much of the area surrounding Orange Walk for the cultivation of sugar, thus introducing that part of the colony to what is now the major agricultural export of Belize. Price and the other settlers also put an end to the Indian raids from Mexico which had been a hindrance to settlement of the Northern District of the British possession for some time. Thus, the Confederates helped to bring political stability and an economic boon to the colony. Tower Hill, near where Louisiana Farm was once located, is now the site of Belize's largest sugar manufacturer.

Notes

1. Perseverance, "The Present and Future," *British Honduras Colonist and Belize Advertiser*, 13 June 1868, 3.

2. Narda Dobson, *A History of Belize* (London: Butler and Tanner, 1973), 223.

3. Rosenberger, 147; Perseverance, 3.

4. W. M. Guild and Co., Agents, "For Sale or Lease," *Daly's Advertising Sheet*, 17 December 1870, 1; Dispatches from U.S. Consuls in Belize, A. C. Prindle to W. A. Seward, No. 125, 4 January 1870, FM T-334 Roll 4.

5. Joe DePriest to author, 9 April 1990.

6. Frank M. Mason to author, 21 August 1990; Daniel Rosenberger and Joe DePriest also made reference to a Colonel Purvis who lived at Corosal. The author has been unable to uncover any information about Purvis. Primary documents place Purvis in Manattee with Maunsel Chapman (refer to R. F. Gray, "British Honduras," *Opelousas Journal*, 4 July 1868, 2).

7. Dobson, 223–24.

8. Information regarding his date of return to the United States is based upon passenger information detailed in *Passenger Lists of Vessels Arriving in New Orleans* (Washington, D.C.: National Archives and Record Service, 1958), M259, Rolls 50–54. For specific information, please consult Appendix D.

9. DePriest, 9 April 1990.

10. Dobson, 224.

11. Emory King to author, 15 January 1990.

12. King to author, 15 January 1990. King was not aware of Archer's full name. I have deduced his name based upon other evidence. King believed that Kevlin was from Missouri.

13. Rosenberger, 157; Hill, 82.

14. "That an Extensive Immigration," *New Era*, 18 March 1871, 3.

15. Andrew B. Booth, *Records of Louisiana Confederate Soldiers and Louisiana Confederate Commands*, vol. 3 (New Orleans: Louisiana Commissioner of Military Records, 1920).

16. King to author, 15 January 1990; Foster, "British Honduras," 1.

17. Pendergast, 64.

18. C. D. [Christopher Hempstead], "British Honduras," *Daily Picayune*, 29 April 1867, 2(E); Rosenberger, 158.

19. Dobson, 224; Emory King to author, 15 January 1990. While it is considered common knowledge that the Confederate soldiers saved the West Indian regiment from certain death, official reports make no mention of their presence at the conflict.

20. King to author, 15 January 1990.

21. Dobson, 224.

22. "Orange Walk," *British Honduras Colonist and Belize Advertiser*, 25 January 1868, 3–4.

23. King to author, 15 January 1990. The author could find no one in Orange Walk as of May 1991 living near the cholera graveyard who was aware of its existence. The exact location is, therefore, unknown.

CHAPTER XIII

Manattee and Other Settlements

The colonial government of British Honduras tried in 1867 to channel most of the expected Confederate settlers toward lands known as the Icacos Grant. The grant, several thousand acres of land between the Deep and Monkey rivers, was deemed appropriate by colonial officials for the demands of the expected agricultural immigrants. As mentioned earlier, James Putnam and his associates planned for a grand relocation of fellow exiles from the southern United States on this large expanse of arable land. The plan, however, was thwarted by higher officials in London as discussed earlier. The lieutenant governor was reprimanded for making such a large grant of land and recalled for his actions while Austin City, named for Lieutenant Governor Austin and planned for Point Icacos, was deemed undesirable.[1] No settler dared to establish himself on a questionable grant of land such as Icacos. Putnam and his associates, in an effort to meet the terms of the grant despite the tremendous setback, began trying to place settlers in other parts of the colony.

To the south of Belize City there were six major attempts, besides the one at Toledo, to establish Confederate settlements along the coast, including along the Manattee River, Mullins River, Sittee River, South Stann Creek, and Deep River. When Charles Swett and his party toured the colony in search of land early that year, they found Dr. F. G. Pew, formerly of Arkansas, clearing land on the Middle River just above Swazie's Landing.[2] Colonel W. H. Martin, Dr. John Thompson, Dr. William Jamieson, and P. C. Perrett had joined Pew by early April.[3] On South Stann Creek, Swett became acquainted with William Cole Chamberlain of Natchez, Mississippi.[4]

Chamberlain, whose personal estate had been valued at more than a quarter of a million dollars before the Civil War,[5] purchased an extensive

Samuel McCutchon (left), *a native of the Ormond Plantation, St. Charles Parish, Louisiana, who was a resident of Pass Christian, Mississippi, at the outbreak of the Civil War, managed the Regalia Estate in British Honduras from 1866 until 1874. His son Azby D. McCutchon* (right) *was seven years old when the family moved to British Honduras. Like many children of the Confederate community in the colony, Azby was sent to the United States for formal education. (Photograph courtesy the McCutchon Family)*

piece of land which ran almost four miles along the sea and extended inland for eight miles.[6] He had already started cutting a road ten miles into the interior when Swett traveled through the area.[7] Chamberlain and the other families at South Stann Creek[8] were neighbored to the north by Samuel McCutchon of Pass Christian, Mississippi.

McCutchon occupied a portion of land along the Sittee River similar in size to Chamberlain's.[9] Unlike many of the other settlers, he did not own the property but served as the manager for the sugar plantation and sawmill known as Regalia Estate, which was owned by Young, Toledo and Company. The employment of McCutchon by the company was evidence of the desire to ensure success of the venture. A similar endeavor in corporate sugar planting that failed in the colony only a few years earlier was said to have been "easily accounted for in the absence of all knowledge of sugar cultivation."[10] McCutchon, having been born on the Ormond Plantation, St. Charles Parish, Louisiana, and considered one of the most knowledgeable men in the industry, was a much sought-after commodity in the colony.[11] He was the most successful sugar planter in British Honduras during the 1860s and has been recognized as the individual who proved the profitability of sugar production in the colony. He manufactured almost as much raw sugar during the first year of his residence at Regalia Estate as had been produced in the entire colony in 1862, only five years prior.[12] The huge operation at Regalia Estate had thirty-five full-time employees by August 1868.[13]

Thirty families are said to have tried to settle along the Moho River.[14] This group, led by Daniel Brown and George Sherrod of Natchitoches Parish, Louisiana, began clearing lands along the river in early 1868.[15] The effort was probably abandoned in short order, however, as Sherrod and Brown are listed as founders of the Toledo Settlement in a letter written late in February 1868.[16]

Of all the ex–Confederates attempting to establish settlements along the coast, including Toledo, the founders of Manattee had the most capital and resources backing their enterprise. The Manattee River bank was originally expected to be the site of a large town. Named for Alfred Usher, who was a land speculator from Belize City, the town was to be auctioned off on Wednesday, 10 July 1867, by Christopher Hempstead. The 3,882 lots were each 100 square feet in size but did not sell as expected.[17] The following month he advertised the town lots in sizes of five to ten acres.[18]

The small lots had little appeal to Southerners who were accustomed to living on large plantations. For example, Maunsel W. Chapman, from Aberdeen, Mississippi, purchased a 12,000-acre plantation in British Honduras.[19] The plantation was called "Aberdeen" after its namesake in Mississippi, at the request of his wife.[20] Twenty-two individuals purchased similar plantations within a five-mile radius.[21] Richard Covington Woods of Louisiana, James G. McCoy of Texas,[22] Lewis Hobbs Hill of Morehouse Parish, Dr. Ade Wilson of Long Beach, Mississippi,[23] and H. B. Britton of New Orleans,[24] were some of the others joining Chapman along the Manattee.

Chapman served as the leader of the fledgling settlement. Extremely well educated, Chapman held a degree from Louisiana University and was fluent in five languages. He was a decorated war veteran and was related to the Beauregard family of Louisiana as well as to the earl of Millwater, Liverpool, England. He was therefore uniquely qualified for such a position of prominence in the newly founded Confederate community.[25] The "large and comfortable dwelling" at Aberdeen,[26] where guests experienced such luxuries as an evening meal served on French china and conversation while reclining on elegantly crafted furniture,[27] was a welcome breath of fresh southern air for the exiles attempting to carve a new life in the harsh and rugged colonial countryside.

Unlike the other Confederate settlements, Manattee planters exported only crops traditionally associated with the colony. Forgoing sugar and cotton, Chapman and the others exported coconuts, pineapples, and bananas. Nature produced a readily accessible supply of crops, yet getting the goods to market profitably and expeditiously was difficult if not impossible.

Labor was as unreliable and expensive in Manattee as it was in Toledo and other parts of the colony. The following is Maunsel Chapman's son's version of the difficulty faced when hiring laborers for the family plantation in Manattee:

> Give a native a cocoanut and a handful of rice and all idea of work was promptly banished — money was no incentive and so it became evident that the indolent nature could not be depended upon. Fruit rotted at the warf [sic] awaiting shipment.[28]

The Chapmans and most other Confederate families in British Honduras apparently had great difficulty making the transition from slave labor to free workers. Difficulty acquiring help was a common complaint and a problem that was not resolved until East Indian laborers arrived in British Honduras during the 1870s, long after the Confederate settlement at Manattee was abandoned.

Nevertheless, labor was not the only reason for the decline of the Manattee settlement. Homesickness plagued the community and was perhaps the primary catalyst for abandoning the effort.[29] The absence of family and friends took a terrible toll on those who tried to settle in the colony as the final lines of a letter written to a friend in Mississippi attests:

> But one thing we lack, and that is the wonted[sic] faces of our brethren and our kinsmen, and this I am persuaded we will ere long. This must be the nucleus of a settlement which will regenerate the tropics. My wife and child are, thank God, in excellent health and happy. My darling Mary often speaks of her Aberdeen [Mississippi] friends with brimming eyes, but this is her only sorrow. She joins me in affectionate remembrance to yourself and wife, and to all friends.[30]

The yearning for the friendly faces of "kinsmen" infected all of the settlements along the coast, including Manattee. By the year 1872, the only families known to remain in the southern region of the colony, outside of Toledo, were the McCutchons and Chamberlains. The Hill and Wilson families moved to Toledo via Corosal; Perrett eventually joined the group at Toledo; and the Britton family moved to Belize City. The rest had returned to the United States by 1872.

The era of group migration came to an anticlimactic conclusion with a handful of families struggling at Toledo and Orange Walk, with McRae at Saturday Creek, Chamberlain at South Stann Creek, and McCutchon on the Sittee River, and a few other families scattered around the colony. Those who were living at Belize City completed the small faction of ex–Confederates, serving as a reminder to all of what might have been.

Notes

1. "Austin City," *Commercial Advertiser*, 17 July 1867, 3.
2. Swett, 36.
3. "Memorable Events," 1–2.
4. Swett, 30.
5. National Archives Microfilm Productions, *Population Schedules of the Eighth Census of the United States, 1860* (Adams County, Mississippi), M653, Roll 577, 41.
6. *Land Titles Register*, vols. 7–8, No. 301, Office of the General Registry, Belize City, Belize.
7. Swett, 30.
8. Gray, "British Honduras," 2; Gray reported that about five families resided at South Stann Creek in June 1868 and Dwight stated in his 30 December 1868 journal entry that about thirty persons had just arrived to join the settlement.
9. *Land Titles Registry* 7–8, No. 328.
10. Pendergast, 63.
11. For information on the business operations of the Regalia and Ormond plantations, refer to the *Samuel McCutchon Papers, 1832–1874* (Bethesda, Maryland: University Publications of America, 1989).
12. Gray, *Publishers Journal*, 2; Pendergast, 63.
13. Samuel McCutchon Papers, 248–49.
14. Hill, 82.
15. "Memorable Events," 1–2.
16. Settlers at Cattle Landing to James M. Putnam, *British Honduras Colonist and Belize Advertiser*, 29 February 1868, 3.
17. Alfred Usher, "Usher's Town, Manattee," *Commercial Advertiser*, 3 July 1867, 3.
18. "Notice," *Commercial Advertiser*, 7 August 1867, 3.
19. Wm. Guild and Co., Agents. "For Sale or Lease," *Daly's Advertising Sheet*, 17 December 1870, 1; Dispatches from U.S. Consuls in Belize, A. C. Prindle to W. A. Seward, No. 125, 4 January 1870, FM T-334 Roll 4.
20. Lt. Col. Robert B. Hardy to author, 9 April 1990.
21. Hill, 82.
22. Rosenberger, 162.

23. Joe DePriest to author, 9 April 1990.

24. Rosenberger, 158; also spelled Brinton.

25. Hardy to author, 9 April 1990.

26. Wm. Guild and Co., Agents, 1; Dispatches from U.S. Consuls in Belize, A. C. Prindle to W. A. Seward, No. 125, 4 January 1870, FM T-334 Roll 4.

27. Hardy to author, 9 April 1990; Hardy has his grandfather's china at his home, "The Cedars," located in Columbus, Mississippi.

28. Letter written by Felix Millwater Chapman to Miss Fan——, 21 October 1947. Located in the personal collection of Lt. Col. Robert B. Hardy, "The Cedars," Columbus, Mississippi.

29. Hardy to author, 9 April 1990.

30. Maunsel W. Chapman, "British Honduras," *Livingston Journal* (Alabama), 22 June 1867, 1.

CHAPTER XIV

Belize City at the Height of the Immigrant Influx

The city of Belize served as the political, economic, and geographic center of the colony. Efforts to colonize the interior radiated from the colonial capital. The predominant concentration of Confederates occurred at Belize City even though not all immigrants entered the colony through the port of Belize.[1] Almost all correspondence referred to travel to the city for social gatherings, worship, and the purchase of supplies.

The city itself impressed the new arrivals. W. A. Love, a former member of the Mississippi legislature from Kemper County, described the city as a "second Venice."[2] In addition to noting the extensive use of water transportation, he was pleasantly surprised by the city's neat appearance. Traveling through Belize City, newly arrived immigrants found modest but well-kept one-story homes,[3] devoid of fireplaces, as several noted, due to the tropical climate.[4] All described the streets as well kept and safe. Southerners were also impressed by the piety shown by the city dwellers. For example, all businesses and shops were closed on the Sabbath. Medicine was the only item sold on Sunday. The Reverend B. R. Duval commented that the day was more "rigidly kept" than in any town in the United States.[5] A correspondent for the *Daily Picayune* wrote that the only sound heard on Sunday was the sound of church bells.[6]

Each arriving vessel during the height of the influx brought with it an additional contingent of exiles to add to the growing community of Confederates. The U.S. commercial agent in Belize City stated, "Generals and Colonels [met] at every turn, for some days after the arrival of each steamer."[7] The commercial agent overstates, perhaps, the social status of the typical immigrant, yet he does give some indication of the perceived impact of the arrivals. The streets of Belize City were teeming with a wide array of Confederate exiles, and the colonial economy flourished. Men preparing for exploration of the interior availed themselves of the city shops stocked with all possible expeditionary supplies. Excited and eager men converged along the docks daily carrying their newly purchased supplies, ready to embark upon their journey into the interior in search of a new home. Women and children were almost always left behind in the colonial capital to await the return of their husbands, fathers, and brothers. For many less fortunate exiles, the streets of Belize City held the promise and hope for a better day. Indeed, many Southerners arrived in the city destitute, with few or no resources and in search of employment. Wandering the streets in hope of stumbling onto some means of subsistence, these exiles joined the ranks of those who had arrived in the colony with some resources only to fall victim to thieves or unscrupulous land agents. The ranks of the destitute swelled also with the casualties of nature: unfamiliar worms which destroyed crops; diseases that wiped out entire families; insects that plagued plants, animals, and humans; and weather which could be mild one moment and at another terribly cruel.

Exiles from New Orleans or other more metropolitan areas of the South who preferred life in an urban setting purchased or rented homes in or near the colonial capital, establishing themselves as permanent fixtures in Belize City. Once the decision was made to remain in town, housing was easily obtained. Large comfortable homes rented in Belize City for $18 (B.H.) per month. Food and supplies were said to be relatively inexpensive. In this tropical climate, fruits were abundant and cheap. Direct steamship service to New Orleans provided access to both necessities and luxury items. News from the United States arrived weekly, and the *Daily Picayune* was readily available. Outside of the city, but within a few hours' walk, small farms with dwellings rented for $300 (B.H.) per year.[8] Letters to relatives spoke of the ease of life along the beautiful Belize River and its tributaries where crops "reached maturity in less than three weeks" and "fruit trees flourished."[9] Some exaggeration should be expected from exiles as their letters attempted to assuage the worries of those at home and convince them of the prosperity to be found in British Honduras if only they, too, would come. Their new life, however, was far from effortless and carefree. British Honduras was not the Old South, and despite their large numbers, Southerners found themselves limited by the laws and customs of the colony and the Crown. The limitations varied according to one's proximity to town. Those establishing settlements in the interior were able to isolate themselves from established colonial laws and customs, but immigrants residing in Belize City soon became intensely aware of the conflict between the two cultures. The unfamiliar social climate, however, did not dissuade those determined to settle in Belize City.

In fact, a number of Confederates became prominent members of the developing urban community. One such success story was W. J. S. Scobell, formerly of New Orleans, who established a newspaper for his compatriots entitled, the *Commercial Advertiser*.[10] "Open to all — Influenced by none!!" was its motto. The publication welcomed new arrivals to the colony by informing them, "No danger that here after years of toil, robber governments will unrest from you the products of your hard earnings."[11] To no one's surprise, Scobell and his associates defiantly referred to themselves as "unreconstructed" individuals.[12] Scobell, for the price of $6 (B.H.) per annum, supplied colonists with the news of the day. More important for Confederates, passenger lists, hotel guest lists, and information regarding naturalization were regular features. Blatantly targeting the new arrivals from the United States, one issue devoted an entire column to the quality of the schools in the colony, the question to which every immigrant's "anxious and fidgetty [*sic*] wife" sought an answer.[13] Scobell's dedication to the interests of the Confederate community in the colony gained him a great deal of notoriety not only in the colony but also back in the United States.

Other notable members of the city's community of Confederates, T. C. Brewer and Mrs. A. Foote, owned well-respected hotels. Foote owned the American Hotel. As a struggling widow with six children, she was the object of much public support. Foote's husband had served as a second lieutenant in St. Mary's Cannoneers, a Louisiana battery mustered into Confederate service in defense of General Butler's attack on New Orleans. The unit was the only one during the Union assault on Fort St. Philip and Fort Jackson in April 1862 that did not experience mutiny, in spite of horrific losses.[14] At the war's end, Mrs. Foote refused to live under the flag of the United States. Newspapers called upon the community to patronize Foote's establishment, which was located at the corner of Orange Street and Duck Lane. The *British Honduras Colonist and Belize Advertiser* requested that sympathetic readers patronize the establishment owned by

> a LADY who has been driven from her once happy home (where she was surrounded by every comfort and luxury), and by the cruel vicissitudes of civil war, forced either to become a dweller in a foreign land, or to live out a life of misery amidst the beastly saturnalia of the new order of things, where the stars are shut out by the blackness of darkness, and the stripes are felt as well as seen![15]

Foote and her family's fight to recover from the loss of her husband and achieve "respectability" were the subject of considerable correspondence in the newspapers.

AMERICAN HOTEL.

NOTICE.

THE Proprietress in returning thanks for the liberal support she has received since opening the above-named Hotel, wishes to acquaint Travellers and others that hereafter her terms w'll be

Monthly Boarders,.....$7 00 per week.
Weekly   do........ 9 00
Day   do........ 1 25
Single Meals,......... 0 50

Large and airy Rooms, civil and attentive Servants, a Table well supplied with all the Market affords.

As for references—she refers to the many Travellers who have patronized her Hotel.

MRS. A. FOOTE,
Proprietress.

Belize, October 8, 1867.

Southern Hotel

—A N D—

RESTAURANT.

THE Undersigned takes pleasure in notifying the Public, that the Restaurant Department of the above Hotel, will be opened on

MONDAY NEXT.

The Mercantile Portion of the Community will find the Restaurant Plan a convenient and pleasant one for obtaining Meals.

Board and Lodging, per day $ 1 50
    "   "   "   " Week, 10 00
Board only, (2 Meals) "   "   8 00
Single Meals,   ..   75

Breakfast, from half-past 7 to 10 o'clock.
Dinner, from half-past 3 to 5 o'clock.

W. S. WIER,
Proprietor.

Belize, Sept. 6th, 1867.

(Left) *Mrs. A. Foote, a Confederate widow from St. Mary's Parish, Louisiana, and owner of the American Hotel, was the subject of sympathetic editorials in the* British Honduras Colonist and Belize Advertiser. *In advertisements like this one on 2 November 1867, Foote thanked the citizens of Belize City for their "liberal support" of her endeavor.* (Right) *The Southern Hotel, the largest and most expensive hotel in Belize City, catered to the most prosperous of the Confederate immigrants arriving in the city. The flood of arrivals in 1867 necessitated the addition of a restaurant, as described in this advertisement, which appeared in the* Colonist *on 14 September 1867.*

Brewer was quite the entrepreneur as well. Before the Civil War, he and his wife, Anna, owned a county newspaper in Wilcox County, Alabama.[16] Upon arrival in Belize City, they purchased a hotel they later named the Brewer's Hotel. It served as a base for several other of Captain Brewer's enterprises, including an auctioneer service and a general commission merchant business. Claiming to have had a great deal of experience as an auctioneer, he guaranteed "satisfaction" in the sale of all types of property including real estate. The hotel, he advertised, possessed adequate storage for any amount of goods along with security if necessary.[17] Next to his hotel, located on Orange Street, Brewer and J. M. Merry established a tinsmithy. Merry operated the shop and promised competent work at a reasonable price. Merry was also a former citizen of the United States and had worked for some time in New York City as a tinsmith.[18] The two remained partners for twenty months until, in November 1868, the partnership was dissolved, and Merry purchased Brewer's interest in the business venture.[19]

T. C. and Anna Brewer were highly admired as "the prince of good fellows" and "the elegant and accomplished lady," respectively, by probably the most intriguing character to join the Confederate community in or near Belize City. Richard Talley Johnson, formerly of Mansfield, Desoto Parish, Louisiana, and a friend, George M. Eldredge, also from Mansfield, arrived in British Honduras in early 1868 with their families. Eldredge settled in the southern region of the colony while Johnson purchased land near Belize City, eventually becoming a frequent topic of conversation for members of the Confederate community in British Honduras and other colonists as well.

Prior to the Civil War, R. T. Johnson had been one of the wealthiest men in Louisiana. Somehow he managed to transport a portion of his wealth to British Honduras. Upon his death on 3 April 1869, Colonel Johnson,[20] possessed a personal estate and effects worth more than $31,000, according to records kept by the colony's officials.[21]

A flamboyant man, Johnson posted the following notice of his intent to reside in the city on the bulletin board at the government offices in Belize:

> The property known as "Martinez Pen" has been purchased by the undersigned, an exile from the United States of America.
>   The purchase was made in consequence of its isolation, adapted to one in bad health, seeking in old age, that peace and repose denied to him in his native land. That part enclosed and embracing the cottage and also the walk in the rear to the terminus of the ridge, after this date will cease to be a public promenade. No fruit will be sold on the Sabbath, and only by the wholesale.
>   Signed,
>   R. T. Johnson

The Pen was located on a sand ridge about a half mile from Belize.[22] Johnson lived there until his death less than one year later. During his short tenure in Belize, Johnson devoted much of his time to writing friends in the United States, encouraging others to settle in the colony.

Colonel Johnson was outspoken about his political beliefs. He expressed these freely to friends in Desoto Parish. "The republicanism of Washington, Jefferson, and Madison has long since been 'played out'; and in confirmation of this assertion you have the evidence transpiring daily before your eyes," he once reported. Like so many of his fellow Southerners following the Civil War, Johnson often stated that he preferred a constitutional monarchy, which he deftly defended by stating the following: "I had rather obey one master in the person of a monarch, yea even the Autocrat of Russia, than to be the slave of hundreds of thousands of sovereigns with no other qualifications to rule than ignorance and brutality."[23] Johnson died a bitter expatriate.

Christopher and Catherine Hempstead were the most visible and also most influential couple of the Confederate community of Belize City. Mr. Hempstead arrived in Belize City during the 1840s and served as U.S. consul under the Polk administration.[24] An ardent secessionist, he remained in the city during the Civil War, eventually becoming a citizen and establishing himself as a prominent businessman.[25] By the war's close he had become an elected member of the legislative assembly, possessed a great deal of authority in the colony, and worked dutifully to encourage his compatriots to establish themselves in the colony. Also involved in the business of merchant and auctioneer, Hempstead maintained offices on Regent Street.[26]

Christopher Hempstead's first wife died rather suddenly in early 1868,[27] and shortly following her death, the widower became a suitor of Catherine McRae, a member of one of the South's most prominent families. One brother, Colin J. McRae, had served as Confederate financial agent in Europe, while another brother, John J. McRae, served as the well-known governor of Mississippi. Catherine arrived in Belize City in May 1868 with her brother John.[28] He died soon after his arrival in Belize City on the last day of May, only a few days before the death of Christopher's wife. The two mourners, Christopher and Catherine, found solace in each other's company and were soon married. The couple had one child, Christabelle Willie Minnie Hempstead.[29]

John J. McRae. (Courtesy Mississippi Department of Archives and HIstory)

Said to be a friend to all Southerners, Christopher Hempstead was often commended for his assistance to those in need. On at least one occasion, he came to the aid of Peter Fisher, the most infamous member of the Confederate population in

Belize. Fisher, formerly of Lafayette County, Missouri,[30] was rumored to be wanted for murder in the United States. Hempstead paid bond for Fisher when he was charged with stealing boards and managed to get the charges dropped for lack of evidence.[31] Unfortunately for Fisher, later when he drew and fired his pistol in a hotel restaurant, British authorities were not so understanding.[32]

Hempstead also drew a great deal of public attention when he assisted the notorious Captain John V. Singer, formerly of Brownsville, Texas, and the brother of M. Singer, founder of Singer Sewing Machine, in his defense against a charge of piracy. John Singer was said to be one of the Confederate heroes of the Civil War as a result of having invented a destructive torpedo. Hempstead accompanied Singer to the hearings and served as his counsel. With the help of Hempstead, Singer was exonerated and a settlement was reached. The trial created a stir in Belize City and became quite the topic of conversation when Singer's scorned wife arrived in town during the hearings to lay claim to her ship, reportedly stolen by Singer and another woman, who also claimed to be his wife. Once released, he fled to Livingston, Guatemala, with the "other woman."[33]

Hempstead's involvement with most Southerners, however, was not so dramatic. During the height of the exodus from the United States, Hempstead served as the agent of Young, Toledo and Company in Belize City.[34] The majority of those deciding to remain in British Honduras settled on lands rented or purchased from this company. Hempstead's offices, as a result of his extreme occupational diversity, became a point of assembly for an assortment of people.

James Mercier Putnam, also a land agent for Young, Toledo and Company, perhaps equaled Hempstead in prominence within the Confederate community of the colony. His contributions toward the establishment of settlements in the interior are documented in other chapters. Putnam, Hempstead, Foote, Brewer, and Scobell were by no means the only immigrants to establish homes in the colonial capital; however, their specific achievements, contributions, and personalities merit recognition.[35] Unfortunately, there is no way to estimate how many Southerners actually established themselves in the city or how many were in residence at any specific time. During the era of group migration, the city became the point of congregation for thousands of transients. The majority returned to the United States within a few months. Most apparently preferred life in the United States rather than face the challenge of the colony's interior.

The influx, however, did bring to the city of Belize a number of formerly high-ranking Confederate officials. The appearance of Lieutenant Governor Benjamin W. Pearce at one of the hotels created quite a sensation during the summer of 1867.[36] Pearce was a former member of the house of representatives in both Arkansas and Louisiana, as well as a former state senator in Louisiana. A senatorial delegate to the Louisiana secession convention in 1861, he was a vocal supporter of the state's move to join the Confederacy. At the outbreak of the war, Pearce left his cotton plantation to organize Company C, Ninth Louisiana Infantry Volunteers, serving as a captain until his election to the office of lieutenant governor in 1862.[37]

At the close of the war Lieutenant Governor Pearce was, like many former Louisiana planters, in debt and disenfranchised. He was the target of much ridicule in his home parish of Bienville as a result of an incident involving representatives of the Bureau of Freedmen, his wife, and an alleged illegitimate daughter, the result of a relationship with one of his former slaves. The humiliation resulting from the incident was surely a contributing factor in the decision by Pearce to consider moving to British Honduras.[38]

During his brief visit to Belize City, Pearce accepted an invitation to visit the legislative assembly and sat at the right hand of the Speaker while the house was in session.[39] He apparently made it known that he and his companions intended to recruit cotton planters to establish a settlement in the interior of the colony, but like so many others, there is no evidence of his return. One reason for his failure to emigrate to the colony may have been poor health as he died less than three years later, but another may have been reports later that year of failures by earlier emigrants to successfully plant cotton in the colony.

Notes

1. Dispatches from U.S. Consuls in Belize, A. C. Prindle to F. W. Seward, No. 1, 1 July 1867, FM T-334 Roll 3; Donald Simmons, Jr., "Prominent Citizens of the Confederate Community in Belize City, 1865–1870," *Belizean Studies* 20, No. 2 (October 1992): 22.

2. W. A. Love, "Social Customs in British Honduras," *Hinds County Gazette* (Mississippi), 9 August 1867, 1; Simmons, 22.

3. Swett, 77; Simmons, 22.

4. Duval, 2.

5. Duval, 38; Simmons, 22.

6. "British Honduras," *Daily Picayune*, 21 March 1866, 11(M); Simmons, 22.

7. Dispatches from U.S. Consuls in Belize, A. C. Prindle to F. W. Seward, No. 15, 1 October 1868, FM T-334 Roll 3; Simmons, 22.

8. "From Honduras," *Mobile Daily Advertiser and Register*, 31 July 1867, 1; Simmons, 23.

9. Texan, "Letter from British Honduras," *Daily Picayune*, 29 July 1867, 2(A); Simmons, 23.

10. "How Things Look in British Honduras," *Daily Picayune*, 23 July 1867, 1(M); Simmons, 24.

11. "Strange Faces," *Commercial Advertiser* (British Honduras), 17 July 1867, 2; Simmons, 24.

12. "Returned," *Commercial Advertiser*, 3 July 1867, 2; Simmons, 24.

13. "A Good Sign," *Commercial Advertiser*, 17 July 1867, 2; Simmons, 24.

14 Arthur W. Bergeron, Jr., *Guide to Louisiana Confederate Military Units, 1861–1865* (Baton Rouge: Louisiana State University Press, 1989), 17–18; Booth, vols. 1–2.

15. "We Have Much Pleasure…," *British Honduras Colonist and Belize Advertiser*, 24 August 1867, 3.

16. National Archives Microfilm Production, *Population Schedules of the Eighth Census of the United States, 1860* (Wilcox County, Alabama), M653, Roll 26, 1044.

17. "T. C. Brewer, Auctioneer," *British Honduras Colonist and Belize Advertiser*, 19 September 1868, 1; Simmons, 24.

18. T. C. Brewer and J. M. Merry, "Tin-Smithing," *British Honduras Colonist and Belize Advertiser*, 7 March 1867, 4; Simmons, 25.

19. "Dissolution," *British Honduras Colonist and Belize Advertiser*, 28 November 1868, 4; Simmons, 25.

20. Johnson, 3.

21. "Last Will and Testament of Richard Talley Johnson," *Probate Records*, Office of General Registry, Belize City, Belize.

22. Dispatches from U.S. Consuls in Belize, A. C. Prindle to F. W. Seward, No. 27, 5 May 1868, FM T-334 Roll 3.

23. Johnson, 3.

24. C.D., "Letter from Belize, Honduras," *Daily Picayune*, 17 September 1868, 2; Dispatches from U.S. Consuls in Belize, A. C. Prindle to Hamilton Fish, No. 116, 19 September 1870, FM T-334 Roll 3; Simmons, 25.

25. Dispatches from U.S. Consuls in Belize, A. C. Prindle to J. L. Cadwaleden, No. 225, 30 August 1875, FM T-334 Roll 4; Simmons, 25.

26. "Last Will and Testament of J. Christopher Hempstead," *Probate Records*, Office of General Registry, Belize City, Belize; Simmons, 25.

27. "Deaths," *British Honduras Colonist and Belize Advertiser*, 27 June 1868, 2.

28. Davis, 88; Simmons, 26.

29. "Last Will and Testament of J. Christopher Hempstead"; Simmons, 26.

30. Dispatches from U.S. Consuls in Belize, A. C. Prindle to Hamilton Fish, No. 73, 17 September 1869, FM T-334 Roll 4; Simmons, 26.

31. "Another Attempt at Robbery," *British Honduras Colonist and Belize Advertiser*, 7 November 1868, 2; Simmons, 26.

32. Dispatches from U.S. Consuls in Belize, A. C. Prindle to Hamilton Fish, No. 119, 26 November 1870, FM T-334 Roll 4; Simmons, 26.

33. Dispatches from U.S. Consuls in Belize, A. C. Prindle to F. W. Seward, No. 44, 16 October 1868, FM T-334 Roll 3; Simmons, 26. The "torpedo" would now be referred to as a mine. For a short description of the use of mines in the Civil War, refer to the *Historical Times Illustrated Encyclopedia of the Civil War*, ed. Patricia L. Faust (New York: Harper & Row, 1986).

34. James M. Putnam, "British Honduras, Central America," *Daily Picayune*, 11 August 1871, 2; Simmons, 26.

35. Simmons, 26. A Mr. Robinson from the United States was mentioned by several members of the Confederate community in Belize. He manufactured candles, soap, and essential oils from his home in Regent Street. It is not known from where he originated in the United States (refer to the *Commercial Advertiser*, 17 July 1867, 2). Robinson told the newspaper that large numbers from his area would soon follow him; Putnam apparently had a residence in Belize and on Ambergris Cay.

36. C. D., "From Belize, Honduras," *Daily Picayune*, 14 June 1867, 1(A); Simmons, 26.

37. "Journal of the Convention of the State of Louisiana," *Louisiana History* 2, No. 1 (Winter 1961): 3–7; *Biographical and Historical Memoirs of Northeast Louisiana* (Nashville: Southern Publishing, 1890), 193–94; Glenn R. Conrad, ed., *A Dictionary of Louisiana Biography* (New Orleans: Louisiana Historical Commission, 1988), 2:636.

38. Ted Tunnell, "Twitchell and the Freedmen's Bureau," *Louisiana History* 33, No. 3 (Summer 1992): 241–263.

39. "Returned," *Commercial Advertiser*, 3 July 1867, 2; Simmons, 26.

CHAPTER XV

Alternatives to Confederate Exile in British Honduras

Many descendants of Confederates who left the United States for British Honduras at the close of the Civil War, only to return some time later, now believe their forefathers lived in Brazil. This is an apparently common error in the genealogy of numerous southern families. The confusion is understandable considering the similar spelling and extensive exposure given to the Confederados of Brazil in recent years. The discovery of this misunderstanding gives rise to three important questions: Why has so much exposure been given to the Confederate settlements in Brazil while similar efforts in British Honduras have gone relatively unnoticed? What factors influenced a family's decision to settle in British Honduras? How were the Confederates in Brazil able to maintain a vibrant, cohesive community which still survives today while their former compatriots failed to do so in British Honduras? There are several reasons why Confederate settlements in British Honduras have been overlooked. The answers lie partially in the geographic sources of the emigrants from the United States. As mentioned earlier, the overwhelming majority of Confederate settlers in British Honduras came from Louisiana and the surrounding states on the Gulf of Mexico. Promoters of this colony specifically targeted the sugar planters of the lower Mississippi Delta region once they realized that cotton could not be raised for profit in British Honduras. Advertisements, letters, and articles promoting the wealth of the colony rarely appeared in publications outside of Louisiana. The resulting effect was, of course, that only a few highly skilled Americans in a concentrated geographic region were ever aware of settlements in British Honduras. Louisianans skilled in the planting of cotton were lured to Brazil.[1]

General interest, publicity, and public awareness do not completely explain, however, America's continued interest in the Brazilian settlements.

The socioeconomic status of immigrants to the two areas differed considerably. Brazil attracted a large number of Southerners but only two high-ranking Confederate officers, General W. W. Wood and General A. T. Hawthorne.[2] Evidence now suggests that perhaps more Confederates immigrated to British Honduras than Brazil, and more high-ranking Southerners chose the former. In addition to General Colin J. McRae and former governors John J. McRae of Mississippi and Benjamin W. Pearce of Louisiana, several state legislators and members of the famous Benjamin and Beauregard families of Louisiana went to British Honduras. It is only natural to assume that the much more impressive array of politicians, military officers, and powerful southern families settling in British Honduras would have attracted the larger share of attention through the years. As that has not been the case, there must be other factors.

One reason for the failure of historians and genealogists to make the connection between British Honduras and the United States may be that the colony was a secondary choice for many Confederates seeking to flee the United States. For example, both Joseph Benjamin and A. N. T. Beauregard, brothers of the well-known Confederate generals, initially sought refuge in Mexico and then in Spanish Honduras, but after finding those destinations unacceptable they established residences in British Honduras. No contemporary published sources, however, refer to any connection between these two individuals and British Honduras. Apparently no effort was made to follow their actions after their arrival in Mexico.[3]

The most obvious reason for the unbalanced coverage of the history and events of the two efforts at Confederate settlement lies in the nature of the communities that evolved following permanent settlement in the two countries. As has been noted earlier, it is now difficult to make distinctions between descendants of Confederates and their fellow Belizeans. Settlers in British Honduras were eventually absorbed into a society where the language, laws, and customs were somewhat similar to those of the United States. After a few generations, the descendants of the former Mississippians, Louisianans, and others have become an indistinguishable part of the culture of modern Belize. With the exception of a small group in Toledo, which maintained a distinctly southern culture, Southerners remaining in British Honduras eventually intermarried with the British or other members of the colonial society or at least became actively involved in the political and social workings of the colony.

Ties to the United States have always been strong for Belizeans. Throughout the history of the former British colony, food, clothing, and agricultural implements from the United States have filled the shelves of local retailers. The connections between the United States and British

Honduras were so close that in the 1860s a colonial monetary unit, the British Honduran dollar, was created in lieu of the British pound. The British Honduran/Belizean dollar has since that time been tied to the value of the United States dollar at a ratio of two to one.

Educational and intellectual ties between the two countries are also still in evidence. Sons and daughters of Southerners in British Honduras attended the same high schools and universities in the United States as did the children of their neighbors in British Honduras. For example, George Price, the first prime minister of Belize, attended schools in Mississippi. The close proximity of the United States has always made educational opportunities in that country exceptionally enticing for Belizeans. Today, Belizeans continue to read publications from the United States in order to follow the financial markets and news, and the ties have been strengthened by television satellite broadcasts to Belize.

In Brazil, the Confederados embarked upon a different adventure. Unfamiliar with the language, laws, and customs of the Portuguese-speaking nation, the settlers formed close-knit English-speaking communities, many of which are still easily recognizable today. The conflicting cultures made assimilation difficult and encouraged the maintenance of the southern dialect and customs. The great distance from the United States discouraged extensive interactions with the United States and allowed the settlers the opportunity to maintain customs and traditions commonly associated with the Old South while living in Brazil. The Fourth of July, for example, is still celebrated in Americana, Brazil.[4]

Although there was an extensive range of socioeconomic status among the various individuals who left for British Honduras and Brazil, all emigrants had one common goal: to escape the postwar environment in the United States. Surprising to some is the fact that efforts to continue the institution of slavery was really of little concern to the Confederates, as is clear by the fact that slavery no longer existed in British Honduras and was being phased out in Brazil. Letters sent home from South America stated that "free labor [was] preferred."[5] Thus, the decisions of particular families to settle in either British Honduras or Brazil depended on a number of factors which varied greatly depending on the particular personalities involved.

To conclude that economic factors were not a consideration when the decision was made to emigrate, however, would be incorrect. Brazil held a slight advantage over British Honduras in that only $20–$30 (U.S.) gold was required for passage to the South American nation.[6] The more frugal emigrant found the price particularly appealing in comparison with the $40 (U.S.) passage required to reach the British colony. There was little noticeable difference in the cost of land and supplies at each destination. The only major difference between the two was the travel distance when emigrating (the voyage to Brazil was much longer and more dangerous) and that one destination successfully promoted cotton and the other, sugar. In conclusion, then, it appears that decisions were reached based upon one's familiarity with cotton culture, promoted by Brazil, or sugar culture, promoted by British Honduras, and the success of advertising in the United States on the part of various recruiters.

Part of the reason why the community of Confederados in Brazil managed to survive into the twenty-first century as a cohesive unit is the size of the community. Thousands of former Confederates settled and remained in Brazil. The sheer number of immigrants that remained ensured the maintenance of a distinct community.

While the long voyage to Brazil and unfamiliarity with local language and customs promoted homesickness, the great distance simultaneously discouraged return to the United States. Those suffering from financial difficulty or bankruptcy found the trip back to the United States lengthy, expensive, and a near-impossibility.[7] The Southerners venturing to Brazil had little recourse other than to make the best of the situation.

Southerners in British Honduras, on the other hand, were less than a week by ship from New Orleans. As previously stated, the *Trade Wind* was even known to carry destitute Southerners free of charge on the short trip. In 1869 the exodus back to the United States was as rapid and extensive as the influx had been to British Honduras. Only a small minority stayed long enough to plant crops. Most Confederates who went to British Honduras remained there less than one year. Some fell victim to swindlers, land speculators, and Indians; others fell victim to cholera, yellow fever, tuberculosis, dysentery, and malaria.

Yet, homesickness was the most difficult test for those who survived the other trials of living in the tropics. British Honduras was not the antebellum South as all soon discovered. The Old South could not be recreated or recovered. The Reconstructed South was, for most, preferable to this vagabond life away from home. Only a small minority, those who had become successful entrepreneurs or planters, refused to return to the United States. In fact, five years after the war's end, less than one hundred Southerners are known to have remained in the British colony.[8] With the exception of the group at Toledo, they were scattered, in remote areas, and not easily recognized as representing a distinct culture or heritage.

Notes

1. Harter, 43–48, 53.
2. *Ibid.*, 17.
3. Evans, 381; in his book Eli Evans quotes correspondence of Judah P. Benjamin in which he often referred to his brother as residing in Spanish Honduras. The only logical explanation for this is that he was trying to protect his brother and McRae, both of whom were wanted by federal authorities, from prosecution. The obituary of A. N. T. Beauregard (*Donaldsonville Chief*, 6 June 1881) refers to his departure to Mexico at the close of the war but makes no mention of his residence in British Honduras.
4. Harter, 97.
5. Houma Civic Guard (of Tenebonne Parish), "From Brazil," *Daily Picayune*, 8 March 1866, 3(M); Harter, 22–23.
6. Harter, 26.
7. *Ibid.*, 65.
8. Dobson, 251.

Conclusion

The largely unsuccessful efforts of Confederate exiles to relocate in British Honduras is a chapter in U.S. history that has been all but ignored by researchers. Only a few lingering reminders of the brief episode remain. A handful of place names, an occasional accent out of place, and the huge sugar fields that dot the nation of Belize are but hints of a long-forgotten episode of the past.

While there was a great deal of diversity among the emigrants who fled the South in favor of British Honduras, some conclusions may be drawn about the type of individual who seized upon the adventure and hope of a new beginning in British Honduras. Typically, the British Hondurans targeted middle-aged gentlemen from the lower Mississippi Delta region or, to be more specific, from Mississippi and Louisiana. The majority were family men of considerable wealth and status in the antebellum South. On the average, these gentlemen were in possession of personal estates valued well in excess of those of the average Southerner prior to the Civil War, and they were residents of counties that voted overwhelmingly in favor of secession.[1] In fact, a considerable number of those fleeing to British Honduras were actively involved in the secession movement prior to the Civil War and held high offices in the Confederate government.

Having failed in their efforts to preserve the society from which they obtained considerable status and wealth, the ex–Confederates attempted to recreate their antebellum society under a different government, one they perceived to be tantamount to the Jeffersonian ideals to which they claimed to aspire. Life under the British Crown, they thought, would be superior to life in the United States after the fall of the Confederacy. These men of wealth and education were openly recruited by colonial officials as the great hope for the future of British Honduras. The Confederates soon discovered, however, that liberties and freedoms in British Honduras were

121

not interpreted in the same manner to which they were accustomed in the antebellum South. The concept of racial superiority, for example, was not given the legitimacy it held in the Old South. Nor were the violent acts committed by Confederates against those they considered socially inferior tolerated by the British Hondurans. The resulting conflict between cultures became increasingly evident with the arrival of more and more Confederates.

Cultural conflict, however, was not the primary reason for the failure of Confederate colonization efforts. After all, the communities in the interior could have isolated themselves quite easily and avoided all but essential contact with the British government. Some Southerners were even encouraged by the interaction between individuals of different races in the colony to reconsider their racial views. The real reason for the failure of the settlements was that Confederates found themselves unfamiliar with the climate and the terrain. Cotton farming was virtually impossible in British Honduras due to the excessive humidity, and sugar was a troublesome crop as dependable labor was difficult to acquire. It was only after Chinese and East Indian laborers, essentially indentured servants, were imported that the few Confederates who had managed to survive during those early difficult years profited from their agricultural pursuits. The Confederates who fled the United States soon discovered that the Old South could not be recreated. That distinctive political, economic, and social foundation had been destroyed by the Civil War. Some Confederates denied the reality of the situation longer than others. Only a few remained unreconstructed until their deaths. While Confederate colonization efforts fell short of their anticipated goals, the long-term impact on the developing economy of British Honduras can be seen today throughout the nation of Belize. Total production of sugar in the colony more than tripled during the first five years of Confederate settlement.[2] The country now depends upon the sugar industry, which was established by the efforts of self-exiled sugar planters from the states of the lower Mississippi Delta region, specifically, Mississippi and Louisiana.

Notes

1. Average age, value of personal estates, and other such data have been ascertained by the author from research materials.
2. Pendergast, 63.

Arrivals at the Hotels

The following listings were taken from an article published in the *Commercial Advertiser* dated 10 July 1867. This article was extremely important in the identification of prominent Confederates who traveled to or resettled in British Honduras.

American Hotel

W. Hustmyre	Alexandria, Louisiana
C. B. Cassidy	Shreveport, Louisiana
J. M. Day	San Marcos, Texas
Joseph Fitzpatrick	
H. Given	Texas
John Rumnondo	Mississippi
Thos. A. Woods	Louisiana
R. W. Broughurst	Texas
J. S. Henderson	Texas

Southern Hotel

Wm. Graves	Hazelhurst, Mississippi
Thos. Stewart	Mississippi
W. C. Chamberlain	New Orleans, Mississippi
T. Daigle	Natchez, Mississippi
Jno. R. Bedsoe, do.	
Wm. Hebert	Evergreen, Louisiana
Geo. Myers	Bolivar, Mississippi
T. J. Lacy	Washington, Louisiana
O. Johnson	New Orleans, Louisiana
Mrs. Byrne	Texas
Mr. Vineyard, lady & child	Texas
Mr. Love	Mississippi

APPENDIX B

Passenger Lists Taken from Various Sources

The lists included here often contradict official immigration sources. In several instances, they give more specific information than can be found in passenger lists kept by customs officials. These lists complement the text and may also assist those seeking genealogical information.

As published 14 July 1866 in the *Colonist*

Passengers arrived in S.S. *Extract* from New Orleans, 11 July 1866

D. Jex and family
G. L. Fuselier
Jas. M. Putnam
John M. Bateman

Geo. O. Foote
Wm. F. Goodrich
L. D. Arnault

Passengers sailed in S.S. *Extract* for New Orleans

Geo. O. Foote
T. E. Williams

W. S. Cary

As published 27 July 1866 in the *Daily Picayune*

The *Extract* arrived last evening with the following passengers

Geo. O. Foote
T. E. Williams
W. S. Cary

Clarence M. Cary
and two steerage passengers

As published 28 May 1867 in the *Daily Picayune*

Passengers arrived in S.S. *General Sherman* from New Orleans, 9 May 1867

H. B. Britton, New Orleans
R. D. Maclin, New Orleans
W. D. Smith, Alabama
J. Howard, New Orleans
T. Nunn, Alabama

J. Finder, New Orleans
T. D. Ball, Alabama
Ramon Olivera, Havana
J. P. Harris, Alabama
August Audoir, La.

D. A. Harris, New Orleans
Thos. Durr, New Orleans

C. P. Littlepays, Texas
R. W. Pearce, La.

As published 10 July 1867 in the *Commercial Advertiser*

Passengers arrived by the steamship *Gen. Sherman* from New Orleans

Edw. Mallon, Jackson, Miss.
Wm. R. Purvis, Concordia Parish, La.
Wm. Dutton, New Orleans, La.
W. J. S. Scobell, New Orleans, La.

H. Beddingliaus, Algiers, La.
W. H. Owen, New Orleans, La.
Edwin E. Overall, New Orleans, La.

As published 17 July 1867 in the *Commercial Advertiser*

The following passengers left for New Orleans by the *Sherman*

P. Toledo, Esq.
J. A. DeBram, Esq.
J. W. Myers
C. A. Hatch
P. Larkins
G. Fearn
R. Fearn
C. Fearn
C. II. Day
Jas. Harley
J. Crevan
J. A. DePras

E. Toomer
T. Dull
H. D. Keeal
J. Cearan
Jas. M. Putnam
Mr. and Mrs. DuBalen
  and three children
Governor Pearce
Dr. Hall
7 seamen from the shipwrecked
  barque *Hilma*

As published 7 August 1867 in the *Commercial Advertiser*

Passengers on board the steamer *Gen. Sherman* on its trip from New Orleans to Belize

F. E. Cevran
G. Lee
P. Lovelace
R. Herman
J. Furman
J. Durrum
S. Rousseau
S. McIntyre
J. Johnston
H. Hyman
L. Ryan
A. Biscoe
W. Cockrell
T. Ormond

P. Trimble
P. McDermott
L. Kousseaus
L. Smith
J. Nedredge
Mrs. Benson
Mitchell Hyman
M. Hyman
Misses McIntyre Hyman
J. Hyman
M. Hyman
S. Hyman
and many others

As published 16 August 1867 in the *Daily Picayune*

Passengers per steamship *Gen. Sherman* from Belize, Honduras, 10 August 1867

W. C. Chamberlain
J. S. Henderson
J. R. Brackle
T. J. Lacey
Theo Daigh
W. A. Love
J. Y. Allen
R. W. Bringhurst
W. Hurstmyer
R. Echelberger

J. E. Cassidy
J. H. Raid
Mr. Herbert
J. R. Bledsoe
Wm. Graves
Thos. Stewart
John Rumeros
J. F. Fitzpatrick
J. S. Van Ingram
and others

As published in 1868 in *A Trip to British Honduras* by Charles Swett

Passengers per S.S. *Trade Wind* from New Orleans, 5 January 1868

Rev. Levi Pearce, Sharon, Mississippi
Col. J. F. Harrison, Tensas, Louisiana
Danl. Swett, Vicksburg, Mississippi
Dr. G. P. Frierson
Dr. G. A. Frierson, DeSoto, Louisiana

Dr. R. F. Gray, Opelousus, Louisiana
Capt. W. Buckner, Tensas, Louisiana
J. S. Peak, Chicot, Arkansas
E. V. Frierson, DeSoto, Louisiana

As published 14 February 1868 in the *Daily Picayune*

Passengers per steamship *Trade Wind* from Belize, Honduras

T. J. Ware
A. W. Bridge
W. L. Tulerlove
T. P. Tulerlove
T. F. Owen
B. H. Wade
Mrs. B. H. Wade
J. C. DeBraam
J. M. Turman
H. M. Turman
R. Turman

S. W. Car__y
T. P. K__
E. M__n
S. W. Kerchemer
Daniel Pugh
J. M. Huffman
C. M. Barrow
Daniel Smith
A. Cousin
J. Caselie
J. Fabre

As published 16 April 1868 in the *New Orleans Crescent*

Passengers per *Trade Wind* from British Honduras

Wm. Fitzgerald
W. W. Rourk
J. M. Davis
C. K. Maddox
A. D. Fuselier
Mrs. C. Fuselier
Master L. Fuselier
H. Wilson
J. Simpson
P. Brooks

W. L. Stanton
Mrs. Stanton
Master Stanton
Z. W. Morrill
M. H. Hope
L. A. Brunor
W. J. S. Scobell
Thomas S. Jordan
J. Y. Allen
N. S. Dickson

R. Rees   Geo. Kuttruff
Louis Arcemeau   G. T. Fuller

As published 26 April 1868 in the *New Orleans Crescent*

Passengers per *Trade Wind* for British Honduras

Mrs. Frierson and family   Robert McCain
Wm. Hayward   James Dothard
B. A. Bangass   A. B. Smith and lady
W. T. B. Butler   Geo. Johnson
Jamelia E. Clard   M. E. Gibson and lady
Asa Jones   John Veneill
Richard Denning   Mrs. J. T. Harrison
Mrs. Mary Talmadge and family   Stewart Harrison
E. M. Harrison

As published 21 May 1868 in the *New Orleans Crescent*

Passengers per *Trade Wind* for British Honduras

Gov. J. J. McRae   Robert Gerards and wife
Miss McRae   Wm. A. Crist
Mr. F. Huffman and family   Wm. Nash and wife
Chas. Kruft and family   Rev. W. C. Stout
N. O. Vineyard and family   Wm. Burns
J. J. Broker, wife, and child

As published 7 June 1868 in the *New Orleans Crescent*

Passengers per *Trade Wind* from British Honduras

J. C. Laurason   Dr. B. F. Gray
W. T. Butler   J. Gentle
Mrs. P. E. Clark   Geo. Johnson
R. McCain   Jos. Dart
Jas. Dolham   Thos. Carr
J. P. Peck   Henry King
D. McCranie   J. Glasscock
J. T. Cellen   Mrs. F. Rochaird

As published 25 June 1868 in the *New Orleans Crescent*

Passengers per *Trade Wind* for British Honduras

Mrs. C. E. Payne and 3 children   Messrs Earnest Trasten
Mrs. J. C. Brock   A. Ward
Mrs. M. E. Trindall   A. Smylie
Miss Hortense Trasten

The Daily Picayune of same date also listed

Mrs. M. J. Rickers

As published 12 July 1868 in the *Daily Picayune*

Passengers per steamship *Trade Wind* from Belize, Honduras

Mrs. Alice Gould
A. H. Mims
Fred Strickley
Daniel Burk
W. M. Burns
J. G. McCoy

M.E. McCoy
P. McCoy
Grayer McCoy
Mr. Vineyard, wife, and family
T. A. Pack, wife and family
A. E. Broadney

As published 23 July 1868 in the *Daily Picayune*

Passengers per steamship *Trade Wind* for Belize, Honduras

Mrs. Degallade
A. D. Hoffman, wife, and 2 children

Mrs. Matthews and 6 children

As published 8 August 1868 in the *Daily Picayune*

Passengers per steamship *Trade Wind* from Belize, Honduras

Chief Justice of British Honduras
  Richard James Corner
Philip James Hankin, Colonial
  Secretary of Sierra Leone
Miss C. Crea
Mr. J. E. Borders
Mrs. M. J. Borders
Mr. A. L. Vannorden

Mr. John Henning
Mrs. S. J. Henning
Miss S. J. Henning
Miss E. A. Henning
Miss E. A. Henning
Miss M. A. Henning
Mr. J. T. Henning

As published 9 November 1868 in the *Daily Picayune*

The steamship *Trade Wind*, Capt. Morrell, arrived yesterday, from Belize, Honduras, with the following named passengers

J. F. Harrison
John McKenzie
Levi Pearce
A. W. Barrow
J. A. Nicholas
T. B. Smiley
R. J. Smiley
J. A. Smiley
Henry White

Miss Maggie Smiley
Jane White
Miss Virginia White
R. Price
Sheldon Price
C. Price
O. Price
M. Price
Patrick Kelly

As published 14 December 1868 in the *Daily Picayune*

The steamship *Trade Wind*, Capt. Morrill, from Belize, Honduras, arrived Sunday evening, and reports having experienced very heavy weather on both outward and inward passage, and was detained thereby for three days, also brings the following passengers

Mrs. H. S. McDermott
Chas. McDermott
Anna Belle McDermott
Margaret McDermott
Chas. J. J. McDermott
Willie McDermott
Scott McDermott
Edw. McDermott
T. E. Carpenter
J. C. Carpenter, Jr.
J. A. Dolsin
Richard McCall
E. Armstrong

Mrs. Mary Putnam
Henry Putnam
Emmett Putnam
___ Putnam
Robert Putnam
Lee Putnam
Mrs. M. E. Merrill
J. _. Merrill
S. _. Merrill
_. L. Campagne
Miss M. E. C__k
W. S. Barc__

As published 24 December 1868 in the *Daily Picayune*

The steamship *Trade Wind*, Capt. Morrill, sailed last evening for Belize, Honduras, with a good freight and the following named passengers

L. Laprade
G. L. Fuselier
Thomas McCrie___

Sam McCutcheon
T. Laprade

As published 12 January 1869 in the *Daily Picayune*

The steamship *Trade Wind*, Capt. Morrill, arrived from Belize, Honduras, with a good freight and the following named passengers

Jas. M. Putnam
W. D. Wall
Jas. Haley
Dr. Quinlan and servant
Dr. Thompson and servant
J. F. Munez
L. Moniga

E. J. Fraston
Jas. Merrill
W. M. Johnson
L. Andise
H. Oladowski
R. Walker
J. P. Peake

As published 6 March 1869 in the *British Honduras Colonist and Belize Advertiser*
tiser

In the British steamer *Mexico* from New Orleans

Mr. R. G. Shaver
Miss A. C. Shaver
Mrs. C. S. Shaver
Mr. J. D. Shaver
Mr. M. N. Shaver
Mr. A. R. Shaver
Mr. R. G. Shaver (jr.)
Mr. J. S. Buck
Mr. J. W. Logan

Mr. R. F. Logan
Mr. J. D. V. Logan
Mr. R. F. Haydon
Mr. A. Layrange
Mr. J. O. Galloway
Mr. E. C. Duff
Mr. H. Behrems
Mr. J. M. Green

In the mail steamer *Trade Wind*

W. B. Massey
C. A. Massey
W. T. Massey
Mrs. Massey
Miss Seaton
J. A. Stoker
Mrs. Stoker
R. Stoker
James Stoker
Albert Stoker
Z. Darnell
Miss Darnell
R. Z. Darnell
N. S. Darnell
J. F. Darnell
S. E. Darnell
N. P. Darnell
G. W. Darnell
L. Darnell
H. Morton
Mrs. Morton
Mrs. Darnell
H. F. Byrd
Mrs. Byrd
A. C. Nixon
W. W. Brown
Molly Rynd
S. F. Rynd
C. H. Rynd
W. N. Rynd

Capt. Daley
Mr. and Mrs. Hubbard
J. Young
Dr. W. Lambert
H. P. Manfred
E. Steven
H. M. Smith
Mrs. Smith
Miss C. Smith
Mr. and Mrs. Miacoo
T. W. Campbell
J. B. Miacco
A. Shaw,
N. Wallace
C. Christie
Miss L. Smith
Chas. Pooh
W. A. Hopper
M. A. Mahley
D. Leathrer
T. W. Foster
J. L. Brown
D. Droke
J. Callea
D. B. Moore
W. Howe
A. J. C. Kaufnesun
Miss Longfield
___ Augustin

Act 18 Vict., Cap. 18, as Published in Two Parts, 20 June 1868 and 27 June 1868, in the British Honduras Colonist and Belize Advertiser

Note: The law, which was in effect after 1855, describes the specific requirements of the Crown for those seeking naturalization.

The following is a copy of the Act 18 Vict., Cap. 18, which passed the Legislature on the 7th February, 1855, received the Royal Assent and proclaimed on the 19th July of the same year — which we promised to lay before our readers in this day's impression: —

An act to declare the rights and privileges of Aliens, within this Settlement, and to facilitate their Naturalization.

Whereas it is expedient to declare the rights and privileges of Aliens within this Settlement, and to provide facilities for their naturalization:

Be it therefore enacted by Her Majesty's Superintendent, by and with the advice and consent of the Assembly, as follows: that is to say;

1. That every person now born or hereafter to be born, out of her Majesty's dominions, of a mother being a natural born subject of the United Kingdom, shall be capable of taking to him, his heirs executors, or administrators, subject to the treaties, tenures, and laws of this Settlement, and any conditions imposed respecting the same, any houses, lands, or personal estate, or any right or interest therein, by devise or purchase, or inheritance of succession.

2. That from and after the passing of this act, every Alien, being the subject of a friendly state, may take and hold, by purchase, gift, bequest, representation, or otherwise, every species of personal property, except chattels real, as fully and effectually, to all intents and purposes and with the same rights, remedies, exemptions,

privileges, and capacities, as if he were a natural born subject of the United Kingdom.

3. That every Alien, now residing in, or who shall hereafter come to reside in any part of this Settlement, and being the subject of a friendly state, may by grant, lease, demise, assignment, bequest, representation, or otherwise, take and hold, subject to treaties, tenures, and conditions as aforesaid, any lands or houses, or any rights therein, for the purpose of residence or occupation by him or her, or his or her servants, or for the purpose of any business, or trade, or usufructuary advantage, for any term of years, not exceeding twenty-one years as fully and effectually, to all intents and purposes, and with the same rights, remedies, and privileges except the right to vote at elections for members of assembly, as if he were a natural born subject of the United Kingdom.

4. That, upon obtaining the certificate of naturalization and taking the oath hereinafter prescribed, every Alien now residing in, or who shall hereafter come to reside in, any part of this Settlement, with the rights and capacities, which a natural-born subject of the United Kingdom can enjoy or transmit; except, that such Alien shall not be capable of becoming a member of assembly, unless, expressly allowed by that certificate, nor of enjoying such other rights and capacities, if any, as shall be specially excepted in and by the certificate of naturalization, to be granted in manner hereinafter to be mention [sic].

5. That it shall be lawful for any such Alien as aforesaid to present to the Superintendent, or officer administering the Government for the time being, a memorial stating the age, profession, trade, or other occupation, of the memorialist, and the duration of his residence in the Settlement, and all other grounds on which he seeks to obtain any of the rights and capacities of a natural-born British subject, and praying the said Superintendent or officer administering the Government to grant to the memorialist the certificate hereinafter mentioned, and such memorial shall be presented through the hands of the Colonel Secretary, who shall see that the requirements thereof are complied with.

6. That every such memorial shall be considered by the said Superintendent or officer administering the Government who shall enquire into the circumstances of each case, and receive all such evidence as shall be offered, by affidavit or otherwise, as he may deem necessary or proper for providing the truth of the allegations contained in such memorials; and that the said superintendent or officer administering the Government, if he shall so think fit may issue a certificate reciting such of the contents of the memorial as he shall consider to be true and material, and granting to the memorialist (upon his taking the oath hereinafter prescribed) all the rights and capacities of a natural-born British subject, except the capacity of being a member of the assembly, unless the same be expressly allowed in such certificate, and except the rights and capacities (if any) specially excepted in and by such certificate.

7. That such certificate shall be enrolled, for safe custody, as of record in the record office of the Settlement, and may be inspected, and copies thereof taken under such regulations as the Superintendent or officer administering the Government shall direct.

8. That within sixty days of the date of such certificate, every memorialist, to whom rights and capacities shall be granted by such certificate, shall take and subscribe the following oath, that is to say: —

"I, A.B., do sincerely promise and swear that I will be faithful and bear true allegiance to her Majesty Queen Victoria, and will defend her, to the utmost of my power, against all conspiracies which may be formed against her or them; and I do faithfully promise to maintain, support, and defend, to the utmost of my power, the succession of the British Crown, which succession, by an act, entitled 'an act for the further limitation of the crown, and better securing the rights and liberties of the subjects,' is and stands limited to the Princess Sophia, Electress of Hanover, and the heirs of her body, being Protestants, hereby utterly renouncing and adjourning any obedience or allegiance unto any other person claiming or pretending a right to that crown. So help me God."

9. Which oath shall be taken and subscribed by such memorialist, and shall be duly administered to him or her before the Superintendent or officer administering the government for the time being, or before any judge of any court of record in the said Settlement, or before the Police Magistrate, or before any other magistrate to whom a dedimus shall be specially directed for that purpose by the said Superintendent or officer executing the government for the time being.

10. And the Superintendent, or other person before whom such oath may be administered, shall grant to the memorialist a certificate of his or her having taken and subscribed such oath accordingly; and such certificate shall be signed by the Superintendent or other person before whom such oath shall be administered; and a memorandum thereof may afterwards be made upon the original certificate of naturalization, or on the record thereof, if desired by the person naturalized, in proof thereof; and such memorandum shall be admitted as proof in every court of the Settlement.

11. That the several proceedings, hereby authorised to be taken for obtaining such certificate as aforesaid, shall be regulated in such manner as the Superintendent or officer executing the government shall, from time to time, direct.

12 That the fees, payable in respect of the several proceedings hereby authorized, shall be fixed and regulated by the Superintendent or officer administering the government.

13. That nothing herein contained shall be construed so as to take away or diminish any right, privilege, or protection, heretofore lawfully possessed by or belonging to Aliens residing in this Settlement under the sanction of any act thereof; but that every such right, privilege, and protection, shall continue to be enjoyed by such Aliens in as full and ample a manner as before the passing of this act.

14. That any woman, married or who shall be married to a natural-born subject or person naturalized, shall be deemed and taken to be herself naturalized, and have all the rights and privileges of a natural-born subject.

15. That this act may be amended or repealed by any act to be passed in the present session, and shall come into operation as soon as her Majesty's assent has been proclaimed thereto.

APPENDIX D

Passenger Lists of Ships Arriving in New Orleans from Belize, Honduras

The following selected information was transcribed from passenger information detailed in *Passenger Lists of Vessels Arriving in New Orleans* (Washington, D.C.: National Archives and Record Servce, 1958), M 259, Rolls 50–54. These lists include, as can be best deduced, only those ships arriving directly or indirectly from the port of Belize.

Report and List of the passengers taken on aboard the <u>AM ST. SHIP EXTRACT of NEW ORLEANS</u> whereof <u>HOWE</u> is Master, burthen <u>288 60/100</u> tons, bound from the Port of <u>RUATAN (LEFT BELIZE)</u> for New Orleans. (Date sworn and subscribed *27* day of <u>JULY</u> 18<u>66</u>)

Names	Age Yr Mon	Sex	Occupation, Trade or Profession	Country to Which Severally Belong	Country of Which They Intended to Become Inhabitants	Died on the Voyage	Part of Vessel Occupied During Voyage
T. W. Williams	30	M	Clerk	U.S.	U.S.		Cabin
J. O. Foote	35	M	Planter	U.S.	U.S.		Cabin
W. S. Cary	38	M	Merchant	U.S.	U.S.		Cabin
C. Cary	18	M	Merchant	U.S.	U.S.		Cabin
Augustine	30	F	Servant	U.S.	U.S.		Cabin
J. Wallas	38	M	Merchant	English	U.S.		Cabin

Report and List of the passengers taken on aboard the <u>BRIG SCHO. VILLAGE GEM</u> of — — whereof <u>ED WARD</u> is Master, burthen — tons, bound from the Port of <u>UTILLA BAY ISLAND H.D. (LEFT BELIZE)</u> for New Orleans. (Date sworn and subscribed <u>6</u> day of <u>DEC</u> 1866)

134

Names	Age Yr Mon	Sex	Occupation, Trade or Profession	Country to Which Severally Belong	Country of Which They Intended to Become Inhabitants	Died on the Voyage	Part of Vessel Occupied During Voyage
J. M. Putnam	48	M	Merchant	U.S.	U.S.		
John Moore	30	M	Merchant	U.S.	U.S.		
Thom Hobbler	28	M	Merchant	U.S.	U.S.		
John Smith	25	M	Merchant	U.S.	U.S.		

Report and List of the passengers taken on aboard the <u>AMER SCH. ELMA</u> of whereof <u>JOHN J. MEARS</u> is Master, burthen — tons, bound from the Port of <u>RUATAN ISLAND, HONDURAS</u> for New Orleans. (Date sworn and subscribed <u>12</u> day of <u>DECEMBER</u> 186<u>6</u>)

Names	Age Yr Mon	Sex	Occupation, Trade or Profession	Country to Which Severally Belong	Country of Which They Intended to Become Inhabitants	Died on the Voyage	Part of Vessel Occupied During Voyage
G. L. Fuselier	66	M	Planter	U.S.	U.S.		

Report and List of the passengers taken on aboard the <u>BR. SCHR. WELCOME</u> of whereof <u>BLOHM</u> is Master, burthen tons, bound from the Port of <u>BELIZE, HONDURAS VIA UTILLA</u> for New Orleans. (Date sworn and subscribed <u>3</u> day of <u>APRIL</u> 186<u>7</u>)

Names	Age Yr Mon	Sex	Occupation, Trade or Profession	Country to Which Severally Belong	Country of Which They Intended to Become Inhabitants	Died on the Voyage	Part of Vessel Occupied During Voyage
A. B. Farmer	32	M	Carpenter	La, US			
Mrs. Farmer	23	F		La, US			
E. Mandace	45	M	Planter	La, US			
E. White	22	M	Planter	La, US			
B. C. Neil	36	M	Merchant	La, US			
F. Agnant	51	M	Merchant	La, US			

Report and List of the passengers taken on aboard the <u>STM. GENL SHERMAN of NEW YORK</u> whereof <u>PENDLETON</u> is Master, burthen <u>294</u> tons, bound from the Port of <u>BELIZE VIA RUATAN</u> for New Orleans. (Date sworn and subscribed <u>10</u> day of <u>APRIL</u> 186<u>7</u>)

Names	Age Yr Mon	Sex	Occupation, Trade or Profession	Country to Which Severally Belong	Country of Which They Intended to Become Inhabitants	Died on the Voyage	Part of Vessel Occupied During Voyage
Jno. S. Graves	32 1	M	Merchant	U.S.	U.S.		Room
Edw. Chapman	19	M	Student	U.S.	U.S.		Room

Names	Age Yr Mon	Sex	Occupation, Trade or Profession	Country to Which Severally Belong	Country of Which They Intended to Become Inhabitants	Died on the Voyage	Part of Vessel Occupied During Voyage
Joseph Peake	40	M	Clerk	England	Honduras		Room
Sarah Peake	35	F		England	Honduras		Room
Lucy Peake	15	F		England	Honduras		Room
Alice Peake	3	F		England	Honduras		Room
Alex Gill	40	M	Pilot	Honduras	Honduras		Room
Etienne Ghivandi	33	M	Clerk	U.S.	U.S.		Room

Report and List of the passengers taken on aboard the STM. TRADE WIND of NEW YORK whereof CHAMPION is Master, burthen 420 tons, bound from the Port of BELIZE for New Orleans. (Date sworn and subscribed 29 day of APRIL 1867)

Names	Age Yr Mon	Sex	Occupation, Trade or Profession	Country to Which Severally Belong	Country of Which They Intended to Become Inhabitants	Died on the Voyage	Part of Vessel Occupied During Voyage
C. T. Hunter	29	M	Merchant	U.S.	U.S.		Cabin
E. L. Wilkins	38	M	Merchant	U.S.	U.S.		Cabin
F. H. Fasten	42	M	Physician	U.S.	U.S.		Cabin
F. Adams	56	M	Planter	U.S.	U.S.		Cabin
J. T. Morill	45	M	Merchant	U.S.	U.S.		Cabin

Report and List of the passengers taken on aboard the AM. SCHR. GREEN-LAND of NEW ORLEANS whereof GEORGE GORDON is Master, burthen 108 tons, bound from the Port of BELIZE HON for New Orleans. (Date sworn and subscribed 20 day of MAY 1867)

Names	Age Yr Mon	Sex	Occupation, Trade or Profession	Country to Which Severally Belong	Country of Which They Intended to Become Inhabitants	Died on the Voyage	Part of Vessel Occupied During Voyage
J. T. Calloway	30	M	Unknown	U.S.	U.S.		Cabin
J. A. Finlay	31	M	Unknown	U.S.	U.S.		Cabin
J. G. Blacknett	19	M	Unknown	U.S.	U.S.		Cabin
H. J. Archer	20	M	Unknown	U.S.	U.S.		Cabin
H. A. Frillen	45	M	Unknown	U.S.	U.S.		Cabin

Report and List of the passengers taken on aboard the <u>STEAM SHIP TRADE WIND</u> of <u>NEW YORK</u> whereof <u>CHAMPION</u> is Master, burthen <u>420 28/100</u> tons, bound from the Port of for New Orleans. (Date sworn and subscribed <u>21</u> day of <u>MAY</u> 186<u>7</u>)

Names	Age Yr Mon	Sex	Occupation, Trade or Profession	Country to Which Severally Belong	Country of Which They Intended to Become Inhabitants	Died on the Voyage	Part of Vessel Occupied During Voyage
R. C. Martin	54	M	Planter	U.S.	U.S.		Cabin
J. Talland	45	M	Engineer	U.S.	U.S.		Steerage
Henry May	24	M	Laborer		Gt. Britain U.S.		Steerage

Report and List of the passengers taken on aboard the <u>AM. S.S. GENL. SHERMAN</u> of whereof <u>PENDLETON</u> is Master, burthen <u>291</u> tons, bound from the Port of <u>BELIZE & RUATAN ISLAND</u> for New Orleans. (Date sworn and subscribed <u>27</u> day of <u>MAY</u> 186<u>7</u>)

Names	Age Yr Mon	Sex	Occupation, Trade or Profession	Country to Which Severally Belong	Country of Which They Intended to Become Inhabitants	Died on the Voyage	Part of Vessel Occupied During Voyage
M. Little	30	M	Doctor	NYK			Cabin
Mrs. Del Brando	28	F		NYK			Cabin
Servant	18	F		Belize			Cabin
D. P. Furguson	33	M	Planter	New Orleans			Cabin
Mrs. H. M. Harraloness	30	F		Texas			Cabin
Miss J. B. Haraloness	16	F		Texas			Cabin
Capt. Ward	40	M	Captain	New Orleans			Cabin
C. Von Nardes	25	M	Sailor	New Orleans			Cabin
Mr. Austin	20	M	Merchant	New Orleans			Cabin
John (Servant)	20	M	Servant	New Orleans			Cabin

Report and List of the passengers taken on aboard the <u>AM. S.S. TRADE WIND</u> of <u>NEW YORK</u> whereof <u>A. CHAMPION</u> is Master, burthen <u>420 26/100</u> tons, bound from the Port of <u>BELIZE, HONDURAS</u> for New Orleans. (Date sworn and subscribed <u>13</u> day of <u>JUNE</u> 186<u>7</u>)

Names	Age Yr Mon	Sex	Occupation, Trade or Profession	Country to Which Severally Belong	Country of Which They Intended to Become Inhabitants	Died on the Voyage	Part of Vessel Occupied During Voyage
B. R. Duval	52	M	Preacher	U.S.	U.S.		Cabin
W. D. Smith	58	M	Farmer	U.S.	U.S.		Cabin
T. Nunn	45	M	Farmer	U.S.	U.S.		Cabin
S. G. Lester	56	M	Farmer	U.S.	U.S.		Cabin
E. P. Watrous	40	M	Lawyer	U.S.	U.S.		Cabin

Names	Age Yr Mon	Sex	Occupation, Trade or Profession	Country to Which Severally Belong	Country of Which They Intended to Become Inhabitants	Died on the Voyage	Part of Vessel Occupied During Voyage
Sauel C. Reid	51	M	Lawyer	U.S.	U.S.		Cabin
L. W. Goldsmith	25	M	Farmer	U.S.	U.S.		Cabin
Sarah Mcalister	23	F		U.S.	U.S.		Cabin
Mary E. Goldsmith	19	F		U.S.	U.S.		Cabin
John Gentle	35	M	Merchant	U.S.	U.S.		Cabin
Rachel Gentle	33	F		U.S.	U.S.		Cabin

Report and List of the passengers taken on aboard the AM. SS GENL. SHER-MAN of whereof JEFF PENDLETON is Master, burthen tons, bound from the Port of BELIZE VIA RUATAN for New Orleans. (Date sworn and subscribed 26 day of JUNE 1867)

Names	Age Yr Mon	Sex	Occupation, Trade or Profession	Country to Which Severally Belong	Country of Which They Intended to Become Inhabitants	Died on the Voyage	Part of Vessel Occupied During Voyage
John M. Davidson	38	M	Lawyer	New Orleans		NONE	Cabin
Edwd. Christy	25	M	Merchant	New Orleans			Cabin
Wm. Dulton	40	M	Merchant	New Orleans			
H. Beddinghaus	40	M	Merchant	New Orleans			
Shusrhen	24	M		Scotland			
E. Eichelberger	23	M		New Orleans			
C. H. Russel	25	M		New Orleans			
John Gauther	28	M		New Orleans			
Wm. T. Buckley	28	M					

Report and List of the passengers taken on aboard the AM. ST. GENL. SHER-MAN of whereof JEFF PENDLETON is Master, burthen tons, bound from the Port of BELIZE H.D. for New Orleans. (Date sworn and subscribed 19 day of JULY 1867)

Names	Age Yr Mon	Sex	Occupation, Trade or Profession	Country to Which Severally Belong	Country of Which They Intended to Become Inhabitants	Died on the Voyage	Part of Vessel Occupied During Voyage
M. P. Toledo	50	M	Merchant		Unknown	NONE	Cabin
J. A. DeBraam	30	M	Merchant		Unknown		Cabin
J. M. Putnam	45	M	Merchant		Unknown		Cabin
J. Fearn	60	M	Merchant		Unknown		Cabin
C. Fearn	30	M	Merchant		Unknown		Cabin
G. Fearn	33	M	Merchant		Unknown		Cabin
Pearce	40	M	Merchant		Unknown		Cabin
Dr. Hall	43	M	Doctor		Unknown		Cabin
Mr. De Pras	22	M	Merchant		Unknown		Cabin
Mr. E. Toomes	38	M			Unknown		Cabin

Names	Age Yr Mon	Sex	Occupation, Trade or Profession	Country to Which Severally Belong	Country of Which They Intended to Become Inhabitants	Died on the Voyage	Part of Vessel Occupied During Voyage
C. A. Hatch	30	M			Unknown		Cabin
J. P. Larkin	28	M			Unknown		Cabin
J. W. Myers	28	M			Unknown		Cabin
H. D. Reene	50	M			Unknown		Cabin
Thm. Durr	23	M			Unknown		Cabin
C. H. Day	27	M			Unknown		Cabin
James Harley	30	M			Unknown		Cabin
Jno. Crenan	32	M			Unknown		Cabin
Jno. Cochran	27	M			Unknown		Cabin
Mr. & Mrs. Du Balen & 3 Children and 6 Seamen Russian Unknown Male Seamen	35	F		French	Unknown		Cabin
Bart C. Gelina			Merchant	French	Unknown		Cabin
Orr Del Balain	4						

Report and List of the passengers taken on aboard the <u>AM. SS. GENL SHER-MAN</u> of whereof <u>PENDLETON</u> is Master, burthen tons, bound from the Port of <u>BELIZE</u> for New Orleans. (Date sworn and subscribed <u>16</u> day of <u>AUGUST</u> 186<u>7</u>)

Names	Age Yr Mon	Sex	Occupation, Trade or Profession	Country to Which Severally Belong	Country of Which They Intended to Become Inhabitants	Died on the Voyage	Part of Vessel Occupied During Voyage
W. C. Chamberlain	55	M	Merchant	Louisiana	Unknown	NONE	1st Cl.
J. H. Racia	25	M	Merchant	Louisiana	Unknown		1st Cl.
J. S. Henderson	40	M	Planter	Louisiana	Unknown		1st Cl.
J. Cassidy	29	M	Farmer	Louisiana	Unknown		1st Cl.
J. R. Brackle	32	M	Clerk	Belize	Unknown		1st Cl.
Wm. Huburt	27	M	Farmer	Louisiana	Unknown		1st Cl.
J. L. Lacy	35	M	Carpenter	Louisiana	Unknown		1st Cl.
J. B. Bledsoe	32	M	Merchant	Mississippi	Unknown		1st Cl.
T. Dagle	37	M	Planter	Mississippi	Unknown		1st Cl.
Wm. Graves	65	M	Planter	Mississippi	Unknown		1st Cl.
W. A. Love	37	M	Planter	Mississippi	Unknown		1st Cl.
Thos Stuart	65	M	Planter	Mississippi	Unknown		1st Cl.
J. G. Allen	48	M	Merchant	Louisiana	Unknown		1st Cl.
John Rumnons	50	M	Farmer	Mississippi	Unknown		1st Cl.
R. N. Benninglaus	26	M	Civil Eng.	Louisiana	Unknown		1st Cl.
T. F. Fitzgerald	25	M	Merchant	Louisiana	Unknown		1st Cl.
W. Hinchmeyer	30	M	Planter	Louisiana	Unknown		1st Cl.
J. S. Van Inra	35	M	Ge——y	Louisiana	Unknown		1st Cl.
R. Eichelberger	18	M	Clerk	Louisiana	Unknown		1st Cl.

Report and List of the passengers taken on aboard the <u>AM. S.S. GEN. SHER-MAN</u> of whereof <u>PENDLETON</u> is Master, burthen <u>291</u> tons, bound from the Port of <u>BELIZE, HONDURAS</u> for New Orleans. (Date sworn and subscribed <u>14</u> day of <u>SEPTEMBER</u> 186<u>7</u>)

Names	Age Yr Mon	Sex	Occupation, Trade or Profession	Country to Which Severally Belong	Country of Which They Intended to Become Inhabitants	Died on the Voyage	Part of Vessel Occupied During Voyage
L. Watkins	57	M	Physician	Georgia	United States	NONE	Cabin
B. L. Watkins	20	M	Planter	Georgia			Cabin
F. Grincans	60	M	Planter	Alabama			Cabin
J. W. Rotchford	41	M	Planter	Louisiana			Cabin
A. H. Biscoe	53	M	Merchant	Texas			Cabin
A. Middlebrook	28	M	Engineer	Mississippi			Cabin
H. Dessant	37	M	ShipMaster	New York			Cabin
G. Watkins	46	M	Physician	Mississippi			Cabin
J. G. Johnston	56	M	Planter	Louisiana			Cabin
W. H. Crockett	48	M	Merchant	Alabama			Cabin

Report and List of the passengers taken on aboard the <u>ST. SHIP TRADE WIND</u> of <u>NEW YORK</u> whereof <u>MORRILL</u> is Master, burthen <u>420 26/100</u> tons, bound from the Port of <u>BELIZE, HONDURAS</u> for New Orleans. (Date sworn and subscribed <i>15</i> day of <u>OCTOBER</u> 186<u>7</u>)

Names	Age Yr Mon	Sex	Occupation, Trade or Profession	Country to Which Severally Belong	Country of Which They Intended to Become Inhabitants	Died on the Voyage	Part of Vessel Occupied During Voyage
M. L. Robinson	55	M	— —	U.S.	U.S.	NONE	Cabin
D. H. Draper	40	M	— —	U.S.	U.S.		Cabin
J. W. Price	30	M	Planter	U.S.	U.S.		Cabin
Mrs. Price	17	F		U.S.	U.S.		Cabin
Mad. L. Esejo	20	F		U.S.	U.S.		Cabin
N. Price	23	M	Planter	U.S.	U.S.		Cabin
Dr. J. C. Dursind	55	M	Doctor	U.S.	U.S.		Cabin
Mrs. M. J. Dickens	40	F		U.S.	U.S.		Cabin

Report and List of the passengers taken on aboard the <u>AM. S. SHIP TRADE WIND</u> of <u>NEW YORK</u> whereof <u>MORRILL</u> is Master, burthen <u>420 26/100</u> tons, bound from the Port of <u>BELIZE, HONDURAS</u> for New Orleans. (Date sworn and subscribed <i>15</i> day of <u>NOVEMBER</u> 186<u>7</u>)

Names	Age Yr Mon	Sex	Occupation, Trade or Profession	Country to Which Severally Belong	Country of Which They Intended to Become Inhabitants	Died on the Voyage	Part of Vessel Occupied During Voyage
G. W. Clifton	22	M	Gent	Virginia	United States	NONE	Cabin
S. M. Grayson	22	M	Gent	Louisiana	United States		Cabin

Names	Age Yr Mon	Sex	Occupation, Trade or Profession	Country to Which Severally Belong	Country of Which They Intended to Become Inhabitants	Died on the Voyage	Part of Vessel Occupied During Voyage
P. E. H. Gowless	57	M	Doctor	Louisiana	United States		Cabin
T. McCannell	55	M	Teacher	Louisiana	United States		Cabin
R. T. McLin	23	M	Gent	Louisiana	United States		Cabin
O. Johnson	25	M	Gardener	Tennessee	United States		Cabin
J. L. Powers	23	M	Gent	Louisiana	United States		Cabin
H. H. Briars	24	M	Planter	Texas	United States		Cabin
L. H. Smith	34	M	Merchant	Georgia	United States		Cabin
J. B. Harris	25	M	Clerk	Louisiana	United States		Cabin
D. A. Harris	21	M	Gent	Louisiana	United States		Cabin
Wm. Schinonerkerin	30	M	Clerk	Louisiana	United States		Cabin
Mrs. Foote	32	F	Lady	Louisiana	United States		Cabin
six children				Louisiana	United States		Cabin
Mrs. Singer	38	F	Lady	Louisiana	United States		Cabin
Miss Sennett	21	F	Lady	Louisiana	United States		Cabin
Louis Barras Gimas	62	M	General	Mexico	United States		Cabin

Report and List of the passengers taken on aboard the <u>AM. S.S. TRADE WIND</u> of <u>NEW YORK</u> whereof <u>MORRILL</u> is Master, burthen <u>420</u> tons, bound from the Port of <u>BELIZE, BRIT. HON.</u> for New Orleans. (Date sworn and subscribed <u>14</u> day of <u>DECEMBER</u> 186<u>7</u>)

Names	Age Yr Mon	Sex	Occupation, Trade or Profession	Country to Which Severally Belong	Country of Which They Intended to Become Inhabitants	Died on the Voyage	Part of Vessel Occupied During Voyage
L. Burguiene	22	M	Merchant	U.S.	U.S.		Cabin
Sophie Burguiene	20	F		U.S.	U.S.		Cabin
Asa Hatch	37	M	Planter	U.S.	U.S.		Cabin
H. Hatch	25	F		U.S.	U.S.		Cabin
C. Hatch	12	M		U.S.	U.S.		Cabin
J. A. Hatch	10	M		U.S.	U.S.		Cabin
C. Bunch	40	F	Servant	U.S.	U.S.		Cabin
F. C. Ledgeaur	45	M	Med. Doctor	U.S.	U.S.		Cabin
H. C. Ledgeaur	22	M	Med. Doctor	U.S.	U.S.		Cabin
J. W. Kuinbraugh	45	M	Planter	U.S.	U.S.		Cabin
F. L. Mullen	19	M	Planter	U.S.	U.S.		Cabin
P. A. Mullen	21	F		U.S.	U.S.		Cabin
Eugenia Mullen	17	F		U.S.	U.S.		Cabin
Phil McDermott	22	M	Planter	U.S.	U.S.		Cabin
J. W. Mullen	15	M	Planter	U.S.	U.S.		Cabin

Report and List of the passengers taken on aboard the <u>SS TRADE WIND</u> of whereof <u>MORRILL</u> is Master, burthen <u>420</u> tons, bound from the Port of <u>BELIZE, BR. HOND</u> for New Orleans. (Date sworn and subscribed <u>17</u> day of <u>JANUARY</u> 186<u>8</u>)

Names	Age Yr Mon	Sex	Occupation, Trade or Profession	Country to Which Severally Belong	Country of Which They Intended to Become Inhabitants	Died on the Voyage	Part of Vessel Occupied During Voyage
Kenney, J. M.	47	M	Planter	U.S.	U.S.		Cabin
Perkins, W.	66	M	Planter	U.S.	U.S.		Cabin
Wood, R. C.	30	M	Planter	U.S.	U.S.		Cabin
McIntosh, L. C.	25	M	Planter	U.S.	U.S.		Cabin
Easter, M. E.	26	M	Planter	U.S.	U.S.		Cabin
Long, J.	28	M	Seaman	U.S.	U.S.		Cabin

Report and List of the passengers taken on aboard the <u>SS TRADE WIND</u> of <u>NEW YORK</u> whereof <u>JONATHAN T. MORRILL</u> is Master, burthen <u>420</u> tons, bound from the Port of <u>BELIZE, BR. HONDURAS</u> for New Orleans. (Date sworn and subscribed <u>14</u> day of <u>FEB.</u> 186<u>8</u>)

Names	Age Yr Mon	Sex	Occupation, Trade or Profession	Country to Which Severally Belong	Country of Which They Intended to Become Inhabitants	Died on the Voyage	Part of Vessel Occupied During Voyage
Ware, T. J.	34	M	Farmer	U.S.	U.S.		Cabin
Carney, S. W.	53	M	Farmer	U.S.	U.S.		Cabin
Bridge, A. W.	55	M	Farmer	U.S.	U.S.		Cabin
Kane, T. P.	28	M	Merchant	U.S.	U.S.		Cabin
Fullerton, W. L.	45	M	Farmer	U.S.	U.S.		Cabin
Fullerton, T. P.	35	M	Farmer	U.S.	U.S.		Cabin
Mallon, E.	46	M	Farmer	U.S.	U.S.		Cabin
Kirchernir, S. W.	38	M	Printer	U.S.	U.S.		Cabin
Owen, T. F.	40	M	Farmer	U.S.	U.S.		Cabin
Pugh, Daniel	18	M	Farmer	U.S.	U.S.		Cabin
Wade, B. H.	25	M	Farmer	U.S.	U.S.		Cabin
Wade, Mrs. S.	23	F	Farmer	U.S.	U.S.		Cabin
Huffman, J. M.	35	M	Farmer	U.S.	U.S.		Cabin
De Braam, J. C.	23	M	Merchant	Holland	Holland		Cabin
Farmer, J. M.	21	M	Farmer	U.S.	U.S.		Cabin
Farmer, V. M.	17	M	Farmer	U.S.	U.S.		Cabin
Farmer, R.	15	M	Farmer	U.S.	U.S.		Cabin
Barrow, C. M.	21	M	Farmer	U.S.	U.S.		Cabin
Daniel Smith	23	M	Merchant	England	England		Cabin
Cruoen, A.	33	M	Merchant	Belgian	Belgian		Cabin
Caselie, Juan	31	M	Merchant	Italy	United States		Cabin
Fabre, Juan	43	M	Merchant	Spain	United States		Cabin

Report and List of the passengers taken on aboard the <u>SS TRADE WIND</u> of whereof <u>JONATHAN J. MORRILL</u> is Master, burthen <u>420</u> tons, bound from the Port of <u>BELIZE, HONDURAS</u> for New Orleans. (Date sworn and subscribed <u>13th</u> day of <u>March</u> 186<u>8</u>)

Names	Age Yr Mon	Sex	Occupation, Trade or Profession	Country to Which Severally Belong	Country of Which They Intended to Become Inhabitants	Died on the Voyage	Part of Vessel Occupied During Voyage
Sweet, Saml	43	M	Merchant	U.S.	U.S.		Cabin
Sweet, Charles	39	M	Merchant	U.S.	U.S.		Cabin
Darnell, Z.	47	M		U.S.	U.S.		Cabin
Turner, Lee	20	M	Farmer	U.S.	U.S.		Cabin
Green, W. N.	21	M	Farmer	U.S.	U.S.		Cabin
Wawn, J. E.	23	M	Farmer	U.S.	U.S.		Cabin
Owen, W. H.	32	M	Farmer	U.S.	U.S.		Cabin
Middlebrook, L. L.	20	M	Farmer	U.S.	U.S.		Cabin
Mercer, Lawrence J.	35	M	C. Engineer	Scotland	Scotland		Cabin
McCandlish, W.	44	M	C. Engineer	Scotland	Scotland		Cabin
Brassell, J. W.	25	M	M.D.	U.S.	U.S.		Cabin
Hamilton, D. C.	30	M	Planter	U.S.	U.S.		Cabin
Shields, W. B.	35	M	Planter	U.S.	U.S.		Cabin
Ryan, P. M.	40	M	M.D.	U.S.	U.S.		Cabin
Williams, J. C.	18	F		U.S.	U.S.		Cabin
Williams, Robert	15	M		U.S.	U.S.		Cabin
Williams, W.	13	M		U.S.	U.S.		Cabin
Ryan, Phil	11	M		U.S.	U.S.		Cabin
Ryan, Mary	8	F		U.S.	U.S.		Cabin
Ryan, Maude	5	F		U.S.	U.S.		Cabin
McAlister, J. H.	39	M	Merchant	U.S.	U.S.		Cabin
Seth, F. O.	26	M	S.B. Capt.	U.S.	U.S.		Cabin
Purdy, J. C.	30	M	Merchant	U.S.	U.S.		CAbin
Mount, S. M. G.	26	M		U.S.	U.S.		Cabin

Report and List of the passengers taken on aboard the SS TRADE WIND of NEW YORK whereof J.T. MORRILL is Master, burthen 420 tons, bound from the Port of BELIZE, HONDURAS for New Orleans. (Date sworn and subscribed 15 day of MAY 1868)

Names	Age Yr Mon	Sex	Occupation, Trade or Profession	Country to Which Severally Belong	Country of Which They Intended to Become Inhabitants	Died on the Voyage	Part of Vessel Occupied During Voyage
Fitzgerald, W.	27	M	Merchant	U.S.	U.S.		Cabin
Morrell, Z. N.	65	M	Minister	U.S.	U.S.		Cabin
Roark, W. W.	20	M	Farmer	U.S.	U.S.		Cabin
Hope, M. H.	20	M	Farmer	U.S.	U.S.		Cabin
Davis, P. M.	32	M	Farmer	U.S.	U.S.		Cabin
Brunner, L. A.	25	M	Farmer	U.S.	U.S.		Cabin
Maddox, C. K.	25	M	Laywer	U.S.	U.S.		Cabin
Scobell, W. J. S.	35	M	Merchant	U.S.	U.S.		Cabin
Fuselier, A. D.	37	M	Planter	U.S.	U.S.		Cabin
Fuselier, Madam C.	34	F		U.S.	U.S.		Cabin
Fuselier, A.	15	M		U.S.	U.S.		Cabin
Fuselier, L.	11	M		U.S.	U.S.		Cabin

Names	Age Yr Mon	Sex	Occupation, Trade or Profession	Country to Which Severally Belong	Country of Which They Intended to Become Inhabitants	Died on the Voyage	Part of Vessel Occupied During Voyage
Fuselier, F.	3	F		U.S.	U.S.		Cabin
Jordan, S. F.	25	M	Merchant	U.S.	U.S.		Cabin
Allen, J. Y.	38	M	Merchant	U.S.	U.S.		Cabin
Dicksen, N. S.	25	M	Merchant	U.S.	U.S.		Cabin
Dicksen, S.	22	F		U.S.	U.S.		Cabin
Ivey, M.	19	F		U.S.	U.S.		Cabin
Thrower, O. A.	20	M	Farmer	U.S.	U.S.		Cabin
Thrower, M. N.	18	F		U.S.	U.S.		Cabin
Wilson, N.	56	M	Farmer	U.S.	U.S.		Cabin
Rees, R.	42	M	Farmer	U.S.	U.S.		Cabin
Simpson, I. L.	60	M	Farmer	U.S.	U.S.		Cabin
Arcemon, Louis	40	M	Engineer	U.S.	U.S.		Cabin
Brooks, T.	34	M	Merchant	U.S.	U.S.		Cabin
Kuttruff, Geo.	30	M	Butcher	U.S.	U.S.		Cabin
Stanten, W. L.	23	M	Farmer	U.S.	U.S.		Cabin
Stanten, L. F.	20	F		U.S.	U.S.		Cabin
Stanten, C. L.	2	M		U.S.	U.S.		Cabin
Miller, C. T.	25	M	Merchant	U.S.	U.S.		Cabin

Report and List of the passengers taken on aboard the <u>STEAM SHIP TRADE WIND</u> of <u>NEW YORK</u> whereof <u>JONATHAN T. MORRILL</u> is Master, burthen <u>420</u> tons, bound from the Port of___ for New Orleans. (Date sworn and subscribed <u>15</u> day of <u>MAY</u> 186<u>8</u>)

Names	Age Yr Mon	Sex	Occupation, Trade or Profession	Country to Which Severally Belong	Country of Which They Intended to Become Inhabitants	Died on the Voyage	Part of Vessel Occupied During Voyage
Hempstead, Honl. Judge C.	54	M	Lawyer	Br Hond.	B. Honduras		Cabin
Gaines, B. P.	64	M	Planter	U.S.	U.S.		Cabin
Kearney, Barrett M. D.	33	M	Surgeon of Her Majesty Victoria	England	England		Cabin
Brinten, A. H.	38	M	Merchant	Br Hond.	B. Honduras		Cabin
Farrar, H. K.	22	M	C. Engineer	U.S.	U.S.		Cabin
Haynoor, W. H.	58	M	Planter	U.S.	U.S.		Cabin
Bavgurs, B. A.	56	M	Planter	U.S.	U.S.		Cabin
Artrurz, L.	31	M	Mechanic	U.S.	U.S.		Cabin
Herman, W. H.	28	M	Mechanic	U.S.	U.S.		Cabin
Truitt, J. W.	33	M	Farmer	U.S.	U.S.		Cabin
Truitt, Mrs. T. E.	20	F		U.S.	U.S.		Cabin
Truitt, M.C.	7	F		U.S.	U.S.		Cabin
Truitt, Robert	5	M		U.S.	U.S.		Cabin
Harlason, A. J.	31	M	Planter	U.S.	U.S.		Cabin
Veritt, E.	35	M	Merchant	U.S.	U.S.		Cabin
Love, W. A.	35	M	Merchant	U.S.	U.S.		Cabin

Names	Age Yr Mon	Sex	Occupation, Trade or Profession	Country to Which Severally Belong	Country of Which They Intended to Become Inhabitants	Died on the Voyage	Part of Vessel Occupied During Voyage
Ferguson, Mrs. V. C.	25	F		U.S.	U.S.		Cabin
Ferguson, W. N.	5	M		U.S.	U.S.		Cabin
Ferguson, D.	1	F		U.S.	U.S.		Cabin
Ward, A.	40	M	Merchant	U.S.	U.S.		Cabin
Dickson, J. D.	40	M	Farmer	U.S.	U.S.		Strge
Glass, F. M.	33	M		U.S.	U.S.		Strge
Glass, Mrs. Mary	30	F		U.S.	U.S.		Strge
Hill, A. J.	26	M	Farmer	U.S.	U.S.		Strge
Hill, H. C.	22	M	Farmer	U.S.	U.S.		Strge
Parkerson, A.	27	M	Farmer	U.S.	U.S.		Strge
Jett, John	25	M	Farmer	U.S.	U.S.		Strge
Maddox, B. R.	23	M	Farmer	U.S.	U.S.		Strge
Jones, J. W.	29	M	Farmer	U.S.	U.S.		Strge
Burford, E. M.	45	M	Farmer	U.S.	U.S.		Strge
Burford, Mrs.	39	F		U.S.	U.S.		Strge
Burford, W.	17	M		U.S.	U.S.		Strge
Burford, Wilson	15	M		U.S.	U.S.		Strge
Burford	13	M		U.S.	U.S.		Strge
Burford, Estes	11	F		U.S.	U.S.		Strge
Burford, Thadeus	9	M		U.S.	U.S.		Strge
Burford, Telulu	7	F		U.S.	U.S.		Strge
Burford, Claudeane	5	M		U.S.	U.S.		Strge
Burford, Joupa	3	M		U.S.	U.S.		Strge

Report and List of the passengers taken on aboard the SS TRADE WIND of NEW YORK whereof JONATHAN T. MORRILL is Master, burthen 420 tons, bound from the Port of BELIZE, HONDURAS for New Orleans. (Date sworn and subscribed 6 day of JUNE 1868)

Names	Age Yr Mon	Sex	Occupation, Trade or Profession	Country to Which Severally Belong	Country of Which They Intended to Become Inhabitants	Died on the Voyage	Part of Vessel Occupied During Voyage
Laurason, J. C.	50	M	Merchant	U.S.	U.S.		Cabin
Buttler, W. T. B.	40	M	Mechanic	U.S.	U.S.		Cabin
Clark, P. E.	59	F		U.S.	U.S.		Cabin
McLain, Richard	60	M	Farmer	U.S.	U.S.		Cabin
Dothard, Jot	56	M	Farmer	U.S.	U.S.		Cabin
Peak, J. P.	37	M	Farmer	U.S.	U.S.		Cabin
McCranie, D.	55	M	Farmer	U.S.	U.S.		Cabin
Richaird, Mrs. F.	46	F		France	France		Cabin
Gray, Dr. R. T.	57	M	M.D.	U.S.	U.S.		Cabin
Gouth, J.	36	M	Merchant	U.S.	U.S.		Cabin
Johnson, Geo.	50	M	Farmer	U.S.	U.S.		Cabin
Dart, Jos.	33	M	Merchant	B. Hond.	B. Hond.		Cabin
Carr, Thomas	56	M	Farmer	U.S.	U.S.		Cabin
King, Henry	20	M	Farmer	U.S.	U.S.		Cabin
Glasscock, J.	19	M	Farmer	U.S.	U.S.		Cabin

Report and List of the passengers taken on aboard the <u>STEAMER TRADE WIND</u> of <u>NEW YORK</u> whereof <u>A. BRIGGS</u> is Master, burthen <u>450</u> tons, bound from the Port of <u>BELIZE, BRITISH HONDURAS</u> for New Orleans. (Date sworn and subscribed <u>13</u> day of <u>JUNE</u> 186<u>8</u>)

Names	Age Yr Mon	Sex	Occupation, Trade or Profession	Country to Which Severally Belong	Country of Which They Intended to Become Inhabitants	Died on the Voyage	Part of Vessel Occupied During Voyage
Allen, Dr. M.	30	M	M.D.	B. Hond	Honduras		Cabin
Grued, Mrs. Alice	25	F		England	England		Cabin
Strully, Fre — —	32	M	Merchant	Honduras	Honduras		Cabin
Mims, H. A.	38	M	Merchant	Honduras	Honduras		Cabin
Brunk, Danl.	50	M	Merchant	U.S.	U.S.		Cabin
Burns, W. M.	51	M	Planter	U.S.	U.S.		Cabin
McCoy, J. G.	36	M	Planter	U.S.	U.S.		Cabin
McCoy, M. E.	35	F		U.S.	U.S.		Cabin
McCoy, P.	8	M		U.S.	U.S.		Cabin
McCoy, Grayer	6(4)	M		U.S.	U.S.		Cabin
Vineyard, N. O.	32	M	Merchant	U.S.	U.S.		Cabin
Vineyard, M. K.	21	F		U.S.	U.S.		Cabin
Vineyard, P. R.	16	M		U.S.	U.S.		Cabin
Vineyard, J. C.	28	M	Merchant	U.S.	U.S.		Cabin
Vineyard, A. W.	22	F		U.S.	U.S.		Cabin
Pack, T. A.	42	M	Farmer	U.S.	U.S.		Cabin
Pack, Mrs. K.	43	F		U.S.	U.S.		Cabin
Pack, B. W.	11	M		U.S.	U.S.		Cabin
Pack, M. E.	4	F		U.S.	U.S.		Cabin
Broadnay, A. E.	38	F		U.S.	U.S.		Cabin

Report and List of the passengers taken on aboard the <u>SS TRADE WIND</u> of <u>NEW YORK</u> whereof <u>A. BRIGGS</u> is Master, burthen <u>450</u> tons, bound from the Port of <u>BELIZE HONDURAS</u> for New Orleans. (Date sworn and subscribed <u>8</u> day of <u>AUGUST</u> 186<u>8</u>)

Names	Age Yr Mon	Sex	Occupation, Trade or Profession	Country to Which Severally Belong	Country of Which They Intended to Become Inhabitants	Died on the Voyage	Part of Vessel Occupied During Voyage
Richard James Corner	64	M	Chief Justice Br. Hond & Barrister of Law	England	England		Cabin
Philip James Hankin	32	M	Royal & Colonial of Sierra Leone	England	England		Cabin
McCrea, Miss C.	30	F		U.S.	U.S.		Cabin
Binders, J. E.	46	M	Planter	U.S.	U.S.		Cabin
Van Norman, A. L.	30	M	Merchant	U.S.	U.S.		Cabin

Names	Age Yr Mon	Sex	Occupation, Trade or Profession	Country to Which Severally Belong	Country of Which They Intended to Become Inhabitants	Died on the Voyage	Part of Vessel Occupied During Voyage
Henniny, John	56	M	Merchant	U.S.	U.S.		Cabin
Henniny, Mrs. S. J.	44	F		U.S.	U.S.		Cabin
Henniny, Miss S. I.	21	F		U.S.	U.S.		Cabin
Henniny, E. A.	19	F		U.S.	U.S.		Cabin
Henniny, M. A.	14	F		U.S.	U.S.		Cabin
Henniny, J. T.	17	M		U.S.	U.S.		Cabin

Report and List of the passengers taken on aboard the <u>STEAMER TRADE WIND</u> of <u>NEW YORK</u> whereof <u>ARCHIE BRIGGS</u> is Master, burthen <u>451 88/100</u> tons, bound from the Port of <u>BELIZE, HONDURAS</u> for New Orleans. (Date sworn and subscribed 5 day of <u>SEPTEMBER</u> 186<u>8</u>)

Names	Age Yr Mon	Sex	Occupation, Trade or Profession	Country to Which Severally Belong	Country of Which They Intended to Become Inhabitants	Died on the Voyage	Part of Vessel Occupied During Voyage
Hailey, Luit. Col. R. W.	38	M	Six Co. of H.B. M.30 W.I. Rgt.	England	England		Cabin
Prindle, A. C.	43	M	U.S. Consul & Agt.	U.S.	U.S.		Cabin
Stuart, Dr. W. C.	44	M		U.S.	U.S.		Cabin
McDermot, Miss C.	18	F		U.S.	U.S.		Cabin
McCutchon, S.	48	M		U.S.	U.S.		Cabin
— —, Miss A.	30	F		England	England		Cabin
Jones, S.	42	M		U.S.	U.S.		Cabin
Hatch, E. F.	27	M		U.S.	U.S.		Cabin

Report and List of the passengers taken on aboard the <u>AM SS TRADE WIND</u> of <u>NEW YORK</u> whereof <u>J.T. MORRILL</u> is Master, burthen <u>451 88/100</u> tons, bound from the Port of <u>BELIZE, B.H.</u> for New Orleans. (Date sworn and subscribed <u>17</u> day of <u>OCTOBER</u> 186<u>8</u>)

Names	Age Yr Mon	Sex	Occupation, Trade or Profession	Country to Which Severally Belong	Country of Which They Intended to Become Inhabitants	Died on the Voyage	Part of Vessel Occupied During Voyage
A. H. Smiley	48	M	Planter	U.S.	U.S.		Cabin
R. S. Smiley	19	M	Planter	U.S.	U.S.		Cabin
C. H. Smiley	18	M	Planter	U.S.	U.S.		Cabin
A. A. Smiley	17	F	Planter	U.S.	U.S.		Cabin
(unidentified)	29	M	Merchant	U.S.	U.S.		Cabin
J. C. A. Hendricks	35	M	Merchant	U.S.	U.S.		Cabin
W. A. Adams	30	M	Mechanic	U.S.	U.S.		Cabin
E. L. Woods	32	M	Planter	U.S.	U.S.		Cabin

Report and List of the passengers taken on aboard the <u>STEAMER TRADE WIND</u> of <u>NEW YORK</u> whereof <u>J.T. MORRILL</u> is Master, burthen <u>451 88/100</u> tons, bound from the Port of <u>BELIZE, HONDURAS</u> for New Orleans. (Date sworn and subscribed <u>9</u> day of <u>NOVEMBER</u> 186<u>8</u>)

Names	Age Yr Mon	Sex	Occupation, Trade or Profession	Country to Which Severally Belong	Country of Which They Intended to Become Inhabitants	Died on the Voyage	Part of Vessel Occupied During Voyage
Harrison, J. A.	50	M	Planter	U.S.	U.S.		Cabin
McKenzie, John	55	M	Merchant	U.S.	U.S.		Cabin
Pierce, Levi	60	M	Minister	U.S.	U.S.		Cabin
Barrow, A. W.	34	M	Farmer	U.S.	U.S.		Cabin
Nicholas, J. A.	38	M	Merchant	U.S.	U.S.		Cabin
Smiley, T. B.	38	M	Farmer	U.S.	U.S.		Cabin
Smiley, E. J.	38	F		U.S.	U.S.		Cabin
Smiley, T. A.	18	M		U.S.	U.S.		Cabin
Smiley, J. A.	7	M		U.S.	U.S.		Cabin
Smiley, Maggie	6	F		U.S.	U.S.		Cabin
White, Henry	38	M	Mechanic	U.S.	U.S.		Cabin
White, Janie	23	F		U.S.	U.S.		Cabin
White, Robert	12	M		U.S.	U.S.		Cabin
White, Emeline	8	F		U.S.	U.S.		Cabin
White, Virginia	6	F		U.S.	U.S.		Cabin
Price, E.	50	F		U.S.	U.S.		Cabin
Price, C.	14	F		U.S.	U.S.		Cabin
Price, Sheldon	18	M		U.S.	U.S.		Cabin
Price, O.	10	M		U.S.	U.S.		Cabin
Price, M.	11	F		U.S.	U.S.		Cabin
Kelly, Pat	13	M		U.S.	U.S.		Cabin

Report and List of the passengers taken on aboard the <u>STEAMER TRADE WIND</u> of <u>NEW YORK</u> whereof <u>J. TUCKER MORRILL</u> is Master, burthen <u>451 85/100</u> tons, bound from the Port of <u>BELIZE HONDURAS</u> for New Orleans. (Date sworn and subscribed <u>14</u> day of <u>DECEMBER</u> 186<u>8</u>)

Names	Age Yr Mon	Sex	Occupation, Trade or Profession	Country to Which Severally Belong	Country of Which They Intended to Become Inhabitants	Died on the Voyage	Part of Vessel Occupied During Voyage
McDermot, Chas.	60	M	Planter	U.S.	U.S.		Cabin
McDermot, Mrs. H. S.	50	F		U.S.	U.S.		Cabin
McDermot, Anne Belle	19	F		U.S.	U.S.		Cabin
McDermot, Margaret	15	F		U.S.	U.S.		Cabin
McDermot, Chas., Jr.	16	M		U.S.	U.S.		Cabin
McDermot, Willie	12	M		U.S.	U.S.		Cabin

Names	Age Yr Mon	Sex	Occupation, Trade or Profession	Country to Which Severally Belong	Country of Which They Intended to Become Inhabitants	Died on the Voyage	Part of Vessel Occupied During Voyage
McDermot, Scott	10	M		U.S.	U.S.		Cabin
McDermot, Edward	7	M		U.S.	U.S.		Cabin
Carpenter, T. H.	30	M	Mechanic	U.S.	U.S.		Cabin
Carpenter, John C., Jr.	22	M	Mechanic	U.S.	U.S.		Cabin
Drinon, J. A.	26	M	Mechanic	U.S.	U.S.		Cabin
McCall, Richard	21	M	Planter	U.S.	U.S.		Cabin
Guntinez, E.	48	M	Merchant	U.S.	U.S.		Cabin
Putnam, Mrs. Mary	44	F		U.S.	U.S.		Cabin
Putnam, Henry	20	M	Merchant	U.S.	U.S.		Cabin
Putnam, Emmet	12	M		U.S.	U.S.		Cabin
Putnam, Edward	9	M		U.S.	U.S.		Cabin
Putnam, Robert	7	M		U.S.	U.S.		Cabin
Putnam, Lee	5	M		U.S.	U.S.		Cabin
Merrell, Mrs. S. E.	40	F		U.S.	U.S.		Cabin
Merrell, L. F.	10	F		U.S.	U.S.		Cabin
Merrell, J. H.	8	M		U.S.	U.S.		Cabin
Merrell, S. N.	3	F		U.S.	U.S.		Cabin
Chick, Mrs. M.E .	19	F		U.S.	U.S.		Cabin
Barelift, W. S.	35	M	Planter	U.S.	U.S.		Cabin
Campagne, D. V. L.	23	M		U.S.	U.S.		Cabin

Passengers on board the Steamship S.S. TRADE WIND bound to NEW ORLEANS. (Date sworn and subscribed 11 day of JANUARY 1869)

Names	Age	Nativity	Color	Occupation
James M. Putnam	45		White	
W. D. Wall	25		White	
James Foley	45		White	
Dr. Tuiquilan & Servant	35/24		White	
Dr. Thompson & Lady	35/27		White	
J. F. Munez	29		White	
L. Moniqa	21		White	
E. J. Fraston	25		White	
James Morrill	17		White	
W. M. Johnson	33		White	
Corrie Audice	28		White	
H. Oladowski	60		White	
R. Walker	19		White	
J. P. Peak	29		White	

Passengers on board the Steamship TRADE WIND bound to NEW ORLEANS, LA. (Date sworn and subscribed 8 day of FEBRUARY 1869)

Names	Age	Nativity	Color	Occupation
S. D. Crankenden	26	United States	White	Gentleman

Names	Age	Nativity	Color	Occupation
H. Alred	26	United States	White	Gentleman
C. Birch	23	United States	White	Gentleman
A. Trasten	58	United States	White	Gentleman
G. L. Fuselier	67	United States	White	Gentleman
N. Johnson	17	United States	White	Gentleman
W. N.——	44	United States	White	Gentleman
M. G. Cheek	23	United States	White	Farmer
Eli Whittaker	18	United States	White	Farmer
W. S. Cary Sen.	46	United States	White	Merchant
C. M. Cary	40	United States	White	
W. S. Cary, Jr.	12	United States	White	
Ella Cary	9	United States	White	
Lilly Cary	6	United States	White	
Mrs. Saunders	29	United States	White	
Mattie Saunders	8	United States	White	

Report and List of the passengers taken on aboard the S.S. TRADE WIND of NEW YORK whereof J.T. MORRILL is Master, burthen 451 85/100 tons, bound from the Port of BELIZE, HOND. for New Orleans. (Date sworn and subscribed 16 day of MARCH 1869)

Names	Age Yr Mon	Sex	Occupation, Trade or Profession	Country to Which Severally Belong	Country of Which They Intended to Become Inhabitants	Died on the Voyage	Part of Vessel Occupied During Voyage
H. P. Manfred	36	M	M.D.	England	England		Cabin
Arteman Hill	75	M	Merchant	U.S.	U.S.		Cabin
Capt. P. H. Thompson	86	M	Civil Eng.	U.S.	U.S.		Cabin
E. C. Thompson	32	F		U.S.	U.S.		Cabin
Z. N. Morrill	65	M	Minister	U.S.	U.S.		Cabin
Z. J. Morrill	15	M	Farmer	U.S.	U.S.		Cabin
H. L. G. Morrill	13	M	Farmer	U.S.	U.S.		Cabin
N. P. Morrill	35	M	Planter	U.S.	U.S.		Cabin
J. Mutter	45	M	Mechanic	U.S.	U.S.		Cabin
Jns. Dawson	28	M	Planter	U.S.	U.S.		Cabin
J. J. Botter	26	M	Merchant	U.S.	U.S.		Cabin
N. H. Botter	21	F		U.S.	U.S.		Cabin
M. L. Botter	1(6)	F		U.S.	U.S.		Cabin
L. Pierce	60	M	Minister	U.S.	U.S.		Cabin
Thos. Henderson	43	M	Farmer	U.S.	U.S.		Cabin
W. Dodsworth	42	M	Merchant	U.S.	U.S.		Cabin
Mrs. W. Dodsworth	39	F		U.S.	U.S.		Cabin
W.E . Dodsworth	13	M		U.S.	U.S.		Cabin
E. B. Jones	24	F		U.S.	U.S.		Cabin
J. D. Harris	60	M	Planter	U.S.	U.S.		Cabin
G. A. Harris	31	M	Planter	U.S.	U.S.		Cabin
L. V. Harris	30	F		U.S.	U.S.		Cabin
W. Williams	24	M	Planter	U.S.	U.S.		Cabin
Jas. Gray	46	M	Planter	U.S.	U.S.		Cabin
W. Gray	9	F		U.S.	U.S.		Cabin
M. Gray	3	F		U.S.	U.S.		Cabin

Names	Age Yr Mon	Sex	Occupation, Trade or Profession	Country to Which Severally Belong	Country of Which They Intended to Become Inhabitants	Died on the Voyage	Part of Vessel Occupied During Voyage
W. Gray	7	M		U.S.	U.S.		Cabin
J. B. Tanner	28	M	Planter	U.S.	U.S.		Cabin
J.B. Tanner	18	F		U.S.	U.S.		Cabin
E. F. Tanner	2	F		U.S.	U.S.		Cabin
C. E. Payne	31	F		U.S.	U.S.		Cabin
Jane Payne	14	F		U.S.	U.S.		Cabin
Harriet Payne	11	F		U.S.	U.S.		Cabin
Jas. Payne	9	M		U.S.	U.S.		Cabin
Mrs. Stibers	37	F		U.S.	U.S.		Cabin
Ophelia Stibers	15	F		U.S.	U.S.		Cabin
Lizzie Stibers	6	F		U.S.	U.S.		Cabin
Harry Stibers	16	M		U.S.	U.S.		Cabin
Geo. Stibers	10	M		U.S.	U.S.		Cabin
Chas. Stibers	8	M		U.S.	U.S.		Cabin
Mrs. Reard	30	F		U.S.	U.S.		Cabin
S. C. White	62	M	Planter	U.S.	U.S.		Cabin
P. White	19	M	Planter	U.S.	U.S.		Cabin
S. White	16	M		U.S.	U.S.		Cabin
Mrs. S. C. White	44	F		U.S.	U.S.		Cabin
Mary White	13	F		U.S.	U.S.		Cabin
Nancy White	7	F		U.S.	U.S.		Cabin
Jno. White	9	M		U.S.	U.S.		Cabin
J. D. White	7	M		U.S.	U.S.		Cabin

Passengers on board the Steamship <u>TRADE WIND</u> bound to <u>NEW ORLEANS, LA.</u> (Date sworn and subscribed <u>13</u> day of <u>APRIL</u> 186<u>9</u>)

Names	Age	Nativity	Color	Occupation
Mr. J. W. Logan	60	United States	White	
Mr. J. L. Buler	42	United States	White	
Mr. J. T. Buck	42	United States	White	
Dr. J. W. Saunders	35	United States	White	
Mr. S. French	58	United States	White	
Mr. Henry B. Richardson	31	United States	White	
Mr. A. O'Luis	26	United States	White	
Master Alinzo Valenzuela	11	United States	White	
Mr. J. A. Stokes	58	United States	White	
Mrs. F. Stokes	31	United States	White	
Mr. M. A. Motley	23	United States	White	
Master R. Stokes	12	United States	White	
Master Ira Stokes	10	United States	White	
Mrs. M. J. Johnston	38	United States	White	
Miss Pauline Johnston	18	United States	White	
Mr. Chas. Aymar	49	United States	White	
Dr. W. A. Ryan	41	United States	White	
Mr. H. R. Reed	37	United States	White	
Mr. Gus Shaw	29	United States	White	
Mr. W. A. Hopper	22	United States	White	
Master W. Hubbard	16	United States	White	
Mr. H. F. Byrd	44	United States	White	

Names	Age	Nativity	Color	Occupation
Mrs. S. F. Byrd	26	United States	White	
Miss Alice Mixon	20	United States	White	
Miss Molly Byrd	9	United States	White	
Miss Flina Byrd	7	United States	White	
Master K. Byrd	3	United States	White	
Master Willi Byrd	1	United States	White	
Mr. Fred Miacco	21	United States	White	
Mr. W. B. Tindall	59	United States	White	
Mrs. M. E. Tindall	40	United States	White	
Mr. W. B. Tindall Jr.	22	United States	White	
Mr. T. R. Tindall	20	United States	White	
M. G. Kuck	30	United States	White	
Mr. H. M. Smith	45	United States	White	
Mrs. H. M. Smith	44	United States	White	
Miss Josephine Smith	25	United States	White	
Miss Cornelia Smith	23	United States	White	
Mr. A. Miacco	23	United States	White	
Mrs. L. Miacco	21	United States	White	
Miss L. Smith	12	United States	White	
Miss Ella Smith	9	United States	White	
Master Frank Smith	7	United States	White	
Master Lins Smith	4	United States	White	
Mr. W. Wallace	31	United States	White	
Mr. T. W. Campbell	25	United States	White	
Ch. P. Smith (Servant)		United States	Colored	

Report and List of the passengers taken on aboard the S.S. TRADE WIND of NEW YORK whereof J.T. MORRILL is Master, burthen 451 85/100 tons, bound from the Port of BELIZE, HONDURAS for New Orleans. (Date sworn and subscribed 11 day of MAY 1869)

Names	Age Yr Mon	Sex	Occupation, Trade or Profession	Country to Which Severally Belong	Country of Which They Intended to Become Inhabitants	Died on the Voyage	Part of Vessel Occupied During Voyage
Col. S. McCutchon	48	M	Planter	U.S.	U.S.		Cabin
Wm. Aymar	36	M	Merchant	U.S.	U.S.		Cabin
C. E. Aymar	49	M	Merchant	U.S.	U.S.		Cabin
R. D. V. Logan	20	M	Planter	U.S.	U.S.		Cabin
Allen Griffen, Sr.	61	M	Planter	U.S.	U.S.		Cabin
Mrs. P. Griffen	58	F		U.S.	U.S.		Cabin
J. A. Griffen	23	M	Planter	U.S.	U.S.		Cabin
J. Griffen	19	F		U.S.	U.S.		Cabin
Allen Griffen, Jr.	19	M	Planter	U.S.	U.S.		Cabin
Miss A. Griffen	15	F		U.S.	U.S.		Cabin
Olivia Griffen	14	F		U.S.	U.S.		Cabin
Thomas Griffen	12	M		U.S.	U.S.		Cabin
George C. Hatch	70	M	Planter	U.S.	U.S.		Cabin
Mrs. E. A. Byrne	44	F		U.S.	U.S.		Cabin
T. C. Brewer	47	M	Merchant	U.S.	U.S.		Cabin
Mrs. T. C. Brewer	24	F	Merchant	U.S.	U.S.		Cabin
T. J. Mooring	35	M	Merchant	U.S.	U.S.		Cabin

Names	Age Yr Mon	Sex	Occupation, Trade or Profession	Country to Which Severally Belong	Country of Which They Intended to Become Inhabitants	Died on the Voyage	Part of Vessel Occupied During Voyage
Julia A. Mooring	29	F		U.S.	U.S.		Cabin
W. Nash	56	M	Carpenter	U.S.	U.S.		Cabin
J. Nash	39	F		U.S.	U.S.		Cabin
H. C. Morton	32	M	Farmer	U.S.	U.S.		Cabin
Mrs. M. Morton	22	F		U.S.	U.S.		Cabin
Mrs. S. F. Manning	50	F		U.S.	U.S.		Cabin
Miss J. Manning	20	F		U.S.	U.S.		Cabin
D.M. Allen	31	M	Merchant	U.S.	U.S.		Cabin
E. de Lautsheer	40	M	Merchant	U.S.	U.S.		Cabin
Revd. D. C. Wells	44	M	Minister	U.S.	U.S.		Cabin
Wm. McLaughlen	32	M	Farmer	U.S.	U.S.		Cabin
W. T. Hightower	23	M	Farmer	U.S.	U.S.		Cabin
Oscar Price	27	M	Planter	U.S.	U.S.		Cabin
Victoria Price	8	F		U.S.	U.S.		Cabin
George Price	6	M		U.S.	U.S.		Cabin
J. H. Coleman	29	M	Farmer	U.S.	U.S.		Cabin
Robert Ferguson	55	M	Merchant	Scotland	England		Cabin
Chas. T. Hunter	31	M	Merchant	Scotland	England		Cabin
Mrs. C. T. Hunter	30	F		Br. Hond.	England		Cabin
Dr. Alex Hunter	27	M	M.D.	Scotland	England		Cabin

Report and List of the passengers taken on aboard the S.S. TRADE WIND of NEW YORK whereof J.T. MORRILL is Master, burthen 451 85/100 tons, bound from the Port of BELIZE, HONDURAS for New Orleans. (Date sworn and subscribed 8 day of JUNE 1869)

Names	Age Yr Mon	Sex	Occupation, Trade or Profession	Country to Which Severally Belong	Country of Which They Intended to Become Inhabitants	Died on the Voyage	Part of Vessel Occupied During Voyage
Mr. Levi Doughty	54	M	Planter	U.S.	U.S.	1 trunk	Cabin
Mr. H. E. Dwight	54	M	Merchant	U.S.	U.S.	1 trunk	Cabin
Mr. J. M. Putnam	45	M	Merchant	U.S.	U.S.	1 trunk 1 bedstead 1 chair	Cabin 2 boxes
Mr. P. L. Kovy	20	M	Merchant	Holland	Holland	1 valise 1 trunk	Cabin
Mrs. M. E. Hatch	43	F		U.S.	U.S.		Cabin
J. E. Hatch	20	M	Farmer	U.S.	U.S.	8 trunks	Cabin
W. A. Hatch	17	M	Farmer	U.S.	U.S.	1 Box	Cabin
J. H. Hatch	11	F		U.S.	U.S.		Cabin
L. Hatch	4	F		U.S.	U.S.		Cabin
J. E. C. Hendrick	35	M	Merchant	U.S.	U.S.	1 trunk	Cabin
Wm. Davidson	35	M	Farmer	U.S.	U.S.	1 pkg	Cabin
W. C. Watrous	22	M	Farmer	U.S.	U.S.	1 trunk	Cabin

Names	Age Yr Mon	Sex	Occupation, Trade or Profession	Country to Which Severally Belong	Country of Which They Intended to Become Inhabitants	Died on the Voyage	Part of Vessel Occupied During Voyage
Mrs. C. Orgen	55	F	Farmer	U.S.	U.S.		Cabin
James Irish	25	M	Farmer	U.S.	U.S.	2 Bdls.	Cabin
Wm. Irish	39	M	Farmer	U.S.	U.S.	4 trunks	Cabin
John Irish	9	M	Farmer	U.S.	U.S.	1 box	Cabin
Dr. R. S. Fasten	29	M	Farmer	U.S.	U.S.		Cabin
Mrs. A. L. Fasten	23	F	Farmer	U.S.	U.S.	1 trunk 1 pkg	Cabin
Henry Brown	13	M	Farmer	U.S.	U.S.	1 trunk	Cabin
G. W. Sherrod	48	M	Farmer	U.S.	U.S.	1 trunk	Cabin

Report and List of the passengers taken on aboard the STEAMER TRADE WIND of NEW YORK whereof J.T. MORRILL is Master, burthen 451 85/100 tons, bound from the Port of BELIZE, HONDURAS for New Orleans. (Date sworn and subscribed 11 day of SEPTEMBER 1869)

Names	Age Yr Mon	Sex	Occupation, Trade or Profession	Country to Which Severally Belong	Country of Which They Intended to Become Inhabitants	Died on the Voyage	Part of Vessel Occupied During Voyage
Mr. C. L. Amalgry	26	M	Planter	U.S.	U.S.	3 valise	Cabin
Dr. John Seay	42	M	M.D.	U.S.	U.S.	3 trunks	Cabin
Dr. Francis Sikon	29	M	M.D.	Austria	Austria	2 trunks 3 boxes	Cabin
Revd. S. C. Littlepage	36	M	Minister	U.S.	U.S.		Cabin
Mr. C. V. Littlepage	42	M	Planter	U.S.	U.S.	3 trunks	Cabin
Mrs. Virginia Littlepage	36	F		U.S.	U.S.	1 valise	Cabin
Effie Littlepage	8	F		U.S.	U.S.	& 3 pkgs	Cabin
Lizzie Littlepage	9	F		U.S.	U.S.		Cabin
Emma Littlepage	5	F		U.S.	U.S.		Cabin
Ellenor Littlepage	3	F		U.S.	U.S.		Cabin
Mr. W. Jameson	28	M	Planter	U.S.	U.S.	3 trunks	Cabin
Mrs. Emma Jameson	25	F		U.S.	U.S.	1 box	Cabin
Mary W. Jameson	2/4	F		U.S.	U.S.	3 pkgs	Cabin
R. T. Jameson	00/4	M		U.S.	U.S.		Cabin
Dr. Vernon	42	M	M.D.	U.S.	U.S.	1 pkg	Cabin
John Hubbard	59	M	Planter	U.S.	U.S.	3 boxes	Cabin
Andrew Hubbard	11	M	Planter	U.S.	U.S.	& 3 pkgs	Cabin
T. A. Woods	33	M	Planter	U.S.	U.S.	1 trunk	Cabin
T. S. Middlebrooks	43	M	Planter	U.S.	U.S.		Cabin
L. A. Middlebrooks	10	F		U.S.	U.S.	5 trunks	Cabin
J. E. Middlebrooks	8	F		U.S.	U.S.	1 box	Cabin
E. Middlebrooks	5	F		U.S.	U.S.	2 pkgs	Cabin

Names	Age Yr Mon	Sex	Occupation, Trade or Profession	Country to Which Severally Belong	Country of Which They Intended to Become Inhabitants	Died on the Voyage	Part of Vessel Occupied During Voyage
Mary Middlebrooks	3	F		U.S.	U.S.		Cabin
Mrs. Nixon	45	F		U.S.	U.S.		Cabin

Report and List of the passengers taken on aboard the <u>STEAMER TRADE WIND</u> of <u>NEW YORK</u> whereof <u>J.T. MORRILL</u> is Master, burthen <u>451 88/100</u> tons, bound from the Port of <u>BELIZE, HONDURAS</u> for New Orleans. (Date sworn and subscribed <u>10</u> day of <u>SEPTEMBER</u> 186<u>9</u>)

Names	Age Yr Mon	Sex	Occupation, Trade or Profession	Country to Which Severally Belong	Country of Which They Intended to Become Inhabitants	Died on the Voyage	Part of Vessel Occupied During Voyage
Dr. Mark Allen	31	M	Merchant	U.S.	U.S.	Baggage	Cabin
Mrs. J. Allen	23	F		U.S.	U.S.	4 trunks	Cabin
M. Allen	3	F		U.S.	U.S.		Cabin
L. Allen	1	F		U.S.	U.S.		Cabin
Alfred F. Giolma	29	M	Minister	Gibraltar	England	2 trunks 1 bag bdle	Cabin
C. de Rodhe	33	M	Merchant	France	France	2 trunks	Cabin
N. T. Thibedaux	26	M	Mechanic	U.S.	U.S.	2 trunks	Cabin
Mrs. C. Thibedaux	26	F		U.S.	U.S.	& 2 chests	Cabin
W. J. Holt	33	M	Mechanic	U.S.	U.S.	2 trunks	Cabin
Mrs. M. Holt	37	F		U.S.	U.S.	1 bed	Cabin
Miss M. Holt	5	F		U.S.	U.S.	1 valise	Cabin
Mrs. Paulman	39	F		U.S.	U.S.	2 trunks 1 box	Cabin
Mrs. E. R. Miller	47	F		U.S.	U.S.	2 trunks	Cabin
Mrs. L. Reuch	45	F		France	France	10 trunks	Cabin
Miss M. Reuch	18	F		France	France	2 boxes 1 bdle	Cabin
W. B. Massey	56	M	Farmer	U.S.	U.S.	4 trunks	Cabin
T. G. Massey	53	F		U.S.	U.S.	1 bdle	Cabin
Chas. A. Massey	19	M	Farmer	U.S.	U.S.	1 bdle	Cabin
W. F. Massey	12	M	Farmer	U.S.	U.S.		Cabin
Miss Sally Deacon	34	F		U.S.	U.S.		Cabin
H. Balis	50	M	Civ. Eng.	England	England	2 trunks 2 cavs.	Cabin
M. E. Gibson	30	M	Farmer	U.S.	U.S.	5 trunks	Cabin
S. Gibson	25	F	Farmer	U.S.	U.S.	2 boxes	Cabin
M. J. Smith	23	F	Farmer	U.S.	U.S.	1 valise	Cabin
John J. Vinceman	20	M	Farmer	U.S.	U.S.	1 pkg	Cabin
H. Brazer	45	M	Farmer	U.S.	U.S.	1 trunk	Cabin
H. Jones				U.S.	U.S.	1 valise	Cabin

Report and List of the passengers taken on aboard the <u>S.S. PERIT of NEW YORK</u> whereof <u>J.T. MORRILL</u> is Master, burthen tons, bound from the Port of

BELIZE TO NEW ORLEANS for New Orleans. (Date sworn and subscribed 20 day of NOV 1869)

Names	Age Yr Mon	Sex	Occupation, Trade or Profession	Country to Which Severally Belong	Destination	Place of Birth	Part of Vessel Occupied During Voyage
W. C. Haller M.D.	39	M	M.D.	Texas	Texas	Louisiana	Rm No. 7
M. C. Haller	28	F		Texas	Texas	Texas	Rm No. 7
Benjamin R. Duval	54	M	Meth. Preacher	Virginia	Virginia	Virginia	Rm No. 2
J. A. Wier	50	M	Merchant	N. Orleans	New Orleans	Nassau N.P.	Cabin
Miss F. A. Wier	20	F		N. Orleans	New Orleans	Mobile Ala.	Cabin
W. C. Chamberlin	57	M	Merchant	Belize Hon.	New Orleans	Mass.	Cabin
L. H. Walker	30	M	Farmer	Belize Hon.	New Orleans	Mississippi	Cabin
Mrs. L. H. Walker	19	F		Belize Hon.	New Orleans	Mississippi	Cabin
— — mon M. Hin	28	M	Asst. Col. Sec. of Brit. Honduras	Belize Hon.	New Orleans	England	
— — —	32	M		Belize Hon.	New Orleans		
Emma — — —	24	M		Belize Hon.	New Orleans		
Jas. Manning	19	M		Aberdeen MS	Aberdeen MS	Aberdeen MS	

Report and List of the passengers taken on aboard the S.S. PERIT of NEW YORK whereof J.T. MORRILL is Master, burthen tons, bound from the Port of BELIZE, BRITISH HONDURAS for New Orleans. (Date sworn and subscribed 13 day of DEC 1869)

Names	Age Yr Mon	Sex	Occupation, Trade or Profession	Country to Which Severally Belong	Destination	Place of Birth	Part of Vessel Occupied During Voyage
Timothy Morris	61	M	Farmer	Br Hond.	New Orleans	New Jersey	Strge.
Mary Morris	52	F					
Jane Morris	24	F				Arkansas	
Sattie Morris	19	F					
John Morris	22	M					
David Morris	17	M					
Geo. Morris	8	M					
Martha Johns	35	F				Illinois	
Mary Johns	11	F				Illinois	
Nancy Johns	10	F				Arkansas	
Wm. Johns	9	M					
Sarah Johns	5	F					
Caroline Johns	3	F					
Caroline Finley	20	F					
Cicero Finley	20	M					
David Finley	2	M					
Marriccio Servanta	50	M				Italy	
Carolina Servanta	2	F				British Honduras	
Pisco Servanta	48	M	Musician			Italy	

Names	Age Yr Mon	Sex	Occupation, Trade or Profession	Country to Which Severally Belong	Destination	Place of Birth	Part of Vessel Occupied During Voyage
J. S. Gibson	52	M	M.D.			Scotland	Saloon
Emily Gibson	44	F				U.S.	
J. S. Gibson	18	M					
John Gibson	15	M					
Elbert Gibson	8	M					
Frank Gibson	4	M					
Catherine Gibson	2	F					
Edward A. Drew	47	M	Gent.			Scotland	
John Della Falline	42	M				France	
Joseph Vandencamp	31	M				Germany	
Carl Senetronson	62	M				Germany	
Joseph Colquit	23	M	Farmer			United States	
Agnes Duval	48	F					
Ida Duval	18	F					
Mary Duval	15	F					
Sedia Duval	12	F					
Wm. Duval	8	M					
Robt. Seabitter	24	M	Farmer				
Newton Young	35	M					
Sally Young	24	F					
Newton Pickett	43	M	Farmer				
(I.?) Gwen Pickett	39	F					
Eva Pickett	16	F					
Jas. Pickett	20	M					
Jas. Pickett	12	M					
Wm. Pickett	10	M					
Newton Pickett, Jr.	8	M					
Calvin Pickett	6	M					
Minnie Pickett	3	F					
Henry Dumas	20	M					
George Eldridge	59	M					
Emma Eldridge	50	F					
Mary Eldridge	22	F					
Marion Eldridge	20	M					
Albert Harrison	22	M	Gent.				2n Cab
Chas Mills	38	M	Planter				2n Cab
Jas. Common	26	M	Traveler			Honduras	Saloon
Henry Dexter	48	M	Civil Service			U.S.	Saloon
Joshua Simpson	60	M	Farmer			England	2n Cab
Susan Simpson	47	F				U.S.	
Samson(?) Mowning	22	M					
Serinson Mowning	20	M					
——Mowning	17	F					
John Mowning	20	M					
(?)Volsmon Mowning	10	M					

Names	Age Yr Mon	Sex	Occupation, Trade or Profession	Country to Which Severally Belong	Destination	Place of Birth	Part of Vessel Occupied During Voyage
Walter — — —	9	M					
Martha Mowning	20	F					
Daniel Brown	72	M					
Sally Brown	32	F					
Jas. Brown	4	M					

Shipwrecked British Seamen Great Britain

Names	Age				
Frank McGentry	26				
Robt. Aitkins	23				
John McDonald	29				
Jas. Frank	26				
S. — — —	23				
Geo. Taylor	34				
Peter Anson	24				
Hugh McCall	28				
Alex Campbell	17				
Stephen Adair	23				
S. McC — —	24				
Jas. Grant	23				
Andrew Easons	23				
Pat Doyle	22				
Frank Pickering	29				
Peter Hay — —	23				
T. F. Carr		Amer. Consul Man			
I. Bert — —					

Report and List of the passengers taken on aboard the <u>S.S. PERIT of NEW YORK</u> whereof <u>J.T. MORRILL</u> is Master, burthen <u>592</u> tons, bound from the Port of <u>BELIZE, BR. HONDURAS</u> for New Orleans. (Date sworn and subscribed <u>8</u> day of <u>JAN</u> 18<u>70</u>)

Names	Age Yr Mon	Sex	Occupation, Trade or Profession	Country to Which Severally Belong	Country of Which They Intended to Become Inhabitants	Died on the Voyage	Part of Vessel Occupied During Voyage
Wm. W. Schernerhorn	28	M	Merchant	U.S.	U.S.		Cabin
C. Hempstead, Jr.	24	M	Merchant	U.S.	U.S.		Cabin
Jno. Garnett	55	M	Planter	U.S.	U.S.		Cabin
Mrs. Garnett	50	F		U.S.	U.S.		Cabin
Mrs. A. T. Beauregard	22	F		U.S.	U.S.		Cabin
Miss Rosa Coleman	24	F		U.S.	U.S.		Cabin
J. Dorian	36	M	Planter	U.S.	U.S.		Cabin
Mrs. Dorian	30	F		U.S.	U.S.		Cabin
W.J. Wetheren	28	M	Planter	U.S.	U.S.		Cabin

Names	Age Yr Mon	Sex	Occupation, Trade or Profession	Country to Which Severally Belong	Country of Which They Intended to Become Inhabitants	Died on the Voyage	Part of Vessel Occupied During Voyage
N——Gibson	72	M	Planter	U.S.	U.S.		Cabin
Doct. J. Hill	35	M	Planter	U.S.	U.S.		Cabin
Doct. D. Gibson	65	M	Planter	U.S.	U.S.		Cabin
Miss Catherine S——	20	F		U.S.	U.S.		Cabin

Report and List of the passengers taken on aboard the S.S. PERIT of NEW YORK whereof J.T. MORRILL is Master, burthen 592 tons, bound from the Port of BELIZE, HONDURAS for New Orleans. (Date sworn and subscribed 7 day of FEB 1870)

Names	Age Yr Mon	Sex	Occupation, Trade or Profession	Country to Which Severally Belong	Country of Which They Intended to Become Inhabitants	Died on the Voyage	Part of Vessel Occupied During Voyage
Wm. Miller	35	M	Planter	U.S.	U.S.		Cabin
Mary Miller	30	F				4 packages	baggs
John Miller	2/06	M					
A. Leckie	35	M	Merchant			2 packages	baggs
———	22	M	Merchant			2 packages	baggs
Mr.———	59	M	Planter			1 package	baggs
A.J. Fo——	59	M	Planter			1 package	baggs

Report and List of the passengers taken on aboard the S.S. PERIT of *NEW YORK* whereof W.H. GARDINER is Master, burthen 595 tons, bound from the Port of BELIZE for New Orleans. (Date sworn and subscribed 12 day of MARCH 1870)

Names	Age Yr Mon	Sex	Occupation, Trade or Profession	Country to Which Severally Belong	Country of Which They Intended to Become Inhabitants	Died on the Voyage	Part of Vessel Occupied During Voyage
Jas. H. Johnson	24	M	Clerk	U.S.	U.S.		Cabin
Louise A. Johnson	22	F	Lady	U.S.	U.S.		Cabin
Wm. H. Sylvester	35	M	Merchant	U.S.	U.S.		Cabin
A. H. Hatch	23	M	Farmer	U.S.	U.S.		Cabin
Milton S. Hatch	29	F	Lady	U.S.	U.S.		Cabin
Christopher J. Hatch	39	M	Farmer	U.S.	U.S.		Cabin
Mary N. Hatch	34	F	Lady	U.S.	U.S.		Cabin
Arthur Halley	29	M	Merchant	England	U.S.		Cabin
H. Harrison	57	M	Merchant	U.S.	U.S.		Cabin
H. Harrison	43	F	Lady	U.S.	U.S.		Cabin
Annie Harrison	22	F	Lady	U.S.	U.S.		Cabin

Names	Age Yr Mon	Sex	Occupation, Trade or Profession	Country to Which Severally Belong	Country of Which They Intended to Become Inhabitants	Died on the Voyage	Part of Vessel Occupied During Voyage
Jas. S. Peak	25	M	Merchant	U.S.	U.S.		Cabin
Richard H. Rousseau	54	M	Lawyer	U.S.	U.S.		Cabin
Isaac H. White	57	M	Farmer	U.S.	U.S.		Cabin
Mary S. White	29	F	Lady	U.S.	U.S.		Cabin
— — McDonald	41	F	Lady	U.S.	U.S.		Cabin
Annie A. Smith	71	F	Lady	U.S.	U.S.		Cabin
Edwd. A. Hubert	30	M	Physician	Canada	U.S.		Cabin
Geo. P. Carr	38	M	Merchant	U.S.	U.S.		Cabin
P. J. O. Osarste	26	M	Merchant	Guatemala	U.S.		Cabin
A. T. Beauregard	42	M	Planter	U.S.	U.S.		Cabin

Report and List of the passengers taken on aboard the <u>BRIT. SCH. JOE KELLY</u> of whereof <u>JAMES BRYAN</u> is Master, burthen tons, bound from the Port of <u>BELIZE, HONDURAS</u> for New Orleans. (Date sworn and subscribed <u>19</u> day of <u>APRIL</u> 18<u>70</u>)

Names	Age Yr Mon	Sex	Occupation, Trade or Profession	Country to Which Severally Belong	Country of Which They Intended to Become Inhabitants	Died on the Voyage	Part of Vessel Occupied During Voyage
Mr. Shavers	40	M	Merchant	U.S.	U.S.	NONE	
Mrs. Shavers	38	F	Merchant	U.S.	U.S.		
Miss Shavers	14	F	Merchant	U.S.	U.S.		
Miss Shavers	12	F		U.S.	U.S.		
Miss Shavers	10	F		U.S.	U.S.		
Miss Shavers	8	F		U.S.	U.S.		
Master Shavers	5	M		U.S.	U.S.		
Master Shavers	3	M		U.S.	U.S.		
Master Shavers	1	M		U.S.	U.S.		
Mr. Darnell	24	M	Merchant	U.S.	U.S.		
Mr. Polk	39	M	Merchant	U.S.	U.S.		
Mrs. Polk	27	F		U.S.	U.S.		
Mr. West	28	M	Merchant	U.S.	U.S.		
Mrs. West	25	F		U.S.	U.S.		

Bibliography

"Agriculture in British Honduras." *Colonist*, 8 April 1865, 4.

"The American News." *Colonist*, 5 August 1865, 2.

AMIGO. "From British Honduras." *Montgomery Weekly Advertiser*, 18 June 1867, 3.

_____. "From Belize, Honduras." *Daily Picayune*, 14 June 1867, 1(M).

"Another Attempt at Robbery." *British Honduras Colonist and Belize Advertiser*, 7 November 1868, 2.

"The Arrival." *British Honduras Colonist and Belize Advertiser*, 7 December 1867, 2–3.

"Austin City." *Commercial Advertiser*, 17 July 1867, 3.

Avet, J. "Belize Honduras." *Daily Picayune*, 25 January 1868, 1(E).

Belize Colonial Secretary's Office. "Memorandum of Revd. R. Dawson's Service for Pension." 11 November 187(?), Public Archives of Belize, 107R681.

"Belize, Honduras." *Daily Picayune*, 21 February 1867, 7(M).

Bergeron, Arthur W. (ed.). *Guide to Louisiana Confederate Military Units, 1861–1865*. Baton Rouge: Louisiana State University Press, 1989.

Bettersworth, John K. *Mississippi: Yesterday and Today*. Austin, Texas: Steck-Vaughn, 1964.

Biographical and Illustrated Memoirs of Northwest Louisiana. Nashville: The Southern Publishing, 1890.

Bolland, O. Nigel. *The Formation of a Colonial Society: Belize, from Conquest to Crown Colony*. Baltimore: Johns Hopkins University Press, 1977.

Booth, Andrew B. *Records of Louisiana Confederate Soldiers and Louisiana Confederate Commands*, vol. 3, no. 2. New Orleans: Commissioner Louisiana Military Records, 1920.

Brackman, _____. "The Belize Hotel." *Colonist*, 29 July 1865.

Brewer, T. C. "Letter from British Honduras." *Mobile Daily Register*, 8 June 1868, 2.

_____. "Tin-Smithing." *British Honduras Colonist and Belize Advertiser*, 7 March 1867, 4.

Brewer, T. C. and J. M. Merry. "Dissolution." *British Honduras Colonist and Belize Advertiser*, 28 November 1868, 4.

"British Honduras." *Colonist*, 16 December 1865, 2.

"British Honduras." *Daily Picayune*, 21 March 1866, 11(M).

"British Honduras." *Daily Picayune*, 31 July 1867, 2(A).

British Honduras. House of Assembly. Message No. 11 to Governor Longdon. 15 March 1869. Public Archives of Belize, 99R160.

Burns, Alan. *History of the British West Indies*. London: George Allen and Unwin, 1954.

Camille, Michael Anthony. "Historical Geography of the U.S. Confederate Settlement at Toledo, Belize, 1868–1930." *Belcast Journal of Belizean Affairs* 3 (June 1986): 39–46.

_____. "Historical Geography of Toledo Settlement, Belize, 1868–1985: A Transition from Confederate Landscape to East Indian." M.A. thesis, Louisiana State University, 1986.

Candor. "We Have Been a Good Deal Amused." *British Honduras Colonist and Belize Advertiser*, 21 September 1867, 3.

Carrington, C. E. *The British Overseas: Exploits of a Nation of Shopkeepers*. Cambridge: Cambridge University Press, 1950.

Chapman, Felix Millwater, to Miss Fan —. 21 October 1947. Located in the personal collection of Lt. Col. Robert B. Hardy, "The Cedars," Columbus, Mississippi.

Chapman, Maunsel W. "British Honduras." *Livingston Journal*, 22 June 1867, 1.

Clegern, Wayne M. *British Honduras: Colonial Dead End, 1859–1900*. Baton Rouge: Louisiana State University Press, 1967.

CONFAB. "To the Editor of the B.H. Colonist." *British Honduras Colonist and Belize Advertiser*, 27 July 1867, 3.

CONFED. "Mr. Editor." *Commercial Advertiser*, 24 July 1867, 2.

Conrad, Glenn R. (gen. ed.). *A Dictionary of Louisiana Biography*. New Orleans: Louisiana Historical Association, 1988.

Cooper, William J., Jr., and Thomas E. Terrill. *The American South: A History*. New York: McGraw Hill, 1991.

Copeland, Jay B. "Correspondence." *Belize Advertiser*, 25 June 1871, 2.

Creath, J. W. D. "Elder Z. N. Morrell." *British Honduras Colonist and Belize Advertiser*, 11 April 1868, 2.

Davis, Charles. *Colin J. McRae: Confederate Financial Agent*. Tuscaloosa, Alabama: Confederate Publishing, 1961.

"Deaths." *British Honduras Colonist and Belize Advertiser*, 16 November 1867, 2.

"Deaths." *British Honduras Colonist and Belize Advertiser*, 27 June 1868, 2.

DePriest, Joe, personal communication to author, 9 April 1990.

Diocese of Baton Rouge Catholic Church Records, 1840–1847. Baton Rouge: Diocese of Baton Rouge Department of Archives, 1986.

Dispatches from U.S. Consuls in Belize. A. C. Prindle to J. D. Cadwaleden. No. 225, 30 August 1875, FM T-334 Roll 3.

_____. A. C. Prindle to Hamilton Fish. No. 73, 17 September 1869, FM T-334 Roll 4.

_____. A. C. Prindle to Hamilton Fish. No. 88, 29 January 1870, FM T-334 Roll 4.

_____. A. C. Prindle to Hamilton Fish. No. 95, 12 April 1870, FM T-334 Roll 4.

_____. A. C. Prindle to Hamilton Fish. No. 116, 19 September 1870, FM T-334 Roll 3.

_____. A. C. Prindle to Hamilton Fish. No. 119, 26 November 1870, FM T-334 Roll 4.

_____. Albert E. Harlan to John Davis. No. 20, 30 May 1883, FM T-334 Roll 4.

_____. C. A. Leas to W. Seward. No. 131, 10 March 1864, FM T-334 Roll 3.

_____. C. A. Leas to W. A. Seward. No. 141, 1 April 1864, FM T-334 Roll 3.

_____. C. A. Leas to W. A. Seward. No. 158, 7 May 1864, FM T-334 Roll 3.

_____. A. N. Miller to W. A. Seward. No.—, 3 September 1866, FM T-334 Roll 3.

_____. A. C. Prindle to F. W. Seward. No. 1, 1 July 1867, FM T-334 Roll 3.

_____. A. C. Prindle to F. W. Seward. No. 15, 10 January 1868, FM T-334, Roll 3.

_____. A. C. Prindle to F. W. Seward. No. 22, 6 March 1868, FM T-334 Roll 3.

_____. A. C. Prindle to F. W. Seward. No. 27, 5 May 1868, FM T-334, Roll 3.

_____. A. C. Prindle to F. W. Seward. No. 44, 16 October 1868, FM T-334, Roll 3.

_____. A. C. Prindle to W. A. Seward. No. 1, 1 July 1867, FM T-334 Roll 3.

_____. A. C. Prindle to W. A. Seward. No. 2, 9 August 1867, FM T-334 Roll 3.

_____. A. C. Prindle to W. A. Seward. No. 3, 1 October 1867, FM T-334 Roll 3.

_____. A. C. Prindle to W. A. Seward. No. 6, 4 December 1867, FM T-334 Roll 3.

_____. A. C. Prindle to W. A. Seward. No. 10, 6 December 1867, FM T-334 Roll 3.

_____. A. C. Prindle to W. A. Seward. No. 22, 6 March 1868, FM T-334, Roll 3.

_____. A. C. Prindle to W. A. Seward. No. 55, 2 January 1869, FM T-334 Roll 3.

_____. A. C. Prindle to W. A. Seward. No. 62, 10 March 1869, FM T-334 Roll 3.

_____. A. C. Prindle to W. A. Seward. No. 64, 7 April 1869, FM T-334 Roll 3.

_____. A. C. Prindle to W. A. Seward. No. 125, 4 January 1870, FM T-334, Roll 4.

Dobson, Narda. *A History of Belize.* London: Butler and Tanner Limited, 1973.

Donohoe, William. *A History of British Honduras.* Montreal: Provincial Publishing, 1946.

Duff, E. C. "Personal." *British Honduras Colonist and Belize Advertiser,* 6 March 1869, 3.

Duigan, Philip B. "British Honduras." *Daily Picayune,* 23 July 1867, 1.

_____. "British Honduras." *Daily Picayune,* 31 January 1868, 1.

Duval, B. R. *A Narrative of Life and Travels in Mexico and British Honduras.* Boston: W. F. Brown, 1881.

Dwight, Charles S. *Journal of Charles S. Dwight (1867–1869).* Manuscript Collections, South Caroliniana Library.

"Emigration to Foreign Lands." *Daily Picayune,* 20 December 1866, 1(M).

"Emigration to Honduras." *DeBow's Monthly Review* 6 (27 October 1867): 262.

"Estate of Colin J. McRae Late of Saturday Creek." *Probate Records.* Office of the General Registry, Belize City, Belize.

Evans, Eli N. *Judah P. Benjamin: The Jewish Confederate.* New York: The Free Press, 1988.

"Every Vessel…" *British Honduras Colonist and Belize Advertiser,* 11 April 1868, 2.

"The Failure of Southern Colonization." *Daily Picayune,* 13 February 1868, 2(M).

"Fire." *New Era,* 13 May 1871, 76.

"The Following Is a Copy of Act 18 Vict., Cap. 18." *British Honduras Colonist and Belize Advertiser,* 20 June 1868, 2.

"The Following Is a List of Passengers." *Daily Picayune,* 12 May 1869, 9(M).

Foote, Mrs. A. "American Hotel." *British Honduras Colonist and Belize Advertiser,* 2 November 1867, 1.

"For Belize, Honduras." *Daily Picayune,* 5 March 1867, 11(M).

Foster, D. W. "British Honduras." *Livingston Journal,* 8 June 1867, 1.

_____. "Statement Touching the Settlement of Toledo." Public Archives of Belize, 107R271.

"From Belize, Honduras." *Daily Picayune,* 22 May 1867, 8(M).

"From Belize, Honduras." *Daily Picayune*, 29 July 1867, 1(E).

"From Honduras." *Mobile Daily Advertiser and Register*, 29 July 1867, 2.

G — — . S — — . or, The Asylum of Refuge. "For Sale." *Colonist*, 17 March 1866, 1.

Genon, W. C., to Lieutenant Governor Longdon. 18 April 1868. Archives of Belize, Belize City, 97R423 (in French).

"A Good Sign." *Commercial Advertiser*, 17 July 1867, 2.

Gray, R. F. "British Honduras." *Opelousas Journal*, 4 July 1868, 2.

_____, to *Publishers Journal*. Reprinted in *Opelousas Journal*, 4 July 1868, 2.

Hanna, A. J., and Kathryn Hanna. *Confederate Exiles in Venezuela*. Tuscaloosa, Alabama: Confederate Publishing, 1960.

Hardy, Lt. Col. Robert B., to author, 9 April 1990.

Harter, Eugene C. *The Lost Colony of the Confederacy*. Jackson: University Press of Mississippi, 1985.

Hempstead, Christopher [C. D.]. "Belize, British Honduras." *Daily Picayune*, 7 July 1866, 1(E).

_____. "British Honduras." *Daily Picayune*, 28 July 1866, 1(A).

_____. "British Honduras." *Daily Picayune*, 22 August 1866, 1(A).

_____. "British Honduras." *Daily Picayune*, 29 April 1867, 2(E).

_____. "From Belize Honduras." *Daily Picayune*, 23 May 1867, 2(M).

_____. "From Belize Honduras." *Daily Picayune*, 14 June 1867, 1(A).

_____. "From Belize, Honduras." *Daily Picayune*, 20 July 1867, 1(M).

_____. "Letter from Belize, Honduras." *Daily Picayune*, 17 September 1868, 2.

_____. "Notice." *Colonist*, 25 August 1866, 2.

Henderson, Thomas [A. A. E.] "Memorable." *British Honduras Colonist and Belize Advertiser*, 11 April 1868, 1.

_____, to James Mercier Putnam. 22 March 1868. Published in *British Honduras Colonist and Belize Advertiser*, 11 April 1868, 2.

Hill, Lawrence F. *The Confederate Exodus to Latin America*. Columbus: Ohio State University, 1936.

Hodge, John, to Lieutenant Governor James R. Longdon. 3 April 1868. Public Archives of Belize, 97R366 (661).

Holdridge, Desmond. "Toledo: A Tropical Refuge Settlement in British Honduras." *Geographical Review* 30 (03 July 1940), 376–393.

"Honduras." *Daily Picayune*, 3 January 1868, 7.

"The Honduras Colony." *New York Times*, 12 July 1868, 4.

Houma Civic Guard (of Tenebonne Parish). "From Brazil." *Daily Picayune*, 8 March 1866, 3(M).

House of Assembly. Message No. 11 to Governor Longdon. 15 March 1869. Public Archives of Belize, 107R271.

"How Things Look in British Honduras." *Daily Picayune*, 23 July 1867, 1(M).

Hunnicutt, W. L. C. "Rev. Levi Pearce." *Christian Advocate*, 6 October 1892, 1.

Hynson, George W. "Honduras." *Daily Picayune*, 12 June 1869, 7(M).

"Important." *British Honduras Colonist and Belize Advertiser*, 7 September 1867, 2.

"In Our Last Week's Issue." *Colonist*, 21 April 1866, 2.

"It Has Constantly Been." *Colonist*, 28 April 1866, 2.

"It Is with Extreme Regret." *Colonist*, 1 September 1866, 2–3.

"It Is with More Than Regret." *Colonist*, 13 October 1866, 2–3.

"It Is with No Little Regret." *British Honduras Colonist and Belize Advertiser*, 24 October 1868, 2.

Johnson, R. T. "British Honduras." *British Honduras Colonist and Belize Advertiser*, 29 August 1868, 3–4.

"Journal of the State Convention." *Louisiana History* 2, no. 1 (1961), 1–106.

Keen, Benjamin, and Mark Wasserman. *A History of Latin America*. Boston: Houghton Mifflin, 1988.

King, Emory, personal communication to author, 15 January 1990.

Krug, Donna D. "The Enemy at the Door in the Confederacy: A Crisis of Honor." Paper presented at the annual meeting of the Southern History Association in Lexington, Kentucky, 9 November 1989.

Land Titles Register, vols. 7–8, no. 301. Office of the General Registry, Belize City, Belize.

"Last Will and Testament of J. Christopher Hempstead." *Probate Records*, Office of the General Registry, Belize City, Belize.

"Last Will and Testament of James Gabrouel Johnston" and "Petition for Probate of Will." *Probate Records*, 1925, no. 24. General Registry of Belize.

"Last Will and Testament of Richard Talley Johnson." *Probate Records*, Office of the General Registry, Belize City, Belize.

Longdon, Governor Robert, to J. H. Faber, Crown surveyor. 16 August 1869. Public Archives of Belize, 107R349.

_____, to unknown person. 6 April 1868. Public Archives of Belize, 97R370.

A Louisiana Planter. "A Merchant of This Town." *British Honduras Colonist and Belize Advertiser*, 14 September 1867, 3.

"Louisiana State Fair." *British Honduras Colonist and Belize Advertiser*, 29 February 1868, 3.

Love, W. A. "Social Customs in British Honduras." *Hinds County Gazette*, 9 August 1867, 01.

McCutchon, Samuel. *Samuel McCutchon Papers, 1832–1874* (Bethesda, Maryland: University Publications of America, 1989.

McPherson, James M. *Ordeal by Fire: The Civil War and Reconstruction*. New York: Alfred A. Knopf, 1982.

McRae, C. J. "British Honduras." *Mobile Daily Register*, 28 September 1868, 2(M).

"Major A. N. Toutant Beauregard" [obituary]. *Donaldsonville Chief*, 11 June 1881, 3.

Mason, Frank M., personal communication to author. 21 August 1990.

"Memorable Events." *British Honduras Colonist and Belize Advertiser*, 11 April 1868, 3–4.

Menn, Joseph Karl. "The Large Slaveholders of the Deep South, 1860." Ph.D. dissertation, University of Texas, 1964.

Minutes from "A Meeting of Merchants and Other Inhabitants of Belize Held in Mr. Cramer's House." 1? March 1867, Public Archives of Belize, 94R48.

Minutes, Legislative Council, 16 March 1868, Public Archives of Belize, 104R1-4.

"Mr. Benjamin, Q.C." *Belize Advertiser*, 28 March 1883.

"Mr. Hodge's Pamphlet." *British Honduras Colonist and Belize Advertiser*, 14 September 1867, 3.

"Monday September 21st." *British Honduras Colonist and Belize Advertiser*, 3 October 1868.

Morrell, Z. N. "British Honduras." *British Honduras Colonist and Belize Advertiser*, 11 April 1868, 2.

_____. *Flowers and Fruits from the Wilderness; or, Thirty-Six Years in Texas and Two Winters in Honduras*. Boston: Gould and Lincoln, 1873.

_____, to James Mercier Putnam. 14 April 1868. Published in *British Honduras Colonist and Belize Advertiser*, 25 April 1868, 2.

National Archives Microfilm Productions. *Population Schedules of the Eighth Census of the United States, 1860* (Wilcox County, Alabama). M653, Roll 26, 1044.

Neumann, Charles J., Brian R. Jarvinen, and Arthur C. Pike. *Tropical Cyclones of the North Atlantic Ocean, 1871–1986*. Asheville, N.C.: National Climatic Data Center, 1988.

"On Monday." *Colonist*, 4 August 1866, 2.

"On Monday Evening." *Colonist*, 14 July 1866, 3, and 6.

"Orange Walk." *British Honduras Colonist and Belize Advertiser*, 25 January 1868.

A Passenger. "Steamer *Trade Wind*." *British Honduras Colonist and Belize Advertiser*, 7 December 1867, 3.

"Passengers." *New Orleans Crescent*, 16 April 1868, 1.

"Passengers per Steamship *Trade Wind*." *Daily Picayune*, 9 February 1869, 7.

Pendergast, David M. "The 19th-Century Sugar Mill at Indian Church, Belize." *Industrial Archaeology* 8 (1982): 57–66.

Perseverance. "The Present and Future." *British Honduras Colonist and Belize Advertiser*, 13 June 1868, 3.

Poole, E. R. "Belize Honduras." *Daily Picayune*, 16 September 1868, 8(M).

_____. "Honduras." *Daily Picayune*, 3 March 1868, 7.

"Prospects of the Cotton Trade." *Colonist*, 17 March 1866, 1.

Putnam, James M. "British Honduras, Central America." *Daily Picayune*, 2 August 1867, 1(A).

_____. "British Honduras, Central America." *Daily Picayune*, 11 August 1871, 2.

_____. "Homes in British Honduras: Free from Taxation." *Daily Picayune*, 7 February 1869, 4(M).

_____, and Wm. S. Cary. "Putnam and Cary, General Commission, Receiving, and Forwarding Merchants." *Colonist*, 29 September 1866, 1.

_____, to Lieutenant Governor Longdon. 13 April 1868. Public Archives of Belize, 97R405.

"The Question of Opening Out Roads." *Colonist*, 10 March 1866, 3.

"Returned." *Commercial Advertiser*, 3 July 1867, 2.

Rolle, Andrew F. *The Lost Cause: The Confederate Exodus to Mexico*. Norman: University of Oklahoma Press, 1965.

Rosenberger, Daniel G. "An Examination of the Perpetuation of Southern Institutions in British Honduras by a Colony of Ex-Confederates." Ph.D. dissertation, New York University, 1958.

"Rumors and Future Prospects." *Colonist*, 23 June 1866, 6.

Sansing, David G. *Mississippi: Its People and Culture*. Minneapolis: T.S. Denison, 1981.

_____. *The University of Mississippi: A Sesquicentennial History*. Jackson: University Press of Mississippi, 1999.

Scarborough, Claude, personal communication to author, 2 February 2000.

Schurer, Harry. "To Let." *Colonist*, 14 July 1866, 2.

Settlers at Cattle Landing to James Mercier Putnam. 22 February 1868. Public Archives of Belize, 101R137. Also published in *British Honduras Colonist and Belize Advertiser*, 29 February 1868, 2.

Settlers at Cattle Landing to Lieutenant Governor J.R. Longdon. 27 March 1868. Public Archives of Belize, 97R583-585 or 97R321.

Ship Registers and Enrollments of New Orleans. Prepared by the Survey of Federal Archives in Louisiana (WPA). Louisiana State University: Hill Memorial Library, 1942.

Simmons Donald, Jr., "Prominent Citizens of the Confederate Community in Belize City." *Belizean Studies* 20, no. 2 (October 1992): 22–29.

"Southern Emigration: Brazil and British Honduras." *DeBow's Monthly Review* 4, no. 6 (December 1867): 537–545.

"Southerners in Venezuela." *Daily Picayune*, 7 May 1867, 2(M).

"The Steamer Extract." *Colonist*, 25 August 1866, 3.

"Steamship *Mexico*." *British Honduras Colonist and Belize Advertiser*, 6 March 1869, 3.

Stovall, Captain W. G. "Indian Corn or Maize." *Colonist*, 11 March 1865, 2.

"Strange Faces." *Commercial Advertiser*, 17 July 1867, 2.

Swett, Charles. *A Trip to British Honduras and San Pedro, Republic of Honduras.* New Orleans: George Ellis, Bookseller and Stationer, 1868.

"T. C. Brewer, Auctioneer." *British Honduras Colonist and Belize Advertiser*, 19 September 1868, 1.

"The Telegrams." *British Honduras Colonist and Belize Advertiser*, 14 September 1867, 2–3.

"Telegraphic Intelligence." *Mobile Sunday Times*, 27 October 1867, 3(M).

Texan. "Letter from British Honduras." *Daily Picayune*, 29 July 1867, 2(A).

_____. "Letter from British Honduras." *Daily Picayune*, 25 September 1867, 2(M).

"There Never Was a More Favorable Opportunity." *Colonist*, 24 June 1865, 2.

"Trade with Honduras." *Daily Picayune*, 9 March 1866, 2(M).

Tunnel, Ted. "Twitchell and the Freedman's Bureau." *Louisiana History* 2, no. 1, 241–263.

Usher, Alfred. "Notice." *Commercial Advertiser*, 7 August 1867, 3.

_____. "Usher's Town, Manattee." *The Commercial Advertiser*, 3 July 1867, 3.

War of the Rebellion: Official Records of the Union and Confederate Armies. Washington, D.C.: Government Printing Office, 1880–1901.

"We Anticipated." *Colonist*, 23 December 1865, 2.

"We Clipped." *Colonist*, 25 August 1866, 6.

"We Have Much Pleasure." *British Honduras Colonist and Belize Advertiser*, 24 August 1867, 3.

"We Understand." *Colonist*, 21 July 1866, 2–3.

Weir, W. S. "Southern Hotel-and-Restaurant." *British Honduras Colonist and Belize Advertiser*, 14 September 1867, 1.

"Who Might Emigrate." *Daily Clarion*, 19 May 1867, 3.

Williams, T. E., and Others. "A Card." *Colonist*, 14 July 1866, 2.

W. M. Guild and Co., Agents. "For Sale or Lease." *Daly's Advertising Sheet*, 17 December 1870.

Yarborough, Marian McCutchon (Pass Christian, Mississippi), personal collection of McCutchon family papers.

Young, Wallace, interview by author, 31 December 1989.

Index

Readers should consider alternative name spellings

Aberdeen, Mississippi 58, 102, 156
Adair, Stephen 158
Adams. F. 136
Adams, W. A. 147
Agnant, F. 135
Aitkins, Robert 158
Alabama 10, 34, 36, 49, 61, 91, 109, 124, 140
Alexandria, Louisiana 123
Algeries, Louisiana 95, 125
Allen, D. M. 153
Allen, Mrs. J. 153, 155
Allen, J. G. 139
Allen, J. Y. 126, 144
Allen, L. 155
Allen, M. 146, 155
Allen, Mark 95, 155
Alred, H. 150
Amalgry, C. L. 154
Ambergris Cay 28
American Hotel, Belize City 49, 108–109, 123
Americana, Brazil 118
Andise, L. 129
Anson, Peter 158
Antigua 19
apiculture 83–84
Arcemeau, Louis 127
Arcemon, Louis 144
Archer, H. J. 95–96, 136
Arkansas 71, 100, 113, 126
Armor, Gelene 90
Armor, James 90
Armstrong, E. 129
Arnault, L. D. 124
Arnoult, Mr. 23
Arnut, Mr. 23
Artrurz, L. 144
Attakapas, Louisiana 20
Audice, Corrie 149
Audoir, August 124
Augustin (last name) 130

Augustine (servant) 134
Aurora (schooner) 23
Austin, John 19, 28, 30–32, 50, 54–55, 87–88, 100
Austin, Mr. 137
Austin City, British Honduras *see* Point Icacos
Avet, J. 39
Aymar, C. E. 152
Aymar, Charles 152
Aymar, William 152

Balis, H. 155
Ball, T. D. 124
bananas 8, 73, 75, 83–84, 88, 103
Bangass, B. A. 127
Baptist Church 78–79
Barlift, W. S. 129–149
Barrow, A. W. 128, 142, 148
Barrow, C. M. 126
Bateman, John M. 124
Batesville, Arkansas 71
Baton Rouge, Louisiana 12
Bavgurs, B. A. 144
beans 73
Beauregard, Armand T. 93, 95–95, 117, 158, 160
Beauregard, Mrs. (wife of Armand) 158
Beauregard, P. G. T. 15, 93
Beddinglaus, R. N. 139
Beddingliaus, H. (*also* Beddinghaus) 125, 138
Bedsoe, J. R. 123
Behrems, H. 129
Belize City, British Honduras 8–11, 17, 20–23, 26, 28–29, 35, 38–39, 41–46, 48–49, 54–58, 60–61, 63–64, 66, 70–71, 84, 87–88, 90, 100, 102–103, 106–113, 125–126, 128–129, 134–148, 150–160

Belize Hotel, Belize City 48
Belize River 54, 63, 87–88
Benjamin, Joseph 64, 89–90, 117
Benjamin, Judah P. 64, 89
Benson, Mrs. 125
Binders, J. E. 146
Birch, C. 150
Biscoe, A. 125
Biscoe, A. H. 140
Black Codes 13
Blacknett, J. G. 136
Blanche, Bruce 13
Bledsoe, J. B. 139
Bledsoe, J. R. 126
Blelock's 39
Bolivar County, Mississippi 123
Borders, J. E. 128
Borders, M. J. 128
Botter, J. J. 150
Botter, M. L. 150
Botter, N. H. 150
Boudreau, E. 95–96
Brackle, J. R. 126, 139
Brackman, Joseph 48
Brassell, J. W. 143
Brazer, H. 155
Brazil 11–13, 16–17, 22, 24, 36, 67, 116–119
Brewer, Anna 61, 109–110, 152
Brewer, T. C. 34, 38, 49, 61, 108–110, 112, 152
Brewer's Hotel, Belize City 49, 108–109
Briars, H. H. 141
Bridge, A. W. 126, 142
Briggs, Archie 146–147
Bringhurst, R. W. 126
Brinten, A. H. 144
British Honduras Colonist and Advertiser (newspaper)

31, 35, 45, 59, 90, 108–109, 129, 131
British Honduras Company Limited 36–37, 96
British Honduras, Legislative Assembly of 26, 39, 73, 88, 113
British seamen 158
Britton, H. B. 102–103, 124
Broadney, A. E. (*also* Broadnay) 128, 146
Brock, Mrs. J. C. 127
Broker, J. J. (and wife and child) 127
Brooks, P. 126
Brooks, T. 144
Broughurst, R. W. 123
Brown, Daniel 72, 76, 102, 158
Brown, Henry 154
Brown, J. L. 130
Brown, Jas. 158
Brown, Sally 158
Brown, W. W. 130
Brunk, Daniel 146
Brunner, L. A. 143
Brunor, L. A. 126
Bryan, James 160
Buck, J. S. 129
Buck, J. T. 151
Buckley, William T. 138
Buckner, W. 71, 126
Buler, J. L. 151
Bunch, C. 141
Burford (unknown male) 145
Burford, Claudcanc 145
Burford, E. M. 145
Burford, Estes 145
Burford, Joupa 145
Burford, Mrs. 145
Burford, Telulu 145
Burford, Thadeus 145
Burford, W. 145
Burford, Wilson 145
Burguiene, L. 141
Burguiene, Sophie 141
Burk, Daniel 128
Burnaby's Laws 8
Burns, W. M. 128, 146
Burns, William 127
Butler, Benjamin F. 27, 57, 108
Butler, W. T. B. (*also* Buttler) 127, 145
Byrd, Flina 152
Byrd, H. F. 130, 151
Byrd, K. 152
Byrd, Molly 152
Byrd, Mrs. 130

Byrd, S. F. 152
Byrd, Willi 152
Byrne, E. A. 152
Byrne, Mrs. 152

Caddo, Louisiana 72, 76
Caldwell, S. B. 21
Callea, J. 130
Calloway, J. T. 136
Campagne, D. V. L. 129, 149
Campbell, Alex 158
Campbell, John 37
Campbell, T. W. 130, 152
Carmichael, John 95
Carney, S.W. 126, 142
Carpenter, John C. (Jr.) 129, 149
Carpenter, T. E. 129
Carpenter, T. H. 149
Carr, George 160
Carr, T. F. 158
Carr, Thomas 127, 145
Cary, Clarence M. 124, 134, 150
Cary, Ella 150
Cary, Lilly 150
Cary, William S. 20–23, 50, 61, 124, 134, 150
Cary, William S. (Jr.) 150
Caselie, Juan 126, 142
Cassidy, C. B. 123
Cassidy, J. E. 126, 139
Catahoula, Louisiana 71
Catholicism 78–79, 93
Cattle Landing *see* Toledo, British Honduras
Cecilia (schooner) 37
Cellen, J. T. 127
Cevran, F. E. 125
Chamberlain, William Cole 63, 100–101, 104, 123, 126, 139, 156
Chamberlain family 103
Champion, A. 136–137
Chapman, E. 135
Chapman, Manusel White 30, 35, 102–103
Cheek, M. G. 150
Chick, M. E. 76
Chick, Miss M. E. 129
Chick, Mrs. M. E. 149
Chicot, Arkansas 71, 126
cholera 43, 72, 96, 119
Christie, C. 130
Christy, Edward 138
Clard, Jamelia E. 127
Clark, P. E. 127, 145
Clifton, G. W. 140
Cochran, Jno. 139
Cockrell, W. 125

coffee 35, 74
Coleman, J. H. 153
Coleman, Rosa 158
Colonist (newspaper) 23–24, 64–65
Colquit, Joseph 157
Commercial Advertiser (newspaper) 29, 59, 61, 108
Common, Jas. 157
Concordia Parish, Louisiana 125
Confederate Flying Cavalry of British Honduras 94, 96
Confederate Medical Department 95
Copeland, J. B. 84
Copeland family 72, 76, 82
corn 65, 73–74, 84
Corner, Richard James 128, 146
Corosal 63–64, 93, 95–95, 103
cotton 8, 17, 20, 28, 35, 64–65, 75, 88, 103, 113, 116, 119, 122
Cotton Tree Bank 89
Cousin, A. 126
Crankenden, S. D. 149
Crea, C. 128
Crenan, Jno. 139
Crescent (newspaper) 88, 90, 126–127
Crevan, J. 125
Crist, William A. 127
Crockett, W. H. 140
Cruoen, A. 142
Cuba 11, 21, 124
Cut and Throw Away Creek 87, 89

Daigh, Theo (*also* Dagle and Daigle) 95, 123, 126, 139
Daily Clarion (newspaper) 14
Daily Picayune (newspaper) 14, 34, 106–107, 124, 126–129
Daley, Captain 130
Darnell, G. W. 130
Darnell, J. F. 130
Darnell, L. 130
Darnell, Miss 130
Darnell, Mr. 160
Darnell, Mrs. 130
Darnell, N. P. 130
Darnell, N. S. 130
Darnell, R. Z. 130
Darnell, S. E. 130

Darnell, Z. 130, 143
Dart, Jos. 127, 145
Davidson, John M. 138
Davidson, William 153
Davis, J. M. 126
Davis, Jefferson 15–16, 89
Davis, P. M. 143
Davis, Varina Howell 38
Dawson, Jns. 150
Dawson, Reverend R. 10, 61
Day, C. H. 125, 139
Day, J. M. 123
Deacon, Sally 155
DeBow's Monthly Review
  (magazine) 36
DeBraam, J. C. 126, 142
DeBram, J. A. (*also*
  DeBraam) 125, 138
Deep River 30, 63, 100
Degallade, Mrs. 128
DeLautsheer, E. 153
Del Balain, Orr 139
Del Brando, Mrs. 137
Denning, Richard 127
DePras, J. A. 125, 138
DeRodhe, C. 155
DeSoto Parish, Louisiana 41,
  71, 110, 126
Dessant, H. 140
Dexter, E. C. 72
Dexter, Henry 157
Dexter family 76
Dickens, M. J. 140
Dicksen, N. S. 144
Dicksen, S. 144
Dickson, J. D. 145
Dickson, N. S. 126
Dieseldorff, Mr. 50
Dodsworth, Mrs. 150
Dodsworth, W. 150
Dodsworth, W. E. 150
Doirn, Mr. 95
Dolham, Jas. 127
Dolsin, J. A. 129
Dominica 19
Dorian, J. 158
Dorian, Mrs. 158
Dothard, James 127
Dothard, Jot 145
Doughty, Levi 153
Doughty, Mr. 95
Doyle, Pat 158
Draper, D. H. 140
Drew, Edward A. 157
Drinon, J. A. 149
Droke, D. 130
DuBalen, Mr. and Mrs. (and
  three children) 125, 139
Duff, E. C. 129
Dull, T. 125

Dulton, William 138
Dumas, Henry 157
Durr, Thomas 125, 139
Durrum, J. 125
Dursind, J. C. 140
Dutton, William 125
Duval, Agnes 157
Duval, B. R. (*also* Duvall)
  14, 34, 87–90, 106, 137, 156
Duval, Ida 157
Duval, Mary 157
Duval, Sedia 157
Duval, William 157
Dwight, C. S. 72
Dwight, H. E. 153

Easons, Andrew 158
Easter, M. E. 142
Echelberger, R. 126
Eichelberger, E. 139
Eldredge, George M. 110; *see
  also* Eldridge
Eldredge family 76
Eldridge, Emma 157
Eldridge, George 157
Eldridge, Marion 157
Eldridge, Mary 157
Elma (schooner) 135
Enterprise (steamer) 73
Episcopal (Anglican) Church
  10, 61, 78
Esejo, L. 140
Evergreen, Louisiana 123
Extract (steamer) 21–21, 28,
  48, 124, 134

Faber, J. H. 23
Fabre, J. 126
Fabre, Juan 142
Falline, John Della 157
Fancy (schooner) 37
Farmer, A. B. 135
Farmer, Mrs. A. B. 135
Farmer, J. M. 142
Farmer, R. 142
Farmer, V. M. 142
Farrar, H. K. 72, 144
Fasten, A. L. 154
Fasten, F. H. 136
Fasten, R. S. 154
Fearn, C. 125, 138
Fearn, G. 125, 138
Fearn, J. 138
Fearn, R. 125
Ferguson, D. 145
Ferguson, Robert 153
Ferguson, V. C. 145
Ferguson, W. N. 145
Finder, J. 124
Finlay, J. A. 136

Finley, Caroline 156
Finley, Cicero 156
Finley, David 156
Fisher, Peter 111–112
Fitzgerald, T. F. 139
Fitzgerald, W. 143
Fitzgerald, William 126
Fitzpatrick, J. F. 126
Fitzpatrick, Joseph 123
Florida 84–85
Foley, James 72, 76, 149
Foote, George O. 124
Foote, J. O. 134
Foote, Mrs. (and six chil-
  dren) 49, 108–109, 112, 123
Foster, David Walker 30,
  76–77
Foster, T. W. 130
Foster family 82
France 46
Frank, Jas. 158
Frasten, E. J. 129, 149
Frasten family 76
French, S. 151
Frierson, E. V. 71, 126
Frierson, G. A. 71, 126
Frierson, G. P. 71, 126
Frierson, Mrs. 127
Frierson, T. C. 71
Frillen, H. A. 136
Fuller, G. T. 127
Fullerton, T. P. 142
Fullerton, W. L. 142
Furguson, D. P. 137
Furman, J. 125
Fuselier, A. 143
Fuselier, A. D. 126, 143
Fuselier, C. 126, 143
Fuselier, F. 144
Fuselier, Gabriel L. 23, 124,
  129, 135, 150
Fuselier, L. (Master) 126,
  143

Gaines, B. P. 144
Galloway, J. O. 129
Gardiner, W.H. 159
Garnett, Jno. 158
Garnett, Mrs. 158
Gauther, John 138
Gelina, Bart C. 139
General Sherman (steamer)
  28–30, 41–42, 124–126, 135,
  137–140
Gentle, J. 127
Gentle, John 138
Gentle, Rachel 138
Georgia 45, 140
Gerards, Robert (and wife)
  127

Ghivandi, Etienne 136
Gibson, Catherine 157
Gibson, Dr. D. 159
Gibson, Elbert 157
Gibson, Emily 157
Gibson, Frank 157
Gibson, J. S. 157
Gibson, John 157
Gibson, M. E. 155
Gibson, N. 159
Gibson, S. 155
Gill, Alex 136
Gimas, Louis Barras 141
Giolma, Alfred F. 155
Given, H. 123
Glass, F. M. 145
Glass, Mary 145
Glasscock, J. 76, 127, 145
Goldsmith, L. W. 138
Goldsmith, Mary E. 138
Goodrich, William F. 124
Gordon, George 136
Gould, Alice 128
Gouth, J. 145
Gowless, P. E. H. 141
Graham, Thomas 63–64
Grant, Jas. 158
Grant, U. S. 11
Graves, J. S. 135
Graves, William 123, 126, 139
Gray, B. F. 127
Gray, Jas. 76, 150
Gray, M. 150
Gray, R. F. 67, 126
Gray, R. T. 145
Gray, W. 150–151
Grayson, S. M. 140
Green, J. M. 129
Green, W. N. 143
Greenland (schooner) 136
Griffen, A. 152
Griffen, Allen (Jr.) 152
Griffen, Allen (Sr.) 152
Griffen, J. 152
Griffen, J. A. 152
Griffen, Olivia 152
Griffen, P. 152
Griffen, Thomas 152
Grincans, F. 140
Grued, Alice 146
Guatemala 23, 30, 77, 112
Guntinez, E. 149

Hailey, R. W. 147
Haley, Jas. 129
Hall, Dr. 125, 138
Haller, M. C. 156
Haller, W. C. 156
Halley, Arthur 156

Hamilton, D. C. 143
Hankin, Philip James 128, 146
Haraloness, J. B. 137
Harlason, A. J. 144
Harley, James 125, 139
Harraloness, H. M. 137
Harris, D. A. 125, 141
Harris, E. B. 150
Harris, G. A. 150
Harris, J. B. 141
Harris, J. P. 124
Harris, L. V. 150
Harrison, Albert 157
Harrison, Annie 127, 159
Harrison, E. M.
Harrison, H. 159
Harrison, J. A. 148
Harrison, J. F. 61, 71, 126, 128
Harrison, J. T. 127
Harrison, Stewart 127
Harrison, Texas 72, 76
Hatch, A. H. 70, 72
Hatch, C. 141
Hatch, C. J. 72, 159
Hatch, Christopher Asa 43, 70, 125, 139, 141, 159
Hatch, E. F. 147
Hatch, George C. 76, 152
Hatch, H. 141
Hatch, Horace 72
Hatch, J. A. 141
Hatch, J. E. 72, 153
Hatch, J. H. 153
Hatch, L. 153
Hatch, M. E. 153
Hatch, Mary N. 159
Hatch, Milton S. 159
Hatch, W. A. 153
Hatch Colony, British Honduras *see* Toledo, British Honduras
Havana, Cuba 21, 124
Hawthorne, A. T. 117
Haydon, R. F. 129
Haynoor, W. H. 144
Hayward, William 127
Hazelhurst, Mississippi 123
Hebert, William 123
hemp 35
Hempstead, Catherine M. 61, 91, 111; *see also* Catherine McRae
Hempstead, Christabelle Willie Minnie 61, 111
Hempstead, Christopher D. 26–27, 34, 61, 102, 111–112, 144

Hempstead, Christopher D. (Jr.) 61, 158
Henderson, J. S. 123, 126, 139
Henderson, Thomas 72, 150
Hendrick, J. E. C. 153
Hendricks, J. C. A. 147
Henning, E. A. 128
Henning, J. T. 128
Henning, John 128
Henning, M. A. 128
Henning, Miss S. J. 128
Henning, Mrs. S. J. 128
Henniny, E. A. 147
Henniny, J. T. 147
Henniny, John 147
Henniny, M. A. 147
Henniny, S. I. 147
Henniny, S. J. 147
Herbert, Mr. 126
Herman, R. 125
Herman, W. H. 144
Hightower, W. T. 153
Hill, A. J. 145
Hill, Arteman 150
Hill, H. C. 145
Hill, J. 159
Hill, Lewis Hobbs 95, 102
Hill family 103
Hilma (wrecked ship) 125
Hinchmeyer, W. 139
Hobbler, Thom 135
Hoffman, A. D. (and wife and two children) 128
Holt, Miss M. 155
Holt, Mrs. M. 155
Holt, W. J. 155
Honduras *see* Spanish Honduras
Hope, M. H. 126, 143
Hopper, W. A. 130, 151
Howard, J. 124
Howard, William Abel 30
Howe, W. 130
Hubbard, Andrew 154
Hubbard, John 154
Hubbard, Mr. 130
Hubbard, Mrs. 130
Hubbard, W. 151
Hubert, Edward A. 160
Huburt, William 139
Huffman, F. (and family) 127
Huffman, J. M. 126, 142
Hunter, Alex 153
Hunter, C. T. 36, 136, 153
Hunter, Mrs. C. T. 153
Hurstmyer, W. 126
Hustmyre, W. 123
Hyman, H. 125

Hyman, J. 125
Hyman, M. 125
Hyman, McIntyre 125
Hyman, Mitchell 125
Hyman, S. 125

Icacos Grant 30–31, 64, 100
Icaiche Indians 93
Indian Church 94
Inglelow, Jean 39
Irish, James 154
Irish, John 154
Irish, William 154
Ivey, M. 144

Jackson, Louisiana 71
Jackson, Mississippi 13–14, 125
Jamaica 19, 82
Jameson, Emma 154
Jameson, Mary W. 154
Jameson, R. T. 154
Jameson, W. 154
Jamieson, William 100
Jett, John 145
Jex, D. (and family) 124
Joe Kelly (ship) 160
Johns, Caroline 156
Johns, Martha 156
Johns, Mary 156
Johns, Nancy 156
Johns, Sarah 156
Johns, William 156
Johnson, Andrew 12–13
Johnson, George 127, 145
Johnson, Jas. H. 159
Johnson, Louise A. 159
Johnson, N. 150
Johnson, O. 123, 141
Johnson, Richard Talley 41, 110
Johnson, W. M. 129, 149
Johnston, J. 125
Johnston, J. H. 83
Johnston, James Gabrouel 83, 140
Johnston, Louise Perrette 83
Johnston, M. J. 151
Johnston, Pauline 151
Jones, Asa 127
Jones, E. B. 150
Jones, H. 155
Jones, J. W. 145
Jones, S. 147
Jordan, S. F. 144
Jordan, Thomas S. 126
Juarez, Benito 16
Judaism 78

Kane, T. P. 71, 126, 142
Kaufnesun, A. J. C. 130
Kearney, Barrett 144
Keeal, H. D. 125
Kelly, Patrick 128, 148
Kemper County, Mississippi 106
Kenney, J. M. 142
Kentucky 67
Kerchemer, S. W. 126, 142
Kevlin, Mr. 95, 97
King, Henry (*also* Keng) 127, 145
Kirchernir, S. W.
Kousseaus, L. 125
Kovy, P.L. 153
Kruft, Chas. (and family) 127
Kuck, G. 152
Kuinbraugh, J. W. 141
Kuttruff, George 127, 144

Laboring Creek 87
Lacey, T. J. 126
Lacy, J. L. 139
Lacy, T. J. 123
Lafayette County, Missouri 112
Lambert, W. 130
Laprade, L. 129
Laprade, T. 129
Larkin, J. P. 139
Larkins, P. 125
Laurason, J. C. 127, 145
Layrange, A. 129
Leas, Charles A. 11
Leathrer, D. 130
Leckie, A. 159
Ledgeaur, F. C. 141
Ledgeaur, H. C. 141
Lee, G. 125
Lee, Robert E. 12, 15–16
Lester, S. G. 137
Lester family 76, 82
Little, M. 137
Littlepage, C. V. 154
Littlepage, Effie 154
Littlepage, Ellenor 154
Littlepage, Emma 154
Littlepage, Lizzie 154
Littlepage, S. C. 154
Littlepage, Virginia 154
Littlepays, C. P. 125
Livingston, Guatemala 112
Logan, J. D. V. 129
Logan, J. W. 129, 151
Logan, R. D. V. 152
Logan, R. F. 129
Long, J. 142

Long Beach, Mississippi 95, 102
Longdon, James Robert 50–51, 54, 73
Longfield, Miss. 130
Louisiana 12–15, 20–24, 28–29, 34–39, 41–45, 49–50, 54–56, 61, 65–68, 70–76, 87–88, 95, 97–98, 101–102, 106–110, 112–113, 116, 121, 123–127, 129, 134–160
Louisiana Farm 95, 97–98
Louisiana State Fair 102
Louisiana University 102
Love, W. A. 57, 106, 123, 126, 139, 144
Lovelace, P. 125

Maclin, R. D. 124
Maddox, B. R. 145
Maddox, C. K. 126, 143
Madison County, Mississippi 72
Mahley, M. A. 130
Mahogany 8, 19–20, 22, 31, 83–84, 89
Mallon, Edward 125–126, 142
Manattee River 56–57, 63–64, 100, 102–103
Mandace, E. 135
Manfred, H. P. 150
Mann, B. L. 38
Manning, J. 153, 156
Manning, S. F. 153
Mansfield, Louisiana 110
Martin, R. C. 137
Martin, W. H. 100
"Martinez Pen" 110
Maryland 54–55
Mason, Frank 85
Mason, James Rogers 85
Mason family 82–83
Massachusetts 59
Massey, C. A. 130, 155
Massey, Mrs. 130
Massey, T. G. 155
Massey, W. B. 130, 155
Massey, W. F. 155
Massey, W. T. 130
Matamoros, Mexico 9
Matthews, Mrs. (and 6 children) 128
Mauger Kaye, British Honduras 22
Maximilian 16
May, Henry 137
Maya 7, 88
McAlister, J. H. 143

McAlister, Sarah 138
McCain, Robert 127
McCall, Hugh 158
McCall, Richard 129, 149
McCandlish, W. 143
McCannell, T. 141
McCoy, Grayer 128, 146
McCoy, James G. 102, 128, 146
McCoy, M. E. 128, 146
McCoy, P. 128, 146
McCranie, D. 127, 145
McCrea, C. 146
McCutchon, Adele 44
McCutchon, Azby 101
McCutchon, Samuel (*also* McCutcheon) 75, 101, 104, 129, 147, 152
McCutchon family 103
McDermott, Anna Belle (*also* McDermot) 129, 148
McDermott, C. 147
McDermott, Charles 129, 148
McDermott, Charles J.J. 129, 148
McDermott, Edward 129, 149
McDermott, H. S. 129, 148
McDermott, Margaret 129, 148
McDermott, P. 125
McDermott, Phil 141
McDermott, Scott 129, 149
McDermott, Willie 129, 148
McDonald, Colonel 31
McDonald, John 158
McGentry, Frank 158
McIntosh, L. C. 142
McIntyre, S. 125
McKenzie, John 48, 128, 148
McLain, Richard 145
McLaughlen, William 153
McLin, R. T. 124, 141
McRae, Catherine 111, 227; *see also* Catherine M. Hempstead
McRae, Colin J. 15, 38, 89–91, 104, 111, 117
McRae, John J. 15, 91, 111, 117, 127
McRae Estate 87, 89–91
Mears, John J. 135
Mercer, Lawrence J. 143
Merrell, J. H. 149
Merrell, L. F. 149
Merrell, S. E. 149
Merrell, S. N. 149
Merrill, J. 129
Merrill, Jas. 129

Merrill, M. E. 129
Merrill, S. 129
Merry, J. M. 109
Methodism (*also* Methodists) 58, 78–79, 83, 85
Mexico 9, 11–12, 14–16, 42, 46, 63, 87, 93, 95, 97, 117, 141
Mexico (steamship) 38, 76–77, 129
Miacco, A. 152
Miacco, Fred 152
Miacco, J. B. 130
Miacco, L. 152
Miacco, Mr. 130
Miacco, Mrs. 130
Middle River 63, 100
Middlebrook, A. 140
Middlebrook, L. L. 143
Middlebrooks, E. 154
Middlebrooks, J. E. 154
Middlebrooks, L. A. 154
Middlebrooks, Mary 155
Middlebrooks, T. S. 154
Miller, C. T. 144
Miller, E. R. 155
Miller, John 159
Miller, Mary 159
Miller, William 159
Mills, Chas. 157
Millwater, Earl of 102
Mims, A. H. 128
Mims, H. A. 146
Mischief (ship) 42
Mississippi 5, 13–15, 27, 35–36, 38, 55, 57–58, 63, 67, 70–72, 74, 89, 91, 95, 100, 102–103, 106, 111, 117–118, 121, 123, 125–126, 139–140, 156
Mississippi Congressional Elections (1866) 13
Missouri 67, 112
Mixon, Alice 152
Mobile, Alabama 10, 36, 91
Mobile Tribune 36
Moho River 63–64, 70, 73, 102
molasses 84
Moniqa, L. 129, 149
Monkey River 30, 83, 100
Monroe County, Florida 84
Monroe County, Mississippi 72
Moore, D. B. 130
Moore, John 135
Moore family 82–83
Mooring, Julia A. 153
Mooring, T. J. 152

Mooring family 76
Morehouse Parish, Louisiana 43, 70, 72, 76, 95, 102
Morill, J. T. 136, 149
Morrell, Z. N. 74, 78–79, 143
Morrill, H. L. G. 150
Morrill, Jonathan Tucker 129, 140–145, 147–148, 150, 152–156, 158–159
Morrill, N. P. 150
Morrill, Z. J. 150
Morrill, Z. N. 150
Morrill, Z. W. 126
Morrill family 76
Morris, David 156
Morris, George 156
Morris, Jane 156
Morris, John 156
Morris, Mary 156
Morris, Sattie 156
Morris, Timothy 71, 156
Morton, H. 130
Morton, H. C. 153
Morton, M. 153
Morton, Mrs. 130
Motley, M. A. 151
Mount, S. M. G. 143
Mowning, John 157
Mowning, Martha 158
Mowning, Samson 157
Mowning, Serinson 157
Mowning, Volsmon 157
Mowning, Walter 158
Mullen, Eugenia 141
Mullen, F. L. 141
Mullen, J. W. 141
Mullen, P. A. 141
Mullins River 63–65, 100
Munez, J. F. 129, 149
Mutter, J. 150
Myers, George 123, 125
Myers, J. W. 125, 139

Nash, J. 153
Nash, W. 153
Nash, William (and wife) 127
Natchez, Mississippi 63, 100, 123
Natchitoches, Louisiana 72, 76, 102
naturalization 51–52, 131–133
Nedredge, J. 125
Neil, B. C. 135
New Era (newspaper) 95
New Orleans, Louisiana 15, 20–22, 28–29, 35–39, 41–43, 45, 50, 54, 61, 66,

73, 76, 87–88, 95, 102,
107–108, 123–127, 129,
134–160
New Orleans Times (newspaper) 35
New Richmond, British
Honduras 14, 54, 63–64,
87–91
New River 93, 95
New York City 21, 16, 50,
109, 135–137, 140–150, 152–
156, 158–159
New York Times (newspaper)
16, 50
New Zealand 89
Nicholas, J. A. 128, 148
Nixon, A. C. 130
Nixon, Mrs. 155
Nunn, T. 124, 137

Oladowski, H. 129, 149
Olivera, Ramon 124
O'Luis, A. 151
Opelousus, Louisiana 71, 126
Orange Grove Estate 85
Orange Walk, British Honduras 63–64, 93, 95–97,
104
Orgen, C. 154
Ormond, T. 125
Ormond Plantation,
Louisiana 101
Oscarste, P. J. O. 160
Oswald, Mr. 90
Otterson daughters 95
Overall, Edwin E. 125
Owen, T. F. 71, 126, 142
Owen, W. H. 125, 143
Owens, William 61
Oxford, Mississippi 91

Pack, B. W. 146
Pack, K. 146
Pack, M. E. 146
Pack, T. A. (and wife and
family) 128, 146
Parkerson, A. 145
Pascagoula, Mississippi 38
Pass Christian, Mississippi
101
Paulman, Mrs. 155
Payne, C. E. (and 3 children)
72, 127, 151
Payne, Harriet 151
Payne, Jane 151
Payne, Jas. 151
Peak, J. P. 145, 149
Peak, J. S. 71, 126, 160
Peak, Lucy 136
Peake, Alice 136

Peake, J. P. 129
Peake, Joseph 136
Peake, Sarah 136
Pearce, Benjamin W. 12, 117,
125
Pearce, F. M. 72
Pearce, Levi (*also* Pierce) 35,
70–73, 76, 78, 85, 126, 128,
148, 150
Pearce, Mr. 138
Pearce, R. W. 125
Pearce family 76, 82–83
Peas 73
Peck, J. P. 127
Pendleton, Jeff 125–126, 135,
137–140
Perit (ship) 156, 158–159
Perkins, W. 142
Perrett family 82
Perrette, P. C. (*also* Perrett)
79, 84–85, 100, 103
Petersburg, Virginia 87
Pew, F. G. 100
Pickering, Frank 158
Pickett, Calvin 157
Pickett, Eva 157
Pickett, Gwen 157
Pickett, Jas. 157
Pickett, Minnie 157
Pickett, Newton 157
Pickett, Newton (Jr.) 157
Pickett, William 157
plantains 73, 88
Point Icacos *see* Icacos
grant
Polk, James K. 26, 111
Polk, Mr. 160
Polk, Mrs. 160
Pooh, Charles 130
Poole, E. R. 37
Potts, Mrs. and child 43
Powers, J. L. 141
Price, C. 128, 148
Price, E. 148
Price, George 118, 153
Price, John Wallace 65,
95–97, 140
Price, M. 128, 148
Price, Mrs. 140
Price, N. 140
Price, O. 128, 140
Price, Oscar 153
Price, R. 128
Price, Sheldon 128, 148
Price, Sterling (General) 87
Price, Victoria 153
Prindle, A. C. 30, 55, 147
Puerto Cortez, British Honduras 89
Pugh, Daniel 126, 142

Punta Gorda, British Honduras 63, 77
Purdy, J. C. 143
Purvis, William R. 125
Putnam, Edward 129, 149
Putnam, Emmett 129, 149
Putnam, Henry 129, 149
Putnam, James Mercier 22,
28, 30, 34–35, 49–50, 65,
70–73, 76, 100, 112, 124–
125, 129, 135, 138, 149, 153
Putnam, Lee 129–149
Putnam, Mary 129, 149
Putnam, Robert 129, 149
Putnam Immigration Association 49, 65

Quinlan, Dr. (and servant)
129

race (attitudes toward) and
racism 56–58, 121–122
Racia, J. H. 139
Raid, J. H. 126
Reard, Mrs. 151
Reconstruction 12, 28, 41, 66
Reed, H. R. 151
Reene, H. D. 139
Rees, R. 127, 144
Regalia Estate, British Honduras 101–102
Reid, Sauel C. 138
Reuch, L. 155
Reuch, M. 155
Rice 35, 73–74
Richaird, F. 145
Richardson, Henry B. 151
Richmond, Virginia 90, 95
Rickers, M. J. 127
Rio Grande, British Honduras 63, 70, 73–74
Roark, W. W. 143
Robinson, M.L. 140
Rochaird, F. 145
Rotchford, J. W. 140
Rourk, W. W. 126
Rousseau, Richard H. 160
Rousseau, S. 125
Rumeros, John 126
Rumnondo, John 123
Rumnons, John 139
Russel, C. H. 138
Russian seamen 139
Ryan, L. 125
Ryan, Mary 143
Ryan, Maude 143
Ryan, P. M. 143
Ryan, Phil 143
Ryan, W. A. 151
Rynd, C. H. 130

Rynd, Molly 130
Rynd, S. F. 130
Rynd, W. N. 130

St. Charles Hotel, New
Orleans 38
St. Charles Parish, Louisiana
101
St. James Hotel, New
Orleans 38
St. Mary Parish, Louisiana
49, 108–109
San Marcos, Texas 123
San Pedro Sula, Honduras
71
San Ramon Estate 93
Saturday Creek 89, 104
Saunders, J. W. 151
Saunders, Mattie 150
Saunders, Mrs. 150
Schinonerkerin, William 141
Scobell, W. J. S. 61, 108, 112,
125–126, 143
Seabitter, Robert 157
Seaton, Miss 130
Seay, John 154
Senetronson, Carl 157
Sennett, Miss 141
Servanta, Carolina 156
Servanta, Marriccio 156
Servanta, Pisco 156
Seth, F. O. 143
Sharon, Mississippi 70, 126
Shaver, A. C. 129
Shaver, A. R. 129
Shaver, C. S. 129
Shaver, J. D. 129
Shaver, M. N. 129
Shaver, R. G. 82, 129
Shaver, R.G. (Jr.) 129
Shaver family 82
Shavers, Master 160
Shavers, Miss 160
Shavers, Mr. 160
Shavers, Mrs. 160
Shaw, A. 130
Shaw, Gus 151
Sherman, W. T. 11
Shernerhorn, William W.
158
Sherrod, G. W. 72, 76, 102
Sherrod, George 154
Shields, W.B. 143
Shreveport, Louisiana 123
Shusrhen, Mr. 138
Sierra Leone 146
Sikon, Francis 154
Simpson, I. L. 144
Simpson, J. 126
Simpson, Joshua 157

Simpson, Susan 157
Singer, John V. 112
Singer, M. 112
Singer, Mrs. 112, 141
Singer torpedo 112
Sittee River 64, 75, 100–101,
104
Smiley, A. A. 147
Smiley, A. H. 147
Smiley, C. H. 147
Smiley, E. J. 148
Smiley, J. A. 128, 148
Smiley, Maggie 128, 148
Smiley, R. J. 128
Smiley, R. S. 147
Smiley, T. A. 148
Smiley, T. B. 128, 148
Smith, A. B. 127
Smith, Annie A. 160
Smith, C. 130
Smith, Charles P. 152
Smith, Cornelia 152
Smith, Daniel 126, 142
Smith, Ella 152
Smith, Frank 152
Smith, H. M. 130, 152
Smith, Mrs. H. M. 130,
152
Smith, J. E. 72
Smith, John 135
Smith, Josephine 152
Smith, L. 125
Smith, Miss L. 130, 152
Smith, L. H. 141
Smith, Lins 152
Smith, M. J. 155
Smith, W. D. 124, 137
Smylie, A. 127
South Carolina 45, 72
South Stann Creek 63–64,
100–101, 104
Southern Hotel and Restau-
rant, Belize City 48–49,
109, 123
Spain 7–8
Spanish Honduras 22, 46,
71, 77, 95, 117
Stanten, C. L. 144
Stanten, L. F. 144
Stanten, W. L. 144
Stanton, Master 126
Stanton, Mrs. 126
Stanton, W. L. 126
Steven, E. 130
Stewart, Thomas 123, 126
Stibers, Chas. 151
Stibers, Geo. 151
Stibers, Harry 151
Stibers, Lizzie 151
Stibers, Mrs. 151

Stibers, Ophelia 151
Stoker, Albert 130
Stoker, J. A. 130
Stoker, James 130
Stoker, Mrs. 130
Stoker, R. 130
Stokes, F. 151
Stokes, Ira 151
Stokes, J. A. 151
Stokes, R. 151
Stout, W. C. 127
Stovall, W. G. 64
Strickley, Fred 128
Strully, F. 146
Stuart, Thomas 139
Stuart, W.C. 147
sugarcane 8, 20, 27–28, 37,
50, 65–68, 72–73, 75, 77,
82–83, 93–96, 98, 101–103,
116, 119, 122
Swazie's Landing 100
Sweet, Charles 143
Sweet, Samuel 143
Swett, Charles 14, 51, 55, 71,
100–101, 126
Swett, Daniel 71
Sylvester, William H. 159

Talland, J. 137
Talmadge, Mary 127
Tanner, E. F. 151
Tanner, J. B. 151
Taylor, George 158
Temple, Robert 36
Tennessee 13, 140
Tensas Parish, Louisiana 61,
71, 126
Texas 11, 27, 56, 72, 74, 76,
78, 102, 123, 125, 137, 140,
156
Thibedaux, C. 155
Thompson, Dr. 129, 149
Thompson, E. C. 150
Thompson, John 100
Thompson, P. H. 150
Thrower, M. N. 144
Thrower, O. A. 144
Tindall, M. E. 152
Tindall, T. R. 152
Tindall, W. B. 152
Tindall, W. B. (Jr.) 152
tobacco 20, 35, 75
Toledo, British Honduras
35, 43, 63–64, 70–87, 93,
100, 102–104
Toledo, M. P. 138
Toledo, Philip 75, 125
tomatoes 73–74
Toomer, E. 125
Toomes, E. 138

Tower Hill Estate 65, 95–96, 98
Trade Wind (steamship) 29–30, 37–38, 41–43, 56, 61, 70, 76, 87–88, 126–130, 136–137, 140–156
Trasten, A. 150
Trasten, Earnest 127
Trasten, Hortense 127
Trial Farm Estate 90
Trimble, P. 125
Trindall, M. E. 127
Truitt, J. W. 144
Truitt, M. C. 144
Truitt, Robert 144
Truitt, T. E. 144
Tuiquilan, Dr. 149
Tulerlove, T. P. 126
Tulerlove, W. L. 126
Turks and Caicos Islands 19
Turman, H. M. 126
Turman, J. M. 126
Turman, R. 126
Turner, Lee 143

United Fruit Company 84
United States Naval Blockade 9–11
University of Mississippi 5, 91
Usher, Alfred 102
Usher's Town, British Honduras 102

Valenzuela, Alinzo 151
Vandencamp, Joseph 157
Van Ingram, J. S. 126
Van Inra, J. S. 139
Vannorden, A. L. 128
Van Norman, A. L. 146
Veneill, John 127
Venezuela 11, 67
Veritt, E. 144
Vernon, Dr. 154
Vicksburg, Mississippi 14, 55, 71, 126
Victoria, British Honduras 64, 93
Village Gem (ship) 135

Vinceman, John J. 155
Vineyard, A. W. 146
Vineyard, J. C. 146
Vineyard, M. K. 146
Vineyard, Mr. (also lady and child) 123
Vineyard, Mr. (also wife and family) 128
Vineyard, N. O. 127, 146
Vineyard, P. R. 146
Virginia 14, 34, 57, 59, 75, 87, 90, 95, 140, 156
Von Nardes, C. 137

Wade, B. H. 126, 142
Wade, Mrs. B. H. 126
Wade, Mrs. S. 142
Walker, L. H. 156
Walker, Mrs. L. H. 156
Walker, R. 129, 149
Wall, W. D. 129, 149
Wallace, N. 130
Wallace, W. 152
Wallas, J. 134
Ward, A. 72, 76, 127, 145
Ward, Captain 137
Ward, Ed 135
Ware, T. J. 126, 142
Warren County, Mississippi 71
Washington, Louisiana 123
Watkins, B. L. 140
Watkins, G. 140
Watkins, L. 140
Watrous, E. P. 137
Watrous, J. A. 72
Watrous, W. C. 153
Watrous family 76, 82
Wawn, J. E. 143
Weir, Robert Lears 30
Weir, W. S. 48
Welcome (ship) 135
Wells, D. C. 153
West, Mr. 160
West, Mrs. 160
West Feliciana Parish, Louisiana 66
Wetheren, W. J. 158
White, E. 135

White, Emeline 148
White, Henry 128, 148
White, Isaac H. 160
White, J. D. 151
White, Jane 128
White, Janie 148
White, Jno. 151
White, Mary 151
White, Mary S. 160
White, Nancy 151
White, P. 151
White, Robert 148
White, S.
White, S. C. 151
White, Mrs. S. C. 151
White, Virginia 128, 148
Whittaker, Eli 150
Wier, F. A. 156
Wier, J. A. 156
Wilcox County, Alabama 49, 109
Wilkins, E. L. 136
Williams, J. C. 136
Williams, Robert 143
Williams, T. E. 124
Williams, T. W. 134
Williams, W. 72, 76, 143, 150
Williams, W. G. 72
Wilson, Ade 95, 102
Wilson, H. 126
Wilson, N. 144
Wilson family, 82, 103
Wood, R. C. 142
Wood, W. W. 117
Woods, E. L. 147
Woods, Richard Covington 102
Woods, Thomas A. 123, 154
World War I 83–84

yams 73
Ycacos *see* Icacos grant
yellow fever 42–43, 70, 119
Young, J. 130
Young, John Alfred 84–85
Young, Newton 157
Young, Sally 157
Young, Toledo, & Company 49, 71, 75–76, 101, 112